WITH HERITAGE SO RICH

WITH HERITAGE SO RICH

A Report of a Special Committee on Historic Preservation

under the auspices of the United States Conference of Mayors

with a grant from the Ford Foundation

ALBERT RAINS, *chairman*

LAURANCE G. HENDERSON, *director*

RANDOM HOUSE NEW YORK

FIRST EDITION

FOREWORD

Mrs. Lyndon B. Johnson

FOR TWO YEARS I HAVE HAD THE PRIVILEGE OF LIVING in one of the great historic homes of the United States. Daily the lives of the President and of my whole family have been affected by tangible mementoes of earlier Chief Executives and their families. The experience has driven home to me the truth that the buildings which express our national heritage are not simply interesting. They give a sense of continuity and of heightened reality to our thinking about the whole meaning of the American past.

I was dismayed to learn from reading this report that almost half of the twelve thousand structures listed in the Historic American Buildings Survey of the National Park Service have already been destroyed. This is a serious loss and it underlines the necessity for prompt action if we are not to shirk our duty to the future.

We must preserve and we must preserve wisely. As the report emphasizes, in its best sense preservation does not mean merely the setting aside of thousands of buildings as museum pieces. It means retaining the culturally valuable structures as useful objects: A home in which human beings live, a building in the service of some commercial or community purpose. Such preservation insures structural integrity, relates the preserved object to the life of the people around it, and not least, it makes preservation a source of positive financial gain rather than another expense.

In the beautification work in which many of us are now engaged, we try to carry on our activities within the sturdy American tradition which seeks the beautiful which is also useful. George Washington and Thomas Jefferson may have disagreed politically. They emphatically agreed, however, that a garden was one of the most "rational" of pursuits because, while throwing a glow of color and charm on everything around it, it also provided food for the body and a place of repose and reflection for the mind. May this tradition of usefulness guide all our beautification work, including that specific important form of beautification, the retention and rehabilitation of our buildings of special historic significance.

I hope that many Americans will read this thoughtful and spirited volume and consider seriously what they can do to help bring its message to fulfillment. The report points out that a number of European countries have long since undertaken extensive programs for protecting the national heritage in highly practical ways. We, blessed with so exciting and meaningful a heritage, should hardly be less active.

Lady Bird Johnson

SPECIAL COMMITTEE ON HISTORIC PRESERVATION
UNITED STATES CONFERENCE OF MAYORS

COMMITTEE MEMBERS

ALBERT RAINS, *Chairman*
former chairman, Housing Subcommittee
United States House of Representatives

EDMUND S. MUSKIE
United States Senator from Maine

WILLIAM B. WIDNALL
United States Representative from New Jersey

PHILIP H. HOFF
Governor of Vermont

RAYMOND R. TUCKER
Professor of Urban Studies, Washington University
former Mayor of St. Louis

GORDON GRAY
Chairman, National Trust for Historic Preservation

LAURANCE G. HENDERSON, *Director*
Director, Joint Council on Housing and Urban Development

EX-OFFICIO MEMBERS

STEWART L. UDALL
Secretary of the Interior
Alternates: WALTER I. POZEN
Special Assistant to the Secretary
GEORGE B. HARTZOG, JR.
Director of National Park Service

JOHN T. CONNOR
Secretary of Commerce
Alternate: REX M. WHITTON
Federal Highway Administrator,
Bureau of Public Roads

ROBERT C. WEAVER
Secretary of Housing and Urban Development

Alternate: WILLIAM L. SLAYTON
Commissioner of Urban Renewal

LAWSON B. KNOTT, JR.
Administrator, General Services Administration

Alternate: WILLIAM A. SCHMIDT
Deputy Commissioner, Public Buildings Service

THE AUTHORS

MRS. HELEN DUPREY BULLOCK, HON. AIA; Director, Department of Information, National Trust for Historic Preservation; editor, *Historic Preservation;* author, *My Head and My Heart; a Little History of Thomas Jefferson and Maria Cosway,* and others.

CARL FEISS, FAIA, AIP; Board of Trustees, National Trust for Historic Preservation; planning and design consultant; consultant on historic preservation; author and lecturer on architecture, city planning; Secretary, Historic Preservation Committee, International Union of Architects.

ROBERT R. GARVEY, JR., Executive Director, National Trust for Historic Preservation; Vice-President, International Council on Monuments and Sites (ICOMOS); Member, Consulting Committee, Registry of National Landmarks, National Park Service.

RICHARD H. HOWLAND, PH.D.; Chairman, Department of Civil History, Smithsonian Institution; architectural historian; archaeologist; author, *The Athenian Agora, The Architecture of Baltimore,* and others.

SIDNEY HYMAN, author of *The American President* and associated with Robert Sherwood in the writing of the Pulitzer Prize biography *Roosevelt and Hopkins.*

CHRISTOPHER TUNNARD, AIA; Director, Graduate Program in City Planning, Yale University; author, *The City of Man, American Skyline, America's Super-Cities, Man-Made America; Chaos or Control,* and others.

WALTER MUIR WHITEHILL, PH.D.; Director, the Boston Athenaeum, librarian, editor; author, *Spanish Romanesque Architecture of the 11th Century, Fleet Admiral King: a Naval Record, Independent Historical Societies,* and others.

GEORGE ZABRISKIE, John Simon Guggenheim Memorial Fellowship (poetry); verse, *The Mind's Geography, Like the Root,* "The Cathedral," text to photographs for *Gloria in Excelsis;* industrial historian; author, *History of Winchester and Potomac Railroad;* technical editor, *A Century of Railroad Folklore.*

CONTENTS

LIST OF PHOTOGRAPHS

Photographers are listed in italic type.

AMERICA: DISAPPEARING SIGHTS *(plates 89-109)*

PREFACE

ALBERT RAINS, *Chairman* and LAURANCE G. HENDERSON, *Director*

On SEPTEMBER 15, 1687, A VENETIAN BOMB FELL ON A Turkish powder keg and blew the Parthenon to pieces. The Venetians who did the bombarding and the Turks who used the Parthenon for a powder magazine did not intend its destruction. But the act of war was decisively final. An edifice which had stood for over 2,000 years as one of the supreme works of Athenian culture, lay in ruins.

We do not use bombs and powder kegs to destroy irreplaceable structures related to the story of America's civilization. We use the corrosion of neglect or the thrust of bulldozers. The result is the same as in the case of the Parthenon. Places where great American voices were heard, or where great acts of valor were performed, are lost. Connections between successive generations of Americans—concretely linking their ways of life— are broken by demolition. Sources of memory cease to exist.

Why then are we surprised when surveys tell us that many Americans, young and old, lack even a rudimentary knowledge of the national past? We ourselves create the blank spaces by doing nothing when the physical signs of our previous national life are removed from our midst.

The Special Committee on Historic Preservation was formed to explore this harsh reality, and to suggest ways of dealing with it.

Members of the Committee have served or continue to serve in various posts at all levels of government, but it is a privately organized body disinterested in all but its objectives in the realm of knowledge.

We on the committee have wanted to know what is happening in the field of historic preservation; the present trends in saving what can be saved, and the losses from destroying what deserves to be saved. We have tried to discover what we must do to rescue from certain destruction what remains of our legacy from the past, and how best to do that rescue work.

We have sought advice in this matter from sources which command respect. We have consulted with members of the

Executive Branch whose various programs—whether in the field of housing, urban renewal, road construction, national parks and the like—have a direct bearing on historic preservation. We have travelled extensively abroad to consult with Europeans and to draw from their experiences such knowledge as can be applied to the American case. We have had the benefit of help rendered by an expert technical staff. We are grateful to all these, and to the Ford Foundation and a generous anonymous donor whose grants of funds made the whole of this project possible.

While the heads of all the Federal departments and agencies whose programs affect historic preservation served as ex-officio members of the Committee, the Committee itself assumes sole and full responsibility for what appears in this report. Much research, many trips, long debates, and above all, an ardent love of country, have gone into its preparation and publication. For the Committee is convinced that an action program for historic preservation cannot be a piecemeal affair or a series of straitjackets. It must be both comprehensive and flexible. It must be designed to allow each interested private and public party to play a role commensurate with his own rights, duties and resources.

The report, therefore, suggests in broad terms certain practical avenues of approach to the problem of conserving places and objects of value in our individual communities and in the nation as a whole. We have not attempted to write the details of any law or laws which are necessary if a program of historic preservation is to attain the object for which it is framed. City councils, state legislatures and the Congress of the United States are and must be the source of the necessary laws. Each of these legislative bodies, in the light of its own best judgment and within the sphere of its own jurisdiction, has an essential part of its own to play in constructing a legal foundation for undertakings in historic preservation.

The Committee, on its own part, hopes that the body of fact it has assembled and the guidelines for action it has set forth, will materially assist our different legislative organs in the discharge of law-making functions they alone can perform. The case is urgent. May the legislative response be both thoughtful and resolute.

EMPIRE FOR LIBERTY

Sidney Hyman

Land without population is a wilderness, and population without land is a mob.

The United States has many social, political, and economic questions, some old, some new,

to settle in the near future; but none so fundamental as the true relation of the land to

the national life. The first act in the progress of any civilization is to provide homes for

those who desire to sit under their own vine and fig tree.

JAMES J. HILL

A NATION CAN BE A VICTIM OF AMNESIA. IT CAN LOSE the memories of what it was, and thereby lose the sense of what it is or wants to be. It can say it is being "progressive" when it rips up the tissues which visibly bind one strand of its history to the next. It can say it is only getting rid of "junk" in order to make room for the modern. What it often does instead, once it has lost the graphic source of its memories, is to break the perpetual partnership that makes for orderly growth in the life of a society.

It is true that small scale things, even important things, can be done by a single generation. It is all the more true, however, that a piece of work cast on an heroic scale needs the labor of generations. It needs the consecutive efforts of grandfathers, fathers and grandsons, "bound in a partnership not only between those who are living, those who are dead, and those who are about to be born." Each generation, by the terms of the partnership, still has a right to express what is unique in itself. Each still has a right to meet its own needs in its own style. But each builds best in its own day when it pays a decent respect to the past and future, and frames its own work to fit in between the growing ends of both.

What we want to conserve, therefore, is the evidence of individual talent *and* tradition, of liberty *and* union among successive generations of Americans. We want the signs of where we came from and how we got to where we are, the thoughts we had along the way and what we did to express the thoughts in action. We want to know the trails that were walked, the battles that were fought, the tools that were made. We want to know the beautiful or useful things that were built and the originality that was shown, the adaptations that were made and the grace-notes to life that were sounded. We want to know the experiments in community living that were tried and the lessons that were taught by a brave failure as well as by a brave success.

1

It is all these things and more like them that we want to keep before our eyes as part of our lived life as a people, and as connecting links between a past which millions of Americans helped make and a future which we must continue to make.

THE TURNING POINT

Yet how can one convey in a few words all there is to see, remember and retain of the partnership among American generations? Where can the account begin? What should be put into the story and what left out? A thousand books would not be enough for the telling, while only a focal point is possible here, and a single starting date must be chosen from any number of equally valid choices.

Let the starting date be the year 1800 when Thomas Jefferson was elected President of the United States, for it was in consequence of his Presidency and that of his hand-picked heir, James Madison, that America began an adventure in nation-building that was without precedent in human history.

Many theorists, some ancient, some fairly new, could be cited to prove in advance that the adventure was doomed. There was Plato who had said that the size of a democracy must be limited to the number of people standing in one place who can hear a speaker's voice. There was Montesquieu who had said that a republic worked best in a limited territory, and was ill-suited for the government of an empire. There was also Adam Smith who had said that "a man is of all sorts of luggage the most difficult to be transportable."

The American, however, had a special theory of his own, and a temperament to go with it. He said that Life was larger than Logic, and he felt that a man finds his best ideals in his obstacles. He had thus brought the Republic to birth despite all high and mighty logicians who told him that he must bend his strength to the end of having everything stand still.

By a law of "natural selection," he presently drew to himself a vast congregation of men and women who shared his special theory, this temperament, and who also could not stand still. Specifically, in the century between the end of the War of 1812 and the onset of the First World War in 1914, some fifty million people left their native Europe to seek new homes in other lands, and of this number fully three-fifths came to the United States. They were called "immigrants," where their pre-Revolutionary War counterparts had been called "settlers," and it took a man like Theodore Roosevelt to make a joke out of the distinction. The term "settler" said he, was "a euphemistic name for an immigrant who came over in the steerage of a sailing ship in the seventeenth century instead of the steerage of a steamer in the nineteenth century." In any case, by whatever name the waves of newcomers were called—and some, at first had a harsh sound—they and their descendants interlaced their

energies with the American population descended from pre-Revolutionary War colonizers. So joined, they made every day in America another "moving day" in a westerly migration whose scope dwarfed the total of all the known tribal migrations on the Eurasian land mass.

It was commonly said of them collectively that "if Hell lay in the West, Americans would cross Heaven to reach it." It could just as well have been said that they were on the constant look-out for a short-cut through Hell in order to reach a Heaven in the West, whether by a water route or overland. With so much land that was vacant, the American could not be expected to be content with what he happened to possess. Somewhere on some unspecified point on the far horizon was the perfect one-hundred-and-sixty-acre-tract. It was made just for him at the beginning of time, and it was lying in wait just for him to find and possess. It had just the right balance between meadows, forests and arable soil. It had a clearer spring for water, a closer river for transportation, a more sheltered and better-drained spot for a home, more wild game for meat, fewer crows to devour his seed grain and no hostile Indians. If the perfect tract could not be found in Kentucky, try Ohio. If not Ohio, try Illinois. If not Illinois, try Iowa.

The individual's search for the perfect one hundred and sixty acres often had its matching piece in the American's recurrent dream about the perfect community in which he wanted to live and help build. If it entailed wandering beyond the boundaries of existing civilization, the gain would be an undefiled stretch of earth where a new-style community could give form and force to his ideal. It might be an ideal of religious (or non-religious) life. It might be an ideal about the modes of work best suited to man, and how best to organize production and distribution. It might be an ideal of social justice. Whatever it was, it was worth a try. And if it turned out in the end that there was a gulf between the ideal and the real, well, so be it. There was no lack of other experiments in community living for him to try out.

Suddenly, though, the continent had been spanned, and the frontier that had run parallel to the ground for so long, as befit a predominantly agricultural society, shot upward in the vertical frontier of an industrialized and urban society. Village crafts which once produced for a local market had become giant and complex factories producing for consumers the world over, and the place where the village stood had become a giant megalopolis. But towering over everything else was the tremendous fact about the American Republic. The union of men, materials, motives, temperaments, convictions—and a kindly Providence—had made of the Republic something unique in the story of man on earth. Here was an infinitely varied people spread in greater number over a greater distance than was the case with the Roman Empire at its height. Here was the first continental democracy, organized along federal lines, differing in its components yet strong in the center. Here was an empire for liberty. Here was a human patriotism distilled from the sum of national and local prides.

APPROACH MARCH TO A NATION OF NATIONS

But now did things stand in the year 1800?

By then, the effort to populate what had become the United States of America had been going on for almost two centuries. Many countries with odd-lot motives—and many odd-lot "corporations" and individuals with motives of their own—had played a part in this effort. Yet in the year 1800—when the population of the British Isles was more than 15 million, and that of the French Republic was more than 25 million—the United States contained only 5.3 million people. Of these, one-fifth were Negro slaves. Of the 4.5 million free whites, less than one million were able-bodied male adults. Of the total population, two-thirds clung to the Atlantic seaboard within fifty miles of tidewater where alone the wants of civilized life could be supplied from various urban centers like Boston, with a population of 23,000, New York with a population of 63,000, or Philadelphia with a population of 70,000.

Nowhere did eastern settlements touch the western. At least one hundred miles of mountainous country held the two regions everywhere apart. The shores of Lake Erie, where alone contact seemed easy, were still unsettled. Western New York still remained a wilderness. Buffalo was not laid out. Rochester did not exist. Utica contained fifty houses, mostly small and temporary. Albany was still a Dutch city with some five thousand inhabitants.

In the region that lay between the western slopes of the Appalachians and the Mississippi River, Indians still represented formidable obstacles to further advances. Powerful confederacies of Creeks, Cherokees, Chickasaws and Choctaws lived and hunted where the states of Mississippi, Alabama and the western parts of Georgia, Tennessee and Kentucky were to extend. In areas that were to form the later states of Wisconsin, Michigan, Illinois, Indiana and one-third of Ohio, there were Wyandottes and Shawnees, Miamis, Kickapoos and other tribes, who could raise in the aggregate a force of some five thousand warriors to fight or hunt. In the south and the north alike, the Indians were ready to offer sharp resistance to any invasion on their domain, exacting life for life, and yielding only as their warriors perished. In this they were being encouraged in the south by the Spanish authorities based in the Florida and Louisiana territories, and in the north by the English authorities in Canada.

Nature itself, however, had created four routes for a flow of traffic from the eastern settlements into the West. To the south,
one rocky route ran from Alexandria to Richmond and from Richmond through the Cumberland Gap into the Kentucky country. It was along this trail that Daniel Boone had blazed the way as early as 1769, and in the course of time it had been widened to a wagon road. A second route lay westward from Alexandria over the mountains and across the Great Kanawha to Boonesboro. In the middle region, three roads, starting from Philadelphia, Baltimore, and Alexandria respectively, converged on Pittsburgh, where the wide waters of the Ohio River offered the emigrant an easy journey into the far country. To the north the Genesee road, beginning at Albany, ran almost due west through level country to Buffalo, on Lake Erie, the principal gateway into the upper reaches of the Northwest Territory.

For a time, the Cumberland road held the primacy. The region into which it led was at the beginning under the governments of Virginia and North Carolina. The road itself was very near the back door of the upland farmers in those states and it beckoned them on to a more fertile soil than their plowshares had so far broken. Moreover, the advance of slave-owning planters from the coast exerted a steady pressure on them, driving them to escape by the Cumberland route from that invasion. On this account, of the 500,000 inhabitants who formed a human wedge driven through the Appalachians into Kentucky and Tennessee with its apex at Nashville and its flanks covered by the Ohio and Tennessee Rivers, the majority were men from Virginia and the Carolinas.

Toward the closing years of the eighteenth century, the routes that first converged on Pittsburgh—not without difficulties—had begun to gather an ever-larger portion of the westward traffic. For as soon as the immigrant family arrived at the headwaters of the Ohio, it could buy almost any kind of boat for the remainder of the trip—a light canoe for two or three, or a ten-ton barge that would carry a score of passengers with household goods, wagons, plows and cattle down the river to the landing points nearest the chosen destination. Since the approach to Pittsburgh lay closest to the settlements of Maryland, Pennsylvania and New Jersey, it was the immigrants from these states who were most likely to travel the Ohio River route.

Another factor contributed to the increase in favor for this route towards the close of the eighteenth century. Until the establishment of the new federal government in 1789, settlers in the region south of the Ohio had been compelled to do their work under the protection of Virginia and North Carolina state governments. The protection was sketchy at best, and the result led to encounters with Indians that made Kentucky and Tennessee a "dark and bloody ground." But not long after his inauguration, President Washington, himself a large holder of western lands, took vigorous measures to organize military expeditions against the Indians on the frontier. His commander,

General Anthony Wayne, after many clashes, brought the leading chieftains to their knees, forcing them in 1795 to sign a treaty which cleared the eastern and southern portions of the Western Reserve and Northwest Territory for white settlement. Grim days, however, still lay ahead.

Meanwhile, the domain of the Western Reserve had been retained as a kind of lien held by Connecticut when it surrendered to the Union its historic land claims. Thus while settlers from other states would leave their mark on the Western Reserve, it was the Connecticut Yankees and their Massachusetts cousins who were in a position to leave the greatest mark. They began to do just that, step by step, in line with General Wayne's work of pacification in the eastern and southern portions of the region. A case in point was Moses Cleaveland who blazed a path to the shores of Lake Erie, and in 1796 established a post that was destined to grow into a great city. Other Connecticut Yankees and their Massachusetts cousins would be flooding the Western Reserve—and after that, the Northwest territory—by the approach march of the Genesee Road running between Albany and Buffalo. After that, with the precision of a drilled army on parade, the town meeting, the Congregational Church, steady-going habits and Massachusetts thrift would be reproduced beyond the mountains once land-hungry sons and daughters of the Puritans began in earnest their rapid advance across northern Ohio, Indiana and Illinois, upward into southern Michigan and Wisconsin and westward toward the great plains. But this would come after 1800, by the route of the Erie Canal as well as the Genesee Road.

Taking the population picture of the country as a whole as it appeared in 1800, America had recovered a fraction of an estimated 300,000 American Tories loyal to the British Crown, who had voluntarily left the country or had been driven out of it, some to England, some to Canada. On the other hand, the *inflow* of wholly new settlers from European shores had been slowed down to a trickle for successive reasons. There was the world turmoil attending the waging of the Revolutionary War. There was America's civil turmoil following the winning of independence, while independence itself brought to an end the English colonial practice of sentencing English convicts to labor for a period of years under a colonial master in America. Then, too, there was the difficulty of reaching the lands available for settlement on the western side of the Appalachian mountains—and in the turmoil to be encountered if those lands were reached. On top of everything else was the trump reason. It was the onset of the French Revolution which spread a contagion of worldwide war that would rage for a generation.

The immediate American byproduct of that world war was the Louisiana Purchase, which removed French power from the North American mainland, gave America control of the Mississippi River, and brought within American possession a tremendous empire fanning out and up from the west bank of the Mississippi River. The further American byproduct of that world war was the War of 1812, whose dismal episodes have tended to obscure the triumphant consequences. The war at its end had produced a set of conditions in which the hostile Indian barrier to westward advance had for all practical purposes been removed throughout the Mississippi Valley. At the same time, it had removed Great Britain as a harassing agent in the northerly part of the region, led to the demilitarization of the U. S.-Canadian border and its clear demarcation up to the Oregon Territory. It had also put Spain in a frame of mind in which it sold the Floridas to the United States in 1819. Still farther, the worldwide war which had engaged and drained Spain's energies made it possible for her colonies in the Western Hemisphere to stage successful revolutions which led to their independence. In this way, Mexico would win her independence and include within her domain the whole of the American Southwest and California, a portion of the domain to fall later to the United States by insurgency, annexation and the Mexican War.

Beginning with the Louisiana Purchase, then, a tremendous area would await settlement, not only by the descendants of the original American colonists, but by newcomers from Europe, once the end of the Napoleonic Wars gave them an opportunity and a spur to start life anew in the United States.

As of 1800, however, the ethnic picture of the American population—save for the loss of the American Tories—was roughly what it had been in 1776. The previous preponderence of the English had served to make English the common language, and to fix governmental institutions and political ideals in an English mold, subject to Americanization. This, in a sense, was the supreme strategic achievement of the "great" migration of 20,000 English Puritans into early New England, and the 150,000 Scotch-Irish Presbyterians who arrived in the eighteenth century and settled in nearly five hundred scattered communities. But as of 1776, fully half the population outside of New England was of non-English background—which explains why Benjamin Franklin, Thomas Jefferson and John Adams jointly proposed that the official seal of the United States bear the national emblems of England, Scotland, Ireland, Germany, Holland and France. In this way, said they, the seal would point out the countries from which these states had been peopled.

Though the three men had overlooked a bit of Sweden and Switzerland, and though in any case other counsels prevailed, the point they had in mind was essentially correct. Men and women from Holland who had colonized New York, and those from Sweden who had helped colonize Delaware had been forcibly absorbed by English power. French Huguenots had settled in virtually all the colonies after the Edict of Nantes had been revoked, while some 200,000 Germans had congregated in the new sections of New York and in the Pennsylvania back country, where they gave rise to the strain called the "Pennsylvania Dutch." There were also congregations of Spanish and Portuguese Jews in Atlantic coast port cities who reached America by way of various stepping stones, and who had woven trading links with Spanish and Portuguese outposts in the New World.

As in the years before 1776, a religious or political motive was often present among the trickle of newcomers who reached America in the years that intervened between 1776 and 1800. So it would often be in all the decades that followed. But the economic urge, operating independently or as a stiffening agent to religious and political conviction, was responsible for most of the settlers. Continuing the pre-1776 pattern, most of the settlers were the poor of Europe. They were the day laborer, the peasant, the artisan and the shopkeeper rather than the nobleman, the squire, the great merchant.

Religious or political persecution, or an unusual chance to acquire wealth, might induce a member of the upper middle class to transplant himself in America. But in the main, America continued to be peopled by the underprivileged who could not even afford to pay for their own passage to America from English and Continental ports. They sold their services to a merchant or ship captain in lieu of paying the transportation fare. Then, after an ocean voyage where they were jam-packed aboard ship under conditions where as many as 50 per cent of them might die en route, they were auctioned off on arrival to the highest bidder for a term of labor extending from two to seven years. People of this description had composed fully half of the total migration before 1776, and the labor-contract system still prevailed in 1800—and would continue to prevail in some states until the third decade of the nineteenth century.

Meanwhile, along the fifty-mile strip of tidewater where the bulk of the American population was to be found in 1800, home construction and town planning had passed through their primitive stages. They continued to show, as in 1776, the differences successive groups of settlers had imported from their points of origin in Europe, subject to modification by local factors of climate, building materials, concepts of communal life and their economic underpinning. It is not possible here to detail all the differences or everything that remains of what was done in the seed-time years of the American Republic. But a picture, drawn in broad strokes, and arranged roughly in the chronological sequence that marked the process by which regions were first opened for colonization, would look like this:

THE VIRGINIA AND MARYLAND COAST

At an early date in the history of the Virginia and Maryland colonies, their legislatures at the request of the Crown had passed various "New Town Acts." These designated the sites for towns, established the method of land acquisition and land valuation, provided for their layout, and made provision for disposition of town lots. The motives stemmed from a desire to promote town life generally as the best means of stimulating the development in the two colonies and the wish to control trade and customs collections for the mother country. Towns which exist to this day—Yorktown, Petersburg, Fredericksburg, Williamsburg, Alexandria and Annapolis—had their seminal source in the ideas that lay behind the "New Town Acts" of colonial times.

In the main, however, the "New Town Acts" failed to conjure up actual towns, and the reasons why not were closely related. First, the Virginia-Maryland coast line was bisected at frequent intervals by rivers that were navigable for many miles inland by the largest merchant ships in general use—a 250- to 400-tonner at the most. Since there were so many excellent and protected anchorages to choose from—and no single site had any marked advantage over the others—the colonial legislatures of Virginia and Maryland were caught in on-going deadlocks and made no decisions whatever about the specific places where a New Town would actually be laid out and built.

Second, the adoption of tobacco as the dominant product of Virginia and Maryland for a growing market in England, had led to a dispersed pattern of settlement in the form of large plantations. Based on slave labor, these proved the most economical and efficient methods of tobacco production. Then as the plantation system matured, individual plantations—almost invariably located close to tidewater channels—became small communities themselves with their own docks and other port facilities, warehouses, shops, slave quarters and the plantation house.

The plantation system did not need any "public" kind of commercial, financial and industrial center. And it was perhaps for this reason that Thomas Jefferson, in his *Notes on the State of Virginia,* extolled the "moral" virtues of agriculture as a way of life and excoriated the "corrupting" influences of city life. The plantation system, however, did need government where titles to land could be recorded, where cases could be argued before a court, where the arm of civil order could be centered, and the means for the common defense mustered. As the county was the basic unit of local government, when towns refused to spring up naturally as county seats, the solution to the needs just mentioned lay in constructing county buildings in as central a location within the county as was possible.

Accordingly, such buildings presently came into existence to form a compound in a rural setting. Some eventually became the centers of present-day Virginia towns, as in the case of Gloucester. Others, such as Virginia's King William Courthouse, stand today as solitary sentinels, symbolic of government. The typical compound was surrounded by a brick wall, inside of which were a courthouse, a jail, a clerk's office, and a row of lawyer's offices. The nearby tavern or ordinary was always part of the complex and often served as a courthouse while the latter was being constructed. The tavern, inn and jail had a year-round use. On the whole, however, these little administrative and legal communities came to life only when the court was in session or other sporadic governmental activities occurred.

State capitals were another matter. Before the Revolutionary War, Georgian architecture had formed the core buildings found in state capitals. But after the Revolutionary War, there was a natural tendency to give effect in building to the independence and vigor of the new Republican state, and a more monumental type of state capital was developed as architects went farther afield in their inspiration.

The new capitol at Richmond as designed by Thomas Jefferson was founded on the plan of the *Maison Carrée* in Nîmes, France; while the new capitol in Washington by Dr. William Thornton was based on the Palladian plans of English country mansions. Here and there, traces of what would presently be called the "Greek Revival" were visible, but the full force of the revival would not be felt in America until the nineteenth century was under-way.

Finally, if the county compounds expressed the form of government that seemed natural to the plantation system in Virginia and Maryland, while the new-style capital buildings expressed the independence of the new Republic, the master's house on the great plantations reflected the social and economic basis of that system. The architectural "envelope" had become formal, balanced, aristocratic, with extended plans, many guest rooms and detached units. It made little difference how far the kitchen might be from the dining room, or how many fireplaces were needed to warm the whole of a house. There were plenty of servants to take the steps from the kitchen, bearing food and to tend the fireplaces when there was a chill in the air. There were also plenty of servants to tend to the area immediately surrounding the manor house with its meadows, sweeping views, rows of trees and gardens. Surviving Virginia examples of the maritime plantation houses include, besides George Washington's *Mount Vernon,* George Mason's *Gunston Hall,* Benjamin Harrison's *Berkeley* near Charles City, *Westover* of William Byrd II, William Byrd Harrison's *Brandon* and Carter Burwell's *Carter's Grove.*

NEW ENGLAND

New England towns and villages, even though they had passed through their rough-hewn days, still continued to show in 1800 the imprint of social forms, ideas and needs that marked their establishment.

It is worth saying here, that the "general welfare" clause in the Federal Constitution of 1789 had one of its early roots in the Mayflower Compact by which the Puritans bound themselves together to promote "the common weal." The individual had rights of his own, but the "common weal" bore within itself the idea of community effort on behalf of those objects needed by and common to all individuals. Nor was this piece of phrasing just a rhetorical flourish. As a minority religious sect that had been persecuted in England, the Puritans had learned that they could survive only through mutual assistance, and this truth was reconfirmed by the needs they faced in the harsh environment of the new world where they planted their first colonies.

By coincidence, the land tenure system with which they were familiar in England, had a form with mutual assistance through communal effort. Specifically, the original Puritan settlers in New England were largely drawn from the English countryside where feudal concepts of community organization and modes of agricultural production still held sway. In that countryside the farmer lived in a village while the strip of field he personally worked as a tenant or freeholder, along with the field he had access to in common with other farmers, lay on the outskirts of the village.

The pattern was transplanted on New England soil. Unlike the vast plantation in the South, or the isolated farmstead that was to be the hallmark of later settlement practices in farmer areas to the west of the Appalachian Mountains, the New England agricultural community centered on the village. All or nearly all farmers lived in it in a relatively compact community and daily went to their fields that stretched outward from the cluster of buildings.

Whereas the county was the basic unit of local government in the South, the basic unit in New England was the township which integrated an urban center with a rural countryside. Homes were constructed on lots near the center of the township, and these were usually grouped around an open space at the front of which the meetinghouse was erected. The outlying fields suitable for cultivation were known as the "common fields" or "proprietors' commons." These had been roughly surveyed, divided into strips, and allotted to the settlers according to agreed upon rules of equity. Land of this description was not open to subsequent settlers unless the newcomers were formally granted commoners' rights. The remaining land, however—pasture and woodland—were held in common ownership by the village. The pasture could be used by all residents of the village, and subject to agreed-upon regulations, residents could fell trees and quarry stone for individual use. Thus the land system of the typical New England village combined individual ownership and ownership in common.

The concentration of people in one place did more than make the village a kind of fortress. It made it easier for the villagers to pool their slender resources in order to provide a library of "serious" books and to maintain a common school where children could be educated. A plantation owner in the South could acquire for his own use or for the use of his friends a personal library far larger and more varied than the total number of books found in several scores of New England villages. He could also set aside among the dependencies surrounding the plantation great house a schoolhouse for his own children, and engage tutors that would give his children a more cosmopolitan education than was the case with New England children. But the difference was, that learning under the plantation system was confined to the few—it could not be until after the Civil War that a public school system was created in the South—whereas in New England there was from the beginning a very high level of literacy and a very broad diffusion of knowledge throughout the population. This head-start in education was to be of material advantage to the sons of New England, and was to make their mind the source of an outlook and values destined to spread throughout most of the Western Reserve, and the Northwest Territory, and the upper reaches of the Louisiana Territory.

What has just been said points to something else. When increases in the population of a New England village—by births or by new immigration—produced a condition where there was no more common land to be subdivided for individual cultivation, the practice was to "hive off" groups of settlers from the old township and to start a new township on newly granted ground nearer the frontier. The "hiving off" process generally involved the youngest sons of a family (and their brides) while the older or oldest sons stayed on to cultivate the lands they were due to inherit from their fathers.

But in 1800, the process of "hiving off" was still limited by several factors. For one thing, the continued uncertainty about where the borderline ran between Canada and the United States posed a risk that a penetration of the frontier along the northwestern part of New England might bring a settler into sharp collision with Canadians who had come to include the Tory refugees from the American Revolutionary War. In another direction, the penetration of the Western Reserve was limited by the extent to which the Indian tribes had been pushed back and their titles to the land extinguished. Then again, there was little profit in bringing new lands under cultivation when there were no waterways or roads over which the produce of those fields could be brought to a market. This latter need was answered in the wedge of 500,000 Americans that had already been driven through the Appalachian mountains into the region bounded by the Tennessee and Ohio rivers. Some sons and daughters of New England had already formed part of that wedge. They tended to favor the lands lying to the north of the Ohio River, and Marietta was their principal "staging area"

for a further northerly advance, destined to intersect with a southerly advance from Cleveland and Cincinnati.

Meanwhile, along the Atlantic coastline, other New England townships, while still retaining their agricultural base, had long before come to look to the sea as a source of food and supplementary income. Food meant the rise of a fishing industry—which led by accident to the rise of the whaling industry. Income meant the rise of a shipbuilding and shipping industry that had been spurred by both the Revolutionary War and the flaring world war that began with the French Revolution. The Revolutionary War had meant the equipping of privateers to prey on British merchantmen, and this work engaged the energies of 90,000 New Englanders more than the total number of Continentals and militia in any year except 1776. The world war that began with the French Revolution meant the equipping of ships to carry cargos for belligerents or for trade that was going by default to the Americans.

Independently of these considerations, there was the need for coastwide shipping—since travel and transport by water along the Atlantic coastline was far more preferable than travel and transport over wretched land routes. There was also the lure of the East Indies—China trade which entailed a voyage around the Horn, then perhaps a voyage up the Pacific coast to the fur trading sea-outposts of the Oregon territory, then on to the East Indies and China with a cargo of fur, and then back around the Horn with the profits from the sale of the furs and with the produce of the East for resale in the United States.

In different degrees, these various aspects of a living drawn from the sea left distinctive marks still visible among New England place names—Boston and Salem, Martha's Vineyard and New Bedford, New London and Nantucket, Fairhaven and Sag Harbor, Portsmouth and Providence, and thirty others of lesser celebrity like Mystic, Conn.

Maritime life not only called for marines and sea-captains; it called for the designers of ships, carpenters who built them, and for the carpenters who signed aboard for a voyage in order to repair damages suffered en route. All these, plus a breed of masons born and trained among the stone quarries of New England, had combined by 1800 to upgrade the style and quality of home construction in New England's seaport towns. From these points, the upgrading process spread into the zones of the interior. A word about this:

In the rural districts of England from which most of the original colonists of New England came, wood was still plentiful and buildings were of the time-honored "half-timber" construction. The frames of such buildings were constructed on the ground, then raised into place and pinned together with heavy dowels. After that, the interstices were filled with wattle and daub or with rough mud, bricks made of clay and straw and called cats. The interior walls were plastered inside with whitewashed clay, and the exterior was covered with a coating of lime.

The early New England colonists were thoroughly familiar with this type of structure, and as they found wood plentiful they used it widely to duplicate the homes they had left behind. But it was not long before there began among them a process of adapting the familiar to the formidable demands of their immediate environment—a process that was to be repeated again and again by other Americans elsewhere. In this case, the New England colonists discovered that wattle and daub, satisfactory in the genial climate of Old England, was not equal to the climate of New England.

Environment thus stepped in to alter the historic architectural procedure. The colonists now rived, split or sawed out a covering of clapboards to sheath the half-timber houses, to shed the water and keep out the cold. The efficacious clapboards were universally adopted, and became an important feature of subsequent American architecture.

Meanwhile, the vigorous climate also accounted for the compact plans of buildings in early New England. The chimney was placed in the center of the house, with fireplaces for various rooms. This arrangement not only conserved heat but stiffened the structural frame. When more room was needed, the house went up instead of out. Most homes faced the south to take advantage of the sun, and most of them had a narrow entrance hall and a stairway hugging the chimney. The floors of the upper rooms were supported by a huge, handhewn summer beam which was supported in turn by the chimney and outside wall.

In New England, as in the South, the winning of independence from Great Britain might of its own accord have released a new spirit that demanded new architectural expressions. Nonetheless, it took more money to build a great house than those people had been accustomed to in colonial days. When money eventually came to those New Englanders who controlled the means of trade in the young nation's seaports, there were available, as noted a moment ago, the designers and craftsmen with finely developed talents in the use of wood or stone.

There were men like Samuel McIntire, the skilled architect and woodcarver, who dominated the construction of some of the finest privately owned and public buildings in Salem which still stand and are in use. Indeed, even the houses built after his death in 1811 reflected his influence. Known as "the Federal style," most of them are square, hip-roofed buildings of white clapboard or brick laid in flawless Flemish bond. Front doors are framed in fanlight and sidelights, shaded by eliptical or oblong porches whose roofs are supported by slender columns. A Palladian window opens into a formal garden in the rear. Most of the interiors are simply arranged, usually four rooms to a floor. But there are three floors instead of the usual two of colonial days and the chimneys have been relegated to the side walls instead of the center of the house. As a crowning touch there is a balustrade around the roof known as "the captain's walk" where householders could look to the sea for incoming ships.

Of equal influence there was the architect Charles Bulfinch whose professional reputation was established in Boston and whose work appears in other communities like Waltham. He was endowed with an experimental turn of mind, the results of which appear in the different forms he gave to the edifices of his design at different stages of his career. Many of the old homes standing on Boston's Beacon Hill and Louisburg Square were his work. In this, he experimented with unified residential blocks whose distinctive feature—representing a break from the traditional austerity of New England architecture—was the bow-front house. It was Bulfinch, too, who designed the Massachusetts State House in 1795 with its long central colonnade and dome, standing on its imposing site.

While men like McIntire and Bulfinch were among the new style setters for the New England beneficiaries of wealth acquired by means of the sea, people throughout the countryside were also beginning to think in terms of more elaborate structures. Into this situation stepped Asher Benjamin, a carpenter from Greenfield, Mass., who is credited with having exerted more direct influence than any other single person on the whole tissue of architecture in New England.

The inspirational idea which gave him this influence began when he recognized a central truth stated by Benjamin Franklin some years earlier. The latter, in reference to the conditions of the Americans, had observed that they were not so miserable as the poor of Europe, but "there are also very few that in Europe would be called rich; it is rather a happy mediocrity that prevails. There are few great proprietors of the soil, and few tenants; most people cultivate their own lands or follow some handicraft of merchandise; very few are rich enough to pay the high prices given in Europe for painting, statues, architecture, and the other works of art, that are more curious than useful." Asher Benjamin, in 1797, had the shrewdness and capacity to prepare and publish a book with this market in mind.

The book was called *The Country Builder's Assistant*. It was not the first book on architecture printed in the United States, but it was the first genuinely American treatment of the subject. It was very much a "how-to-do-it" book, since it contained plans and detailed drawings for various private and public structures. Carpenters throughout the northeast, being of Puritan stock, were a literate breed. They acquired Benjamin's book and began to pattern their construction work on his plans. The First Congregational Church in Bennington, Vt., one of the most admired of all New England churches, was built by the carpenter Lavius Fillmore and closely resembles one of the designs found in *The Country Builder's Assistant*. Most of the local carpenters had souls of their own, fortunately, and they were not given to automated reproductions of what they saw in Benjamin's book. They added their own improvisations. But the total result is a pervasive pattern which continues to give New England its distinctive flavor.

THE MIDDLE ATLANTIC STATES

In the year 1800, the role the Dutch had played in opening up New York for settlement was clearly visible in the Hudson Valley, and so was the patroon system of landowners and development which marked the Dutch effort. Less visible was the evidence of the role the Dutch had played in the founding of the city of New York (under their own title of Nieu Amsterdam) on the island of Manhattan. Dutch hegemony throughout New York, or more precisely, the hegemony of the West India Company, had been a brief experience. If the founding of Albany in 1623, following Henry Hudson's earlier exploration, can serve as a starting date, it ended in a conquest by England in 1664, except for a brief revival from 1672 to 1674.

As conceived by the West India Company, the city of New York—to call it by its post-1664 name—was supposed to have an orderly relationship between the town and the country. The town was to be a neatly symmetrical arrangement within a large five-pointed fortification. Everything was specified in detail—the location of homes within the fortress, the sizes of lots, the size and location of the market squire, the location of the school, hospital and church. Outside the fortress area, similar detailed regulations were set forth governing the location of the farms, how they were to be divided among the tenants of the patroon, how they were to be served by a drainage system, and so on.

The patroon system was based upon slavery—and the tenants were the slaves. They were Dutch peasants who in the new world paid rent to the patroon for the use of the land he owned, and for the use of facilities like flour mills which he provided. It was a feudal practice imported from Europe and it was fated to undergo a sharp modification, less from the British conquest and far more from the availability of land in the West when that region opened up for settlement. The tenant would see little point in paying rents to an overlord when he could own his own land in the West. When access routes were opened up, and especially after the Erie Canal was built, Dutch tenant farmers would head for the West (along with new immigrants from the Netherlands) to establish a string of Dutch-flavored villages in the Western Reserve and Northwest Territory.

In the original plan for New York City—to return to it—the fortress enclosure was planned on a scale which exceeded by far the resources, needs or interests of the settlers on the ground. They built a much smaller fort which contained a few houses and essential municipal structures, and let the city spread beyond its walls. In other words, the East India Company's plan became a dead letter at the outset, and New York City began to grow with no over-all plan for its development.

New streets were laid out from time to time as they were needed, usually following the lanes that had sprung up naturally as men and animals followed the most convenient paths between houses, farms and the fort. The result was a pattern of growth in which the streets were irregular in their alignment and width. There was Wall Street, originally built to serve the wall of palisades hurriedly erected in 1633 when an English attack threatened. There was, at the foot of the fort, a green patch that came to be called Bowling Green. Leading off from it, there was the great axial street which came to be called Broadway. Then beyond the city proper, there were a number of villages with their clusters of farms, villages like the Bowery and Harlem.

After the British assumed control of the region and gave it the name of New York, they established the corporate existence of New York City on a charter basis. At the end of the seventeenth century, the original charter was supplemented by the so-called Dongan Charter which extended the city's municipal jurisdiction over the entire island of Manhattan. It further granted ownership to the city of all land between high- and low-water marks, thus fixing the basis for a system of municipal piers and wharfs. Then again, it also granted to the city ownership of all lands not yet allotted to individuals as well as all lands occupied by public buildings or used for streets, lanes or alleys. This wholesale land grant to the municipal corporation of New York thereby established the basis for a vast plan to extend the city at the start of the 1800's. In the intervening century, however, no comprehensive plan of growth was followed. Instead, on a street-by-street and lot-by-lot basis, small parcels of land were surveyed and sold by property owners following their own whims as to design.

During the Revolutionary War, the occupation of New York by British troops led to a suspension of normal commercial land development activities. Two disastrous fires had also destroyed large portions of the city, so that from a pre-war population of 20,000, New York by 1783 had declined to a civil population of 10,000. But at the end of the decade, when New York briefly served as the home of the new federal government, the expansion of the city had regained the momentum it had under English rule. In 1800 it was, as already noted, a city of 63,000, the second largest in the land.

In that same year, Washington Irving made his first trip up the Hudson where the magic of the old Dutch life and its charming fables still seemed vital and alive—alive enough to bear fruit in Irving's *The Legend of Sleepy Hollow,* and the *Head-*

less Horseman. If Irving at that time had stopped at Kinderhook and gone into a certain tavern which was also the village polling place, he would have seen one of his future benefactors —then a seventeen-year-old youth, born in the place, who was destined to be the first President of the United States not born a British subject. This was Martin Van Buren.

"My family," so Van Buren would write, "was from Holland, without a single marriage with one of different extraction from the time of the first emigrant to that of the marriage of my eldest son, embracing a period of over two centuries and including six generations." The immigrant, Marten Cornelissen Van Burrmalsen, came over in 1631 as a servant indentured to Van Rensselaer, the first patroon, and later changed his surname to Van Buren. The young Martin Van Buren of 1800 did not stay for long in the tavern helping his father, though he would presently win a dubious celebrity as "Blue Whiskey Van" because he could drink large quantities of whiskey without the customary effects. He was already studying law on the side, would come to be known as "The Flying Dutchman," "The Little Magician" or as the "Red Fox of Kinderhook." He would prosper mightily in the practice of the law. He would go on to become, besides Secretary of State, Vice President and President, the prophet of organized national party politics in the democratic age that dawned in 1828 with the election of Andrew Jackson as President.

In 1800, the Dutch patroon system which his first immigrant forebear was part of as an indentured servant, was still in strong evidence on all sides, as it is to this day. There was the Van Cortland Manor at Croton-on-the-Hudson, the Van Rensselaer Manor at Claverack, the Schuyler Mansion in Albany where Alexander Hamilton was married, and where "Gentleman Johnny" Burgoyne was confined after his surrender at Saratoga. There was also Fort Crailo in Rensselaer, a brick building first constructed in 1705 as a fortress against Indians, and where Dr. Richard Shuckburgh is supposed to have written the words of "Yankee Doodle."

Above all, there was Philipse Castle in Tarrytown, that had been taken from its Tory owner during the Revolutionary War. What was involved here was a 25,000-acre estate whose manor house built in 1683 served as home, office and fortress to the owner. The stone walls of the house—to speak of the place in the present tense—are two feet thick, with gun ports in the cellar walls to protect the manor against river pirates. A ramp which was used to take cattle indoors to safety during raids leads to the cellar, which has a diary, a storeroom for a year's supply of food, and a kitchen with an enormous fireplace. Nearby are the slave houses, the smoke house, a mill looking over a river wharf where Philipse's ships once landed their cargoes.

Tenant farmers brought their grain to the mill, paid their rent, then made their purchases at the trading post. The typical Dutch house of the people who inhabited the region was a compact and thrifty structure that preserved the medieval flavor of their prototypes in Holland. It was generally a two-story and loft building made of stone, with an entrance stoop. Usually two rooms deep, it was crowned by a roof of low slope with deep projections front and rear. The overhang had come to be extended in such a way as to form a porch, or as later called in New York, a piazza. By whatever name, it is considered to be the origin of the American veranda or porch and marched westward into the interior of the United States, just as did the "Captain's walk" that had appeared on the roof of New England coastal homes.

Upstate New York, however, was not all Dutch, nor was the manor system confined just to the heirs of the original patroons. There was also English "lords of the manor," and one of these in the year 1800 is better known for his son than for himself. Himself was Judge William Cooper, "a testy and choleric gentleman easily wrought into passion." An old school politician of high Federalist persuasion, a vigorous, even truculent embodiment of the stake-in-society principle of statecraft, Judge Cooper was smitten with the common itch for large lands in the baronial fashion. He had founded Cooperstown in the lake region of the New York frontier. In the year 1800 he "set up" a claim to having placed the plough upon more acres than any other man in America, and in late life recalled that "there were 40,000 souls holding land, directly or indirectly under me." This was the father of America's first great novelist, James Fenimore Cooper, who received his first schooling from the rector of St. Peter's in Albany, and whose *Leatherstocking Tales,* set in part against the background of the Mohawk Valley were to earn him world-wide celebrity.

Upstate New York with its lakes, river basins and valleys, was a natural invasion route and battleground for forces moving down from or up to Canada, and one is tempted to dwell on all the fierce battles that were fought here by the French, the English, the Indians, the Revolutionary War Tories and loyalists. Two different kinds of "invasion," however, that had occurred between the end of the Revolutionary War and the year 1800, deserve at least a brief mention.

First, in the year 1792, Thomas Jefferson and James Madison of Virginia had journeyed up the Hudson River on what they called a botanizing expedition. They doubtless stopped along the way to pick a few flowers. But their real purpose was to establish contact with local political leaders in New York City and on up to Albany. It was out of this "botanizing expedition" that there was first brought into being an intersectional entente, anchored on Virginia and New York, which presently matured into what now goes by the name of the Democratic Party, the oldest political party in the world.

The second "invasion" had no comparable significance for the future of the nation. Far, far from it. Yet it has a title of right to be noticed, as the symbol of "utopian" communities of various kinds that would presently dot the backwoods areas of the United States.

The motives of the people who tried to create these utopias differed from case to case. Their form was equally varied. So was their fate. Some came into being and passed away without leaving a trace of their existence. Some, in whole or in part, survive to this day in brick and mortar—and even more so in books on political theory. Some that have survived owe their survival to the fact that they shed their ideological origins and allowed themselves to become or be absorbed by more conventionally organized communities. Others survive because the heirs of the first believers were equal to the task of re-interpreting and applying original principles to new circumstances. In any case, these experiments in forming an ideal community stand out as intriguing punctuation marks on the terrain of American history. Whether they form a story of success or failure, of great reasonableness or the occult, they deserve the dignity of being remembered.

There was, for example, the case of the Shakers, known as the United Society of Believers in Christ's Second Appearing, and as the "Millennial Church." The Shaker sect originated in England in 1747 during a Quaker revival, and its original tenet was the distinctive merit of celibacy. They did not prohibit marriage but refused to accept it as a Christian institution and considered it less perfect than the celibate state.

Under the stress of persecution and in response to a revelation, "Mother" Ann Lee who had succeeded the original founders as the head of the sect, led a band of six men and two women to America. They arrived in New York in August 1774, and after a stay there of two years, settled in the woods of Watervliet, not far from Albany. In 1780 there was a religious revival in New Lebanon, N. Y., and some of the converts became disciples of Ann Lee. At this place, in 1787, the first Shaker Society in the United States was organized; the society at Watervliet was organized immediately afterward. Ann Lee went from place to place preaching her new doctrine and became known as a faith healer. When she died in 1784 she had disciples not only in New York but in Massachusetts and Connecticut. At the time of the Kentucky revival of 1800-02, the Shaker community at Mt. Lebanon in New York sent three of its number to Kentucky to bear witness to the people. Bitterly opposed at first, these Shaker preachers made a sufficient number of converts to found five societies during that revival period. Two of the societies were in Kentucky, two in Ohio, one in Indiana.

The theological doctrine of the sect, as developed by Ann Lee before her death, was to this effect. God was both male and female: Adam having been created in the image of God had in him the nature of both sexes, Christ as he appeared in Jesus, the son of a Jewish carpenter, represented the male principle; in Ann Lee, the female principle of Christ was manifested, and in her, the promise of the Second Coming was fulfilled.

The practical ideals of the Shaker community, as expressed first in its New York settlements and extended elsewhere, were the common possession of property, a life of celibacy, confession of sin, a power over disease and separation from the world. Disease they regarded as a sin against God. Their separateness from the world was indicated in their manner of living in families of 30 to 90 individuals. Each family had its own house, the stories being divided between the men and women. They made no room for adornments in the way of pictures or other works of art. In their prescribed mode of dress for men and women they also protested against the fashions of a vain world.

For a time in New York they wove their own cloth and made their own clothing. To supplement their income they made leather in New York for several years, but were more successful in selling an odd assortment of other things: herbs and garden seeds, applesauce, Shaker-woven linen and Shaker-knitted underwear. The sect at its height (1784) was represented by 58 specially organized communities, embracing 2,415 members in all, and located in seven states. Their aggregate land holdings at the time amounted to 100,000 acres, but the number of the communities by the mid-twentieth century had dwindled to five with less than a hundred souls in all.

Though the year 1800 is being used here as a point of departure and return for everything being said, mention should be made of a post-1800 "utopian" community that took root in New York, and that reversed one of the salient tenets of the Shakers. The counterpart community in question was that of the Oneida Perfectionists.

The sect was originally founded in 1842 at Putney, Vt., by John Humphrey Noyes, a graduate of Dartmouth College. Converted at a revival he entered Yale Theological Seminary where his Bible studies convinced him that Christ came a second time in 70 A.D. and absolved Christians from the necessity of sin. Called a perfectionist, he barely escaped expulsion from the Seminary before graduation, and later was deprived of his license as a Congregational minister. He and his followers established a commune at Putney, eventually pooling all property, renouncing all religious observances and instituting "complex marriages." Monogamy was antagonistic to their earnest interest in eugenics. For they sought to make practical application of what scientific information they possessed, endeavoring by chance and experiment to produce the best possible offspring.

In 1847, when dissention brought the sect before the courts

and their theories and practices before the public, they were forced to leave Putney. They purchased near Oneida, N. Y., 600 acres of forest land which proved extremely productive. They planted orchards, lumbered, blacksmithed, farmed, made steel traps and Oneida Community silver—their most profitable industry. In January 1847, their first annual inventory revealed them to be worth about $74,000. They were mostly New England farmers and mechanics, and they had the reputation of being excellent citizens—except for their practice of "complex marriages." After 25 years of increasing public hostility on the latter point, the community at Oneida was voluntarily dissolved as a communitarian experiment and Noyes and a few of his adherents removed to Canada, known as the Oneida Community, Limited, and so passed off the stage of American history.

In the year 1800, how did the state of Delaware look at that stage? The pioneering Swedes who had settled on the Delaware River in 1638 never reached a community of more than 600 persons before they were overrun and absorbed by the British. The great migration of families to America from Sweden and the other Scandinavian countries would come in the nineteenth century. But that handful of 600 original settlers on the Delaware River is generally credited with having introduced to America a type of dwelling that marked the first stage of any settlement process where there were forests that had to be cleared before any kind of crop could be grown. The structure, of course, was the log cabin.

Delaware in 1800 had generally passed beyond the log cabin stage, but the structure known to the men and women of Sweden in their original homeland had been adopted by the pioneering Germans of Pennsylvania, and by the Scotch-Irish elsewhere. It was exactly what the pioneer needed, and it became the universal structural form in all pioneer, wood-bearing sections of the country. It was a type of dwelling that could be built of materials taken from the land in clearing it for cultivation. It could be put together with the same tool used in felling trees. It represented a combination of economy and convenience admirably adapted to the westward movement. Houses, jails, schools, churches and courthouses alike were built in this manner. When the first stage of pioneering had been passed, the early cabin of one or two rooms graduated into a log structure of one or two stories with a stone foundation and a stone or brick chimney. After clapboards became available, many houses of log cabin construction were converted to what appeared to be a frame house.

So it was in Delaware in 1800. But there was more to the picture than that. Industry had been coming to some of the states comprising the infant republic, but nowhere was it more noticeable than along the busy banks of the Brandywine Creek that ran through Delaware. The Delaware *Gazette* in 1793 reported that on Brandywine Creek fifty mills were grinding corn and wheat alone, and listed more than thirty of other types. Four of these were paper mills, which were largely responsible for a phenomenon that astonished Duc de La Rochefoucauld who was in the area at the time. "All these people busy themselves with much politics," he observed, "and from the landlord down to the housemaid, they all read two newspapers a day."

If the flour mills along the Brandywine set the price of wheat for the country, there had arrived in the United States in the year 1792 a certain gentleman from France, whose son in 1802 would lay the first cornerstone of an enterprise at Wilmington, Del., that would eventually produce more than 1,200 products.

The gentleman from France was Pierre Samuel Dupont de Nemours, one of the founders of the French school of "physiocrats," a distinguished economist, educator and political leader, a friend of Thomas Jefferson, and a man who emigrated to the United States for the first of several times after his house in Paris was sacked by a mob. His son, Eleuthère Irénée had learned to manufacture gunpowder under the renowned French chemist, Antoine Lavoisier. He had also studied the fact that explosions, along with British manufacturers, had put most American powder mills out of business. So he bought a 96-acre tract along the Brandywine and went into the gunpowder business, constructing his mills with an open wall facing the river in order to direct explosions away from the little community which lay behind the mills.

In neighboring New Jersey in the year 1800, one could see many traces of the human elements that entered into its colonization, and of the cultural and religious influences that had swept over them. There were Dutch and English settlements in New Jersey. There were enclaves of Quakers, of Congregationalists and of Presbyterians.

The site of the first Universalist Church ever built was in Ocean County, its founding date being 1779. At Brotherton (Indian Mills) was what was perhaps America's first Indian reservation, the founding date being 1785. In Trenton and in Princeton, there were two places noteworthy to Revolutionary War veterans, because it was there that George Washington's forces—previously at the end of their tether—won crucial battles that stiffened the fibre of the revolutionary cause. Princeton, too, evoked other memories of the late war. It was there that the Continental Congress was in session when it received the news that victory was won and peace had come. It was there that Washington received the formal thanks of the Congress for his leadership in the war and the place where he wrote his farewell letter to his troops.

There was a connection between these later events at Princeton and a further fact about the place. Briefly, all the principal denominations of the colonies stood in need of colleges where clergymen could be trained. The respective branches of Puritanism had their Harvard and Yale, and the Anglicans had their William and Mary in Virginia. The Presbyterians of the middle colonies wanted a college of their own to rank with these others. Different sites were experimented with in the period between 1739 and 1752, but in the latter year, the site of Princeton was selected.

While additional funds were being collected in Great Britain, work was begun in Princeton in 1754 on the first college building, Nassau Hall. Designed by Robert Smith, the architect of St. Peter's Church in Philadelphia, Nassau Hall at the time of its completion in 1756 was the largest academic building in the American colonies. The central location of New Jersey among the other colonies and the physical facilities of Nassau Hall made Princeton a logical place for the Continental Congress to sit.

But there may have been another reason which operated in the matter. Presbyterians were so much at the forefront of the agitation for independence from Great Britain that in some quarters the Revolutionary War was known as the "Presbyterian War." And on this account, perhaps, the theological center of the Presbyterians in America may have appealed to the members of the Continental Congress as a place where they 'should assemble near the end of the war. It would be pleasing to the Presbyterians of the North. It would be just as pleasing, if not more so, to the Presbyterians of the South. For the great number of young men from the South who had once come here to prepare for the Presbyterian ministry—James Madison, for example had studied theology in the school—gave Princeton a distinctly southern flavor. Indeed, it would not be entirely accidental that another Southerner, destined to be President of the United States, was chosen at the end of the nineteenth century to be Princeton's President. This was Woodrow Wilson, of Virginia, the Presbyterian son of a Presbyterian clergyman.

But to return to the year 1800. As of that time, one could see at Paterson, N. J., a "ghost town" destined to stand for many years as a monument to Alexander Hamilton's "folly"— though the ghost eventually sprang to life. The story to be told is this. As Secretary of the Treasury, Hamilton's most frequent criticism of American businessmen was, that once they had hit upon a way of making money, they tended to become timid, unadventurous and impervious to new ideas. They seemed, said he, to be mere creatures of habit, fond of following the course of least resistance in their quest for profits and dominated by "the fear of want of success in untried enterprise." Obviously, therefore, something more than his *Report on the State of Manufactures* was required to persuade businessmen to abandon "the certainties they enjoy" for "probabilities de-

pending on untried experiments." He must himself show the way by establishing not a single factory but a whole city of factories—this because he felt that manufacturing would flourish only if it were undertaken on a vastly larger scale than had hitherto been the case, and only by corporations more heavily capitalized than had yet appeared in this country.

To prove all the points he had in mind, Hamilton proposed to establish the Society for Useful Manufactures, a corporation capitalized for $1 million—a sum larger than the total assets of all the existing joint-stock manufacturing concerns in the United States. As the site for this experiment, Hamilton chose Paterson. The state itself was comparatively thickly populated, with cheap and abundant supplies of food and water power. It was rich in minerals, but without commerce or western lands to serve as distractions to factory workers. Manufacturing, therefore, could be carried out under the closest approximation of ideal conditions that were to be found in the United States. Besides, the proximity of Paterson to New York and Philadelphia was expected to attract the investment capital of these cities to the new city. In this village, Hamilton declared there was "a moral certainty of success" in the manufacture of such articles as paper, sailcloth, linen, cotton cloth, shoes, thread, stockings, pottery, ribbons, carpets, brass and ironware.

The prospectus of this million-dollar colossus among American business corporations was written by Hamilton in the late summer of 1791, and Governor William Paterson undertook to steer it through the New Jersey legislature. In due course, the corporation, known as the S. U. M., was granted the necessary charter. Further, thanks in part to the assiduous salesmanship of William Duer, the governor of S. U. M., stock to the value of $600,000 was quickly sold. Since textiles were the least advanced, the most precarious and yet, to Hamilton's mind, the most important branch of American manufactures, he felt it would be wise at first to concentrate on this particular industry. He also meant to concentrate on the introduction of the latest labor-saving machinery from Europe, and to aid the emigration of British workmen, engineers and managers to the United States.

Hamilton's plans, however, suffered a miscarriage from the beginning. It is enough to say briefly that William Duer, the governor of the S. U. M., became deeply enmeshed in wild speculative ventures. He was ruined when the country went through one of its episodic cycles of boom and bust. It was never fully known how deeply he had tipped his hand in the S. U. M. till in the course of his juggling, but he had been entrusted with $10,000 of the Society's money specifically to procure workmen and machinery from Europe, and it was believed he had "borrowed" heavily from the funds of the Society to finance his other speculations which had crashed. Duer was to spend the rest of his life in prison, the first great American speculator in stocks and bonds to do so.

The S. U. M., meanwhile, suffered from other causes. The bounties and premiums expected from the New Jersey state legislature were not forthcoming. The directors were reluctant to nurse this "infant industry" with their own funds. True, things seemed briefly to change for the better when Hamilton himself took over active direction of the S. U. M.'s affairs. He brought Major L'Enfant to lay out the "capital scene of manufactures" on the Passaic. Buildings were erected and machines installed. Skilled workers were brought in to operate the new-fangled devices. Hamilton personally inspected the sites selected for the various factories, paying special heed to the effective utilization of waterpower.

But all of Hamilton's skill and energy was to no avail. The project suffered from the Ten Plagues: lack of capital, too heavy an outlay on installation, insufficient money to cover operating expenses, frequent changes of plans, indifference wealthy men showed to manufacture in comparison with less risky forms of capital investment, the inability of the S. U. M. to bring in enough foreign artisans, the incompetence of the self-styled "experts," the inexperience most Americans had in operating power-driven machinery, their inexperience in managing the kind of industrial complex that had been created at Paterson, the decision to concentrate energy and capital upon cotton manufacture. All these proved to be ruinous.

By 1795 the heavy losses incurred by the S. U. M. led the directors to abandon the attempt to create an industrial empire in New Jersey. All operations ceased at Paterson, and the city reverted to the status of an agricultural village. The stark, untenanted buildings of the S. U. M. were in 1800, and for many years afterward, an object of curiosity to travelers. The "ghost town" was regarded as a monument to Hamilton's "ill-founded" optimism that large-scale industry could be made to thrive in the United States.

A wholly different picture presented itself in neighboring Pennsylvania. In the year 1800 few Americans would dispute the assertion that William Penn's "holy experiment" in political and religious toleration had proven itself a thumping success from every standpoint. The state, with its mixed population of English, back-country Germans and Scotch-Irish, stood before all eyes as the example of the most successful English colonization effort in the new world.

What was true of the state generally came into sharpest focus in the city of Philadelphia. It was not only the first city in the land from the standpoint of size, but it was also the first from the standpoint of urban design and the quality of life that went with it. It is true that the city had departed in some respects from Penn's original careful design. That design had called for an orderly grid pattern and the separation of homes from each other so as to reduce the hazards of fire. It had called for a series of square-shaped greens around which units of private and public structures would be grouped, with the right of access to these greens being available to all of the city's residents and not merely those whose property faced on the square. Despite any backsliding in these points of detail, Philadelphia remained a city in which the human figure was never dwarfed by either the plan or the buildings. All parts of the city could be reached comfortably on foot, and even the chief buildings were almost domestic in size. It remained a compact yet uncrowded settlement with a sharp distinction between its urban core and the surrounding rural region.

One of its structures—the Pennsylvania State House, later called "Independence Hall"—had been the stage for more great events and the echo chamber for more great voices than any other spot in America. It was here that John Hancock, following the news of Lexington and Concord, had called the Second Continental Congress to order. It was here that the Declaration of Independence was signed. It was here in 1787 that the Continental Convention was drafted and the charter signed. While a single structure like this belonged to "history," Philadelphia itself in 1800 surpassed any city of its size on either side of the Atlantic for most of the comforts and some of the elegancies of daily life.

Largely due to the efforts of Benjamin Franklin, it was well paved, partly drained, had a water-pipe system, and a model market and jail. Also due to Franklin's efforts, it was the best lit and policed city. It had America's first fire department, insurance company and circulating library. It also had an informal club which had become the American Philosophical Society in 1743—with a membership list that later included fifteen signers of the Declaration of Independence, eighteen signers of the Constitution, and still later, twelve Presidents of the United States.

In and about the city flourished industries considerable for 1800. The ironworks were already important. Paper, gunpowder, pleasure carriages and many other manufactures were produced on a larger scale than elsewhere in the Union. It was a center of national finance and its civic spirit, radiating outward over the state, accounted for more public works than to be found elsewhere. More roads and canals were being built. A new turnpike ran from Philadelphia to Lancaster, and the great highway to Pittsburgh was a more important artery of national life than was controlled by any other state.

Meanwhile, in the interior of Pennsylvania, one could find in 1800 scores of settlements by different religious sects that had originated in Germany or in other parts of central Europe. It is possible here to mention only the Moravians, otherwise known as the Church of the United Brethren. The Moravians had originated in Bohemia in the fifteenth century, but following various religious wars and persecutions, they emigrated to Saxony. Here again they were plagued by persecutions, and in 1734, a few Moravians embarked on the long journey to America. Some landed in Philadelphia; others went first to the Virgin Islands and Georgia and then made their way northward to Pennsylvania. In 1741, on a site about fifty miles northwest of Philadelphia, on the Lehigh River, work was begun on the town of Bethlehem.

All of the buildings constructed at Bethlehem apparently were located only after careful deliberation. By 1757 the settlement was a busy, thriving community, virtually self-sufficient in industrial output. A bakery, tailor shop, shoemaker, spinning and weaving establishment, grist mill, carpentry shop, blacksmith, potter, gunsmith and other crafts were all represented. Schools, dormitories for single members of the congregation, a tavern and other buildings completed the town. All residents worked under general church direction in a communal form of organization. The profits from their industrial efforts were used to help distressed brethren in other lands, in forming new settlements, and in defraying the expense of the missions for the purpose of propagating the gospel among the Indians, not only those nearby but those in distant places.

Other Moravian towns followed the initial settlement. The Pennsylvania settlements included Nazareth and Lititz. Then, after the Moravian Brethren in 1753 took possession of a tract of nearly 100,000 acres in the Piedmont region of North Carolina, the first settlers were dispatched from Pennsylvania in order to clear land for their first town and its surrounding farms. The town in North Carolina on which the colony centered at first was named Betharbara. There was also a settlement at Bethania. In due course, it was felt that a central town was needed. Many sites were examined. After a winnowing process, the names were written on "lots," one side of which was blank. Then, calling upon the Lord for assistance, the Board of Elders drew one of the "lots." In this way the site of what is now Salem, N. C., was chosen in 1766.

Salem was not intended as an agricultural village. The instructions concerning the town plan reflected the growing Moravian dissatisfaction with communal living, for the instructions warned against close buildings or tall apartments, and proposed that each family should have its own yard and garden in the rear, for the benefit of the children, yet the lots should not be so large that the settlement would sprawl. The governing aim was to develop a self-contained industrial village.

But until the village industry and handicrafts should develop, each family was to be provided with farm lots so that they could provide their own food. In Salem, as in Bethlehem and in other places, the Moravians built well. Designed for a limited population and for a closed society, but not for a close-minded society (much of the work of the great German composers reached the United States through them), Moravian towns were admirably suited for their purpose at the time of their founding. They remained so in 1800 and afterward.

THE CAROLINAS AND GEORGIA

The Carolinas had been the scene of the first effort the English had made to form a colony in the new world, the time being 1585 and the place, Roanoke. But the first efforts had failed, and nothing happened for 68 years. When something did happen, and a colony was established in 1653 on the Cowan River, in what is now North Carolina, it was the work of migratory Virginians moving southward. The event foreshadowed the way much of North Carolina and part of South Carolina would be peopled. It would be a project largely undertaken by the movement of settlers already in America.

The city of Charleston in what is now South Carolina felt some of this influence, but its origin was different. Direct colonization from England had begun in South Carolina in 1669, and a small settlement called Albemarle Point was formed a little inland from the coast near the mouth of the Ashley and Cooper Rivers. The place proved unhealthy and after 13 years of struggle, the colony was removed to a better location on the peninsula between the two rivers whose confluence, according to Charlestonians, forms the Atlantic Ocean. Here the town of Charleston was laid out on the side of the peninsula that fronted the mouth of the Cooper River. It had a clear landing area that could be made into port installations, and was accessible to settlers from outlying districts. It was easy to defend for a fort built on high ground could command the avenues of approach from both the Ashley and Cooper Rivers.

The town so situated had become by 1800 the seat of a slave-owning aristocracy that drew its wealth from rice plantations and indigo, and which made its homes among the most elegant in the United States, and its city one of the most important intellectual and commercial centers in the land.

In the case of Georgia to the south, the slave system had been slow to come to the state, and was of but limited extent in 1800. The reason went back to the circumstances under which it had been colonized.

Georgia, the last of the English colonies to be formed, owed its original existence to two factors. One was the desire of the British government to protect South Carolina from invasion by the Spaniards in Florida and by the French in Louisiana. The other was the desire of James Edward Oglethorpe, imperial philanthropist, to found a refuge for the persecuted Protestant sects and the unfortunate but worthy indigent classes in England, including those who spent much of their time in and out of debtor's prisons. A charter was granted in

1732 to "the trustees for establishing the colony of Georgia in America," and the parliament gave 10,000 pounds sterling for the enterprise. The first settlement was made at Savannah in 1733 under the personal supervision of Oglethorpe. The early colonists were English, German, Salzburgers, Piedmontese, Scottish Highlanders, Swiss, Portuguese and Jews.

The colony was successful as a defense bulwark against the Spanish, but it was a failure from an economic standpoint. The trustees had desired that the colony should grow wine grapes, hemp, silk and medicinal plants, for which England was dependent upon foreign countries. They required the settlers to plant mulberry trees, and forbade the sale of rum, a chief commercial staple of the colonies. They also forbade the introduction of Negro slaves. The industries planned for the colony did not thrive, and as sufficient labor could not be obtained, the importation of slaves was permitted in 1749. About the same time, the prohibition was removed on the sale of rum. In 1753 the charter of the trustees expired and Georgia became a royal province.

Savannah and the rest of the colony began to prosper, but the "cotton culture" that was to become its foundation had to await the arrival in Savannah in 1792 of a young man from Massachusetts who had recently graduated from Yale. His name was Eli Whitney.

Whitney, who had already shown marked mechanical abilities, had accepted an invitation to spend some time on the plantation of Mrs. Nathanael Greene, the widow of the Revolutionary War general. He was still undecided on his future course, but while mulling over what he was to do with himself, he constructed for Mrs. Greene some ingenious household devices. Mrs. Greene, enchanted, introduced him to some gentlemen who were discussing the desirability of a machine to separate the short staple upland cotton from its seeds. In a few weeks, Whitney produced a model. It consisted of a wooden cylinder encircled by rows of slender spikes set one-half inch apart, which extended from the bars of a grid set so closely together that the seeds could not pass, but the lint was pulled through the revolving spikes; a revolving brush cleaned the spikes, and the seed fell into another compartment. The machine was worked by hand and could clean fifty pounds of lint a day. Now everyone was enchanted.

Not long afterward, Whitney returned to New Haven where he formed a partnership with Phineas Miller and built at New Haven a factory for the manufacture of the cotton gin, on which a patent had been granted in March of 1794. The demand for their product was so great that they were unable to meet it and country blacksmiths entered the picture with designs of their own. Patent infringement suits promptly followed and Whitney's claim was eventually validated. But he became disgusted with the protracted legal struggle, so he built a new factory near New Haven for the manufacture of firearms, introduced into it the division of labor and the standardization of parts, and secured profitable government contracts. Thus this one man, by inventing the cotton gin, which made the growing of cotton with slave labor a highly profitable venture, and by introducing the mass production of firearms, almost single-handedly set the stage for both the spread of slavery and its climax in Civil War.

In the year 1800, however, the burning issue in Georgia was the way the federal government had just settled assorted claims rising over the "Yazoo Land Frauds." Briefly, in 1795 the Georgia legislature had granted to four land companies, for a cost of $500,000, a territory comprising what is now the whole state of Mississippi and more than half of Alabama. The following year a new state legislature rescinded the land contracts on the ground that they had been fraudulently obtained. Meanwhile, the U. S. Senate had appointed a commission to inquire into Georgia's claim to the land in question, and as this committee pronounced the claim invalid, the federal government in 1800 established a territorial government over the region. The Georgia legislature remonstrated, but could only ratify the cession.

All this while, there had been going on in North Carolina, South Carolina and Georgia a two-way population movement. From one direction, tens of thousands of English, Scottish Highlanders, Scotch-Irish and Germans had moved down from the Piedmont region of Virginia and the backwoods of Pennsylvania to occupy lands in North Carolina, South Carolina and Georgia. Here they mingled with others of their kind who came straight from England. The settlement pattern, and the different modes of economic production tended to divide these states between "slave soil" and "free soil." It also tended to divide them between a lowland with an aristocratic way of life reinforced by the strong influence of the Anglican church, and a highland with a democratic way of life reinforced by the strong influence of the Presbyterian, Baptist and Methodist churches, as well as by lesser religious denominations. In 1800, as in the immediately preceding years, neither "the party of the lowlands" nor the "party of the highlands" had been able to win a clear upper hand in the struggle between them. Nor had they been able to compromise their conflict in terms that suggested a satisfactory final solution.

There was, however, a marked similarity in the political outlook of the backcountry settlers on a line extending from Pennsylvania, Virginia, North and South Carolina and Georgia. Most of them rallied around the political standard raised by Thomas Jefferson and James Madison, who were themselves Piedmont men (though Jefferson, through his mother, a Randolph, was connected with the great households of the Virginia aristocracy).

Further, it would be hard to overstate the historic role the upland men from Virginia and the Carolinas were destined to play in the second of the two-way population movements—the expansionist drive to the west. By 1800 as has already been noted, many of these upland men, feeling the pressures of the slave-owning interests in the East, had removed themselves to the Kentucky-Tennessee triangle and formed the bulk of the 500,000 people found within it. Not all, to be sure, were "free-soilers." Some were slave-owners, and meant to carve out plantations for themselves on ground more fertile than the ground they had left behind. Some, too, were already toying with the idea of establishing a new Republic that would no longer look to the Atlantic for its commercial outlet but would look to the mouth of the Mississippi River and the whole of the north shore of the Gulf of Mexico. Others, on the other hand, being bound by family ties to both the South and the Middle Atlantic states, were among the staunchest Union men. All, however, were expansionists.

Until they were irreconcilably divided from within by the cotton-growing agriculturalists and the grain-growing agriculturalists, they were largely responsible for a salient fact in the American political dynamo until the decade before the Civil War—namely the alliance between the South and the West. The names of political leaders born in or near the Piedmont region tell part of that story. There was the future President, Andrew Jackson, born near the border between Union County, N. C., and Lancaster County, S. C., and transplanted to Tennessee. There was the future President, James K. Polk, born in Mecklenburg County, N. C., and transplanted to Tennessee. There was the future Vice President and President Andrew Johnson, born in Raleigh, N. C., and transplanted to Tennessee. There was Henry Clay, born in Hanover County, Va., and transplanted to Kentucky. There was also Thomas Hart Benton, the authentic voice of frontier democracy, and for decades the most forceful exponent of Manifest Destiny with its corollaries, a transcontinental railroad and a Homestead Act for the settlement of the West. He had been born in Hillsborough, Orange County, N. C., was transplanted to Tennessee, and replanted himself in St. Louis, Mo.

BREAKOUT FROM THE NEST

With the increase of American settlement on the western side of the Appalachians, the freedom of the Mississippi River had become of vital importance to the western settlers since it was the only way they could get their produce to a market. Spain had recognized these interests in its treaty with the United States of 1794 by guaranteeing freedom of navigation and the privilege of deposit at New Orleans. But the imminent transfer of Louisiana from a weak neighbor like Spain to a powerful and ambitious state like Napoleonic France was naturally un-welcome to the United States. Thus, after Jefferson became President, he instructed Robert R. Livingston, the U. S. Minister in Paris, to prevent the consummation of the retrocession by Spain to France of the Louisiana Territory. Failing to prevent the retrocession, Livingston was instructed to try to buy the Floridas (either from France if they passed with the transfer, or from Spain) or at least West Florida and if possible New Orleans. This would give the United States a secure position on the Mississippi River and ensure its commerce.

In his preliminary conversations at the Paris end of things, Livingston lightly suggested a cession of Louisiana to the United States in order to satisfy certain claims of American merchants for spoliations by French cruisers. He more seriously pressed a demand that France should pledge observance of the Spanish treaty concerning U. S. trade on the Mississippi. Napoleon gave that pledge. But then, during the negotiations, several things happened. For one, the Spanish governor of Louisiana suspended the U. S. Right of Deposit at New Orleans—and this fact roused great indignation in America. For another, there were reports out of London that the British meant to mount an expedition against New Orleans. Livingston turned this report to good account by pressing for a cession to the United States of West Florida, New Orleans and Louisiana north of the Arkansas River. Meanwhile, the collapse of Napoleon's American colonization schemes—as the collapse came into focus by the revolt against the French in Santo Domingo—persuaded him that he could not hold New Orleans against the British. He thus suddenly offered to Livingston the whole of the Louisiana province. At this stage, James Monroe had become associated with Livingston in the negotiations. Louisiana was thus acquired under circumstances which played hob with Jefferson's theories of government, but which he laid aside in favor of gaining a tremendous if undefined territory.

On December 20, 1803, the United States took possession of the lower part of the Province of Louisiana, and on March 9, 1804, the upper part. The entire region contained at the time possibly 80,000 residents, some Spanish, some French, and a mixed lot of fur-traders and mechanics of different nationalities. There was thus absorbed into the United States a whole new set of ethnic strains, community forms of settlement and architectural styles.

The treaty of cession required the incorporation of Louisiana into the union and the admission of its inhabitants "as soon as possible, according to the principles of the Constitution, to the enjoyment of all the rights, the advantages and immunities of the citizens of the United States." Out of the great domain that had been acquired there would be carved the states of Louisiana, Missouri, Arkansas, Iowa, North and South Dakota, Nebraska and Oklahoma in their entirety, and most of Kansas, Colorado, Wyoming, Montana and Minnesota. With good reason, Jefferson, at the time of the purchase, said:

> The addition of a country so extensive, so fertile, as Louisiana, to the great republican family of this hemisphere, while it substitutes for our neighbors, brethren and children in place of strangers, has secured the blessings of civil and religious freedom to millions yet unborn. By enlarging the empire of liberty, we multiply its auxiliaries and provide new sources for the renovation, should its principles, at any time, degenerate in those portions of our country which gave them birth.

The same acquisition gave new force and meaning to a project mounted by Jefferson even before the Louisiana Purchase was formally consummated. The project involved an expedition by Meriwether Lewis, Jefferson's private secretary, from 1801 to 1803, and Lewis's old friend and former army comrade, Lieut. William Clark, (whose older brother, George Rogers Clark had won celebrity for his Revolutionary War triumphs at Kaskaskia and other British forts).

TRAIL BLAZING

Over a preceding span of centuries, Europeans had dreamed of finding an all-water "northwest passage" to the Orient, and Columbus' accidental discovery of America was part of the effort to make the dream come true. During that same period, there had been many explorations at the Pacific end of things— including explorations by New England sea captains—to find river mouth openings on the Pacific coast that might be part of the northwest passage being sought. But the water northwest passage proved elusive, and it would never be found until a U. S. submarine, propelled by atomic energy, discovered the route under a polar icecap.

Jefferson, like other men with a curious turn of mind, had shared this interest in finding a northwest passage. But the gravitational center of his thoughts had turned on finding a route that could be traveled partly by water in the interior of the American continent, and if necessary, partly by an overland route to the Pacific. Even while serving as minister plenipotentiary to France after the Revolutionary War and before the new Constitution was adopted in the United States, he spent much time collecting Spanish, French and English maps and as much other information as was available about the interior of the North American continent. Not much information actually was available, and the little in existence was either jealously guarded by fur traders or made no clear distinctions between the place where fact ended and fantasy began. The interior of the North American continent as it appeared on maps, resembled the notations the ancient cartographers used to crowd into the margins of their charts when they had exhausted their knowledge of the known, saying "beyond this lies nothing but the sandy deserts full of wild beasts, unapproachable bogs, Scythian ice or a frozen sea."

To force darkness into light, Jefferson, while still in Paris, had worked out a plan whereby the Connecticut traveler John Ledyard was to go eastward through Siberia to the Pacific Northwest and then venture overland across North America to Virginia, but the venture was frustrated by the Empress Catherine of Russia. Back in America as Secretary of State in Washington's cabinet, Jefferson arranged for the French scientist, André Michaux, to explore the Pacific Northwest under the auspices of the American Philosophical Society. This plan likewise failed when Michaux became involved in the filibustering intrigues of the French ambassador Genet. It was not until Jefferson was inaugurated President in 1801 that he was in a position to do something about his long-standing interest. In a message to the Congress, he requested an appropriation of $2,500 to finance a "scientific" exploration of the interior of the North American continent.

The word "scientific" represented no abuse of language. But there was more to the story. A responsible statesman was not likely to forget that geographical knowledge was a necessary preliminary to economic penetration and eventual domination. Scientific knowledge was to be sought for the fur trade.

The aggressive North West Company of Montreal was expanding westward across Canada; Alexander Mackenzie had reached the Pacific in 1793 and British fur traders were already established far down into present Minnesota and the Dakotas. American trappers had to be encouraged to move into this area as an offset to the British, whose strong economic position might easily lead to the extension of their sovereignty over most of the trans-Mississippi. The best means of inducing American fur companies to enter the area was to make it profitable for them, and this in turn meant finding a better trade route than the British could command. Jefferson, in his message to the Congress, pointed out that the Canadian route along the line of lakes and rivers from Montreal to the Rocky Mountains "could bear no competition with that of the Missouri," which was shorter, offered a continuous water route without portages, and might possibly lead to the Pacific with only a short land carriage over the mountains.

Congress appropriated the necessary funds. The Lewis and Clark expedition was organized in late 1803 near St. Louis, Mo. It consisted of the two leaders, Clark's Negro servant York, plus nine young Kentuckians, 14 U. S. Army Regulars, two Frenchmen and Lewis' Newfoundland dog. On May 14, 1804, they began what turned out to be a journey of 4,000 miles, an expedition lasting two years, four months and nine days, during which they only lost one man. Many place names, like Council Bluffs, Iowa, first were named by them, and the same was true of many rivers like the Jefferson, Madison and Gallatin. What they saw, did and learned along the way, and the storehouse of information they brought back with them, stands on a plane of its own in the drama of U. S. exploration. Regretfully, it cannot be retold here. One can only repeat what Thomas Jefferson said in his report to the Congress on December 2, 1806, after the explorers were safely back in civilization:

> The expedition of Messrs. Lewis and Clarke, for exploring the river Missouri, and the best communications from that to the Pacific Ocean, has had all the success which could be expected, they have traced this Missouri nearly to its source, descended the Columbia to the Pacific Ocean, ascertained with accuracy the geography of that interesting communication across our continent, learned the character of the country, of its commerce and inhabitants: and it is but justice to say that Messrs. Lewis and Clarke and their brave companions have by this arduous service deserved well of their country.

In point of fact few men could or would follow the Lewis and Clark trail to the Pacific in the early days of expansion. For one thing, the prospect of an advance up the Missouri to the area where American fur traders might come to grips with the British, faded when the hostility of the Blackfoot Indians effectively closed the waterway. For another thing, the effort to find a commercial route over the Continental Divide and down the Columbia to the Pacific failed because of the difficulties of the terrain. Even Meriwether Lewis admitted that 340 miles of land carriage, 140 miles of it "over tremendious mountains which for 60 miles are covered with eternal snow" would be necessary along the most practicable communications across the continent by way of the Missouri and the Columbia.

But these practical difficulties were of minor consequence beside Jefferson's continental breadth of vision, and the way the Lewis and Clark expedition fired the imagination of Americans. It was a drama that embodied the future. It gave tangible substance to what had been merely an idea, and established the image of a highway across the continent so firmly in the minds of Americans that repeated failures could not shake it.

American fur traders, marching in the van, were now determined to penetrate the northern Rockies. They were finally to succeed in 1826 when Jedediah Strong Smith led a party through the Platte Valley and over South Pass, across "Great Shining Mountains." Even so, for the next two decades American trappers would be worsted in their struggle with the British for economic domination of the Northwest. They were fighting the greatest mercantile empire in the world, and after 1821 they faced in the Hudson Bay Company (which had absorbed the North West Company) an adversary enjoying the advantages of vigorous government support as well as the practical experience of more than two centuries of British-chartered trading companies.

As long as the contest for Oregon remained in the stage of imperial rivalry based on the fur trade, the British would remain impregnable. On the other hand, the discovery by Jedediah Strong Smith of the overland route that was to become the Oregon Trail had an ultimate consequence of far greater moment than the fur trade. When the frontier farmer looking longingly for free land learned that he could take his family all the way to the Pacific with no more equipment than his rifle, his wagon and his livestock, new energies would be thrown into the contest against Britain in the Northwest. Beyond the South Pass there would be the Mormon Trail, the Oregon Trail and the California Trail. Within five years after the first significant migration of American settlers to the Willamette Valley the Hudson Bay Company would give up and quit, and the Treaty of 1846, establishing the boundary where it is now at the forty-ninth parallel, would merely record officially the fact that the American agricultural frontier had been pushed to Oregon.

CONSOLIDATIONS

Though the Louisiana purchase had added an empire for liberty to America's dominions, an advance onto it was fiercely contested by Indians even in territories lying in the eastern side of the Mississippi that were already part of the United States.

Trouble with Great Britain on the high seas during the Napoleonic Wars triggered trouble with the British and their Indian allies on the western frontier, and with the Spanish in the Floridas who were using the Indians to play a game of their own. The result was a great Indian uprising known as Tecumseh's Uprising. It extended from the Great Lakes all the way down to Alabama, and its opening shots at Tippecanoe were fired *before* Great Britain and the United States clashed head-on in the War of 1812. Within the interior of the United States, Tecumseh's Uprising became a war within a war. It was ended in the North by American victories on the Great Lakes and the death of Tecumseh in the Battle of the Thames. It was ended in the South when the so-called Creek War was won by frontiersmen led by Andrew Jackson who crushed the Creeks and their allies in their final stand at Horseshoe Bend in Alabama.

The treaty of peace following the War of 1812, the forceable removal of the Indian Tribes on the western frontier to their lands, the end of the Napoleonic Wars in Europe, all combined to two effects. They now made possible a swift American advance westward, and they now provided population feeder lines from Europe to the United States.

TIDAL WAVES

There had been an inflow of not more than 250,000 people from Europe in the 25-year period from the ratification of the Constitution to the close of the War of 1812 and the end of the Napoleonic Wars. But now, the totals began to shoot up, reaching half-a-million in the 1830's, over a million-and-a-half in the 'forties and two-and-a-half in the 'fifties. The bulk of the immigrants consisted of Germans and Irish, but appreciable contingents of English, French, Scots, Swiss and Scandinavians accompanied them. These stocks, though now mixed in altered proportions, were still pretty much the same as in earlier times.

The Germans, fleeing from bad crops, avaricious landlords and bad politics, furnished one-and-a-half million in the period of 1830-60. The majority settled in the Middle West. They gave Cincinnati its German character and pioneered in the newer parts of Ohio. They took up the hardwood lands of Wisconsin along Lake Michigan, making a capital of Milwaukee. They went in sizeable bands to Indiana, Michigan, Illinois, Missouri and the river towns of Iowa. Some even colonized in Texas on the eve of its annexation, and after the Mexican War. The group contained a high percentage of educated and forceful leaders, who contributed signally to the spiritual and educational progress of their communities. In the face of the general disapproval of the native-born, the Germans also introduced a saving element of sociability with their singing societies, gymnastic clubs and beer gardens.

The Irish arrived in even greater numbers, totalling nearly two million in the decades between 1830-60. Over half migrated after the potato famine in 1846 and later years. Originating in the central and southern parts of the island, they were peasants by occupation and Roman Catholics by religion. In unfamiliar surroundings they preferred urban jobs to farming, in order to be both near their kin and near their priests. Many, hard-pressed for cash, sought work in construction camps, for these were the years of new modes of transportation—canals and especially railroads—being hurriedly built to meet the expanding needs of industry and trade. One such migrant, from County Cavan, settled at Somerset in Ohio, where his son grew up to become General "Phil" Sheridan, the leader of Union cavalry in the Civil War.

The congested life in the Irish quarters of eastern cities excited the pity and dismay of the older residents. Those who were dismayed bitterly attacked the Irish as being the agents of a "foreign conspiracy" against the United States. The dismayed, furthermore, who saw Catholic churches, schools, convents, priests and nuns appear on the horizon for the first time, reacted violently by organizing militant secret societies. Mobs attacked religious edifices, the wildest rumors of "Popish" plots were believed by otherwise sensible men. Out of all this hubbub, the "Know Nothing" movement was born as the political striking arm of "nativists" who were anti-Catholic and anti-foreign-born.

Those who pitied what they saw among the impoverished Irish living in hopeless squalor in eastern cities gave impetus to the many humanitarian movements that marked the times—temperance, public education and labor reforms. There was, as well, a very considerable attempt by Roman Catholics in England, Ireland and on the continent to provide transportation for the Irish Catholic immigrant and large tracts of land for the establishment of farming communities in America. A considerable number of such Catholic colonies were established although few survived. Closely ruled, paternalistic communities were not suited to the twin standards of democracy and individualism which ruled the American west, and the religious bond was not enough to hold the communities together.

The one great exception to this settlement effort had to await the enactment of the Homestead Act during the Civil War, the railroad building boom in the west after the war, and the presence of a man "with enough idealism to render him impervious to the previous failures and enough realism to enable him to find a way for industrious immigrants to earn a fair living from the hard ground of the west." The man was John Ireland, Bishop Coadjutor of St. Paul, who would never tire of reminding urban Catholics that "man made the city but God made the country." Between 1876 and 1881 he would establish in five counties of western Minnesota, ten rural villages and farming communities—De Graff, Clontarf, Graceville, Minneota, Ghent, Currie, Avoca, Iona, Fulda and Adrian. In most of these colonies the land would be furnished by land-grant railroads, and Bishop Ireland himself would be named a land agency by five railroads who understood that it was possible for good citizens to be at the same time good Church members and frequent railroad patrons. The settlers themselves, while Irish in the main, would include Catholics from England, Belgium, Germany and French Canada. Out of this experience, its trials and triumphs, Bishop Ireland would leave a deep imprint on Roman Catholicism throughout the northern frontier, and would teach American Catholics everywhere the means by which the Catholic Church in America could be both an agency of Americanization and custodian of the faith.

NEW UTOPIAS

The westward advance after the end of the War of 1812 and the Napoleonic Wars, coincided with an intensification of the industrial revolution in Europe, and with the first serious human encounters with the industrialization process in the United States. American and European political theorists alike had begun to evolve what they hoped would be plans for a better ordering of society under the impact of the machine. The plans differed from each other in points of detail. But all had a common element in that they tried to reformulate the terms of man's relationship to his environment, to his modes of production, and to the basic units of society. Besides, there were groups of men and women who were prepared to join an effort to live by such plans in newly-formed "utopian communities."

There were also lands available—for purchase for a relatively small price—where such communities could be formed on American soil.

One of these efforts was an extension of the thinking of the English industrialist and social reformer, Robert Owen, and was financed in good part by him on a site in Indiana that had previously been cleared and settled by the Harmonists. The latter, a German sect devoted to the coming of the Millenium, were followers of Father George Rapp and his son. They had first come to America from the Würtemberg area of Germany in 1803. They acquired 5,000 acres about 25 miles north of Pittsburgh. Here they founded the town of Harmonie, named after the Harmonist Society of which they were members. The location was not found to their liking and a move was in order.

Some 30,000 acres were purchased in Posey County, Ind., and by the summer of 1815 the entire colony moved to the new location on the banks of the Wabash River, to which they gave the name New Harmony.

Their buildings were well constructed of squared logs and later of brick. The Harmonists developed a system of standard sizes of framing members and lumber, identified by number. When they built a house they drew upon a common warehouse what they needed of each size. They insulated floors and walls so well with a kind of packing material of clay, straw and wood subsequently known to outsiders as "Dutch biscuits," that their houses were warm in winter and cool in summer.

The community prospered in Indiana. Their grain grew well, their vineyards flourished; they made pottery; manufactured cloth and wallpaper; their fine felt hats and other goods found a wide market; and a brewery and two distilleries provided beer for themselves and whiskey for sale—far away from New Harmony.

For a variety of reasons which need not be gone into here, the Harmonists, despite their success in Indiana, decided to return to Pennsylvania in 1824. There they built their third and most elaborate town, Economy, north of Pittsburgh. It still survives within the modern industrial bridge-building city of Ambridge and is administered by the Pennsylvania Historical and Museum Commission.

But before leaving, they had a buyer for New Harmony in the person of Robert Owen, a successful industrialist of New Lanark, Scotland; probably the most notable philanthropist and reformer mid-nineteenth century England produced. Owen among other strands of thought he had produced, had pointed out that the general misery and stagnation of trade in Europe resulting from the end of the Napoleonic Wars was to be found in the competition of human labor with new machinery. Hence the only effective remedy was the united action of men, and the subordination of machinery to men.

To put his ideas to the test, he came to America and used a substantial part of his fortune to buy New Harmony in 1824 from Father Rapp and his followers. The rich and developed farm lands of the Harmonists, their mills, distilleries, manufactories and orderly town of sturdy log, frame and brick buildings offered a ready-made setting for a new social order.

By the spring and summer of 1825 some 900 colonists had arrived. His son, Robert Dale Owen, later described them as a "heterogenous collection of radicals, enthusiastic devotees to principle, honest latitudinarians, and lazy theorists, with a sprinkling of unprincipled sharpers thrown in."

The enthusiastic devotees included a brilliant galaxy of scientists, educators, artists and social reformers from Europe and the older cities of the United States. They included Dr. William Maclure, geologist; Thomas Say, zoologist; Charles Alexander Leseur, painted-naturalist; and Constantine Rafinesque, naturalist. Madame Fretageot, Phiquepal, d'Arusmont, Frances Wright and Joseph Neef led a group of educational reformers who forwarded a Pestallozzian method of education.

After contributing four-fifths of his personal fortune to this experiment Owen withdrew from the hurly-burly and dissensions that developed and gave his share in the noble experiment to those who wished to remain and carry it forward. In many ways called a failure, it is now acknowledged that these "impractical idealists" pushed forward the frontiers of scientific knowledge, and many of their wildest dreams are the firm foundations upon which most of today's social and educational philosophy are erected.

From this small community came the program which resulted in the first geological survey of the United States. Its leader David Dale Owen was also one of those responsible for chartering that great organization for the diffusion of useful knowledge, The Smithsonian Institution.

From this yeasty soil on the banks of the Wabash there was a continuing ferment of ideas. Among all the backwoods Utopias that dot the United States this is the first community of its type to be named a National Registered Landmark, and one of thirteen to date in this category. It was named in the broad thematic group of "Social and Humanitarian Movements." It could have been honored as well in "Scientific Discoveries and Inventions."

In August 1965 Secretary Udall gave the bronze plaque to New Harmony at ceremonies fittingly attended by the present head of the Smithsonian Institution S. Dillon Ripley, Governor Roger Branigin of Indiana, Congressman Winfield K. Denton, state and local officials, descendants of the Owen family and other townspeople who have organized an active New Harmonie Associates.

The bronze plaque was placed on a brick wall near a town bench at the intersection of Church and Main Streets. Above it is a limestone tablet quoting the words of Robert Owen, still optimistic in his disappointment: *If we cannot reconcile all opinions let us endeavor to unite all hearts.*

Not far from this intersection stands The Roofless Church, a testament to yet another movement that has taken place in this incredible little town. It was designed by Philip Johnson, FAIA, and features a bronze sculpture "Descent of the Holy Spirit" by Jacques Lipschitz who also designed its great ornamental gates. Its name was inspired by George Sand who once remarked only one roof—the sky—is vast enough to hold all worshipping humanity. It was erected by the Robert Lee Blaffer Trust and around it in garden settings are some reassembled and adapted Harmonist houses for the educational and religious activities of their program.

Nearby is the Paul Tillich Park, named for the eminent German-born theologian who loved the natural beauty of this Indiana countryside, and its long tradition of spiritual and intellectual challenge. His ashes will be placed there and by his special wish some linden trees will be added to the native growth.

In a compilation of his sermons *The Shaking of the Foundations* he lamented man's increasing alienation from nature. It is in this setting that he raises the question of whether communion between man and nature is possible in our time:

> Is nature not completely subject to the will and wilfulness of man? This technical civilization, the pride of mankind, has brought about a tremendous devastation of original nature, of the land, of animals, of plants. It has kept genuine nature in small reservations and has occupied everything for domination and ruthless exploitation. And worse: many of us have lost the ability to live with nature. We fill it with the noise of empty talk, instead of listening to its many voices, and, through them, to the voiceless music of the universe. Separated from the soil by a machine we speed through nature, catching glimpses of it, but never comprehending its greatness or feeling its power. . . .

In addition to Owen's efforts there were a string of Utopian experiments stretching straight across the continent from Massachusetts to Texas and California, all owing their inspirational source to the theories of François Marie Charles Fourier.

It was Fourier's conviction that the existing organization of society imposed innumerable restrictions upon the free development of human desires. Misery and vice were the consequence of these unnatural restraints. Society therefore had to be reconstructed in order to restore to the individual the natural harmony within his spirit that had been taken away from him. Only so could full scope be given to his natural will to cooperate with his fellow man to the harmonious evolution of human nature.

Society, on Fourier's scheme, was to be divided into departments or *phalanges,* each phalange numbering about 1,600 persons. Each phalange could inhabit a *phalanstère* or common building, and would have a certain portion of soil allotted to it for cultivation. The phalanstères would be built after a uniform plan and the domestic arrangements would be laid down in detail. The stable industry would be agriculture but the various *series* or groups into which the members were divided, could devote themselves to such occupations as were more to their taste, nor need any occupation become irksome from constant devotion to it. Any member of a group could vary his employment at pleasure and could pass from one task to another. The task regarded as menial or degrading in ordinary society would be rendered attractive if advantage were taken of the proper principles of human nature.

It was not necessary that private property be abolished, nor was the privacy of family life to be denied. Each family could live in separate apartments and there could be richer or poorer members. But the rich and the poor would be locally intermingled in order that the broad distinction between them might become almost imperceptible.

Fourier's ideas were introduced into the United States by his disciple, Albert Brisbane, the father of Arthur Brisbane who was to win fame as a great editor and columnist for the chain of newspapers William Randolph Hearst was to build.

The first fruits of the elder Brisbane's influence was the formation in 1841 at West Roxbury, Mass., of an institute of agriculture and education known as Brook Farm. Its leader was the Reverend George Ripley, a former Unitarian minister, who edited *The Dial,* a critical literary monthly to which the leading intellectuals of New England were contributors. Many of the same contributors were either members of the Brook Farm experiment, shareholders in it or keenly interested visitors. The list included Nathaniel Hawthorne, Ralph Waldo Emerson, Charles A. Dana, Theodore Parker, Orestes A. Bronson and William Henry Channing.

It was their desire to combine the thinker and the worker, to guarantee the highest mental freedom, to prepare a society of liberal, intelligent and cultivated persons whose relations with each other would permit a more wholesome and simple life than could be led amid the pressure of competitive institutions. There was no religious creed. Truth, justice and order were the governing principles. Each individual was free insofar as he did not violate the rights of others. Nor was the community confined to intellectuals. Included in it were carpenters, shoemakers and printers as well. Everyone was paid a dollar a day for his mental or physical work, and all the necessities of life were provided to the members at close to actual costs. Many experiments in the education of the young, now called "modern" were first tried out here.

For a while, it looked as though the ideal of the founders

would have something of a practical realization. But a series of mishaps afflicted it and though the colony struggled on for a while, "the enterprise faded, flickered, died down and expired." The land and its buildings were sold at auction on April 13, 1849. This, however, did not mean the end of experiments based on theories of Fourier. The latter had another disciple in the person of Victor Prosper Considerant who arrived in the United States after the French Revolution of 1848. There were the vast new lands of Texas available for settlement, and it was at San Antonio that Considerant formed his short-lived communitarian colony of La Réunion.

It remains to be said further that Texas was not limited to the role of an experimental ground for just the disciples of Fourier. Robert Owen also had his disciples and despite failures at New Harmony they were of a mind to prove his theories right.

One of these disciples was Etienne Cabet who evolved in France certain theories on progressive taxation, on compulsion to work, old age pensions and the division of the products of industry. These he set forth in a book called *Voyage en Icarie*. Then like Owen and encouraged by him, he bought a tract of land on the Red River in Texas and drew up a scheme for the intended colony, community property being the distinctive principle of society.

In 1848 an expedition of 1,500 "Icarians" sailed to America. But unexpected difficulties arose on the Texas site and the complaints of the disenchanted settlers soon reached Europe. Cabet went out in 1849, but on his arrival, finding that the Mormons had been expelled from their city Nauvoo in Illinois, he transferred his settlement there. He remained there as the dictator of his little society until dissensions arose. So now, with about 200 members of the community, Cabet left Nauvoo to form a new settlement of Icaria near St. Louis, Mo. Still other Icarias sprang up afterward in California, but none survived along the lines Cabet said they should. To offset all these failures in Utopian Socialism there was the case of the Mormons. Here were a group of people, adherents to a native-born religion, who combined in their practices certain elements of socialistic economic planning for production and distribution, and who triumphed in the end over every adversity.

Their story began in 1827 on a hill near Palmyra, N.Y., where Joseph Smith said he had found the golden tablets inscribed with sacred writing. There years later, Smith and the members of the church he founded were forced by the hostility of their neighbors to start a trek that was to continue for 16 years across the continent. It was a trail marked by bloodshed, hatred and hardship without parallel in American history. Joseph Smith was only one of the many who died along the way.

The first Mormon settlement in the west was made at Kirttand, Ohio. Here they were left in peace until 1838 when they were forced to move on, this time to Independence, Mo. Soon the mobs were at their heels again. The Governor announced they must be driven from the state and they headed east to Commerce, Ill., renamed Nauvoo. By 1841 they had built a prosperous city of 15,000 on the Mississippi banks. That year trouble struck up again. Joseph Smith and his brother Hyrum were taken to jail in Carthage and killed by a mob. But eight years before he died, he had a prophecy to make that was to be confirmed when the Civil War broke out in the United States. As Brigham Young recalled for the benefit of a great Salt Lake Congregation three weeks before Fort Sumpter was fired on:

> I heard Joseph Smith say nearly thirty years ago, they shall have mobbings to their hearts' content, if they do not redress the wrongs to the Latter-Day Saints. Mobs will not decrease but will increase until the whole Government becomes a mob, and eventually it will be state against state, city against city, neighborhood against neighborhood, Methodist against Methodist, and so on. It will be Christian against Christian and man against man; and those who will not take up the sword against their neighbors, must needs flee to Zion.

After the murder of Joseph Smith and his brother the other Mormons had to decide whether they should stand or flee. One leader, James Jesse Strang, took a group north to Voree, Wis., and then on to Beaver Island, Mich. Most of the people, however, decided to follow 43-year-old Brigham Young who felt that the only place the Mormons could find repose was in an isolated, untainted spot far beyond civilization. From John C. Frémont's account of his 1842 expedition, Young knew that such a place existed beside Great Salt Lake.

Beginning late in 1845 the Mormons began preparations for their migration, and early in February of the following year the first band set out across the Mississippi to Iowa where they established Camp of Israel, the first of many way stations along the route. Party by party left Nauvoo and by June of 1846 the place was deserted. Brigham Young and a group of pioneers went ahead, establishing way stations like Garden Grove and Mount Pisgah in Iowa. By the time the last covered wagon and handcart had left Nauvoo, Young was at his winter quarters in Missouri. Here where winter food and fuel proved scarce, 600 persons died of a plague. But on April 9, 1847, Young and his pioneer band set off once again. Beyond the South Pass they met Jim Bridger who directed them across the Wasatch Mountains and the red-walled cliffs of Echo Canyon. Finally, as Emigration Canyon broadened, they caught sight of the land Brigham Young had promised them. "This is the place," he said. But the brethren could see little to confirm the words of the great hymn that had been composed by one of their number en route:

> Come, come ye saints. . . .
> All is well! All is well!

The site chosen, where Salt Lake City now stands, was "a broad barren plain hemmed in by mountains, blistering in the burning rays of the midsummer sun. No waving fields, no swaying forest, no verdant meadows, but on all sides a seemingly interminable waste of sagebrush." What they could not have known at the time, they presently learned. It was, that while they had meant to get out of the United States, the "place" in Utah had put them astride the highroad of empire. The overland rush for newly-discoverd California gold, begun two years after the Mormons settled in their new home, rushed past their doors. By 1860 the pony express was operating through Great Salt Lake City and it was not long before rail connections farther east at Omaha, Neb., brought the Atlantic seaboard within a week's trip. In 1869 Ogden, Utah, was the place where a gold spike was driven into a railroad tie to signal the junction between the Union Pacific and the Central Pacific, thus completing the first transcontinental railroad system in the United States.

Of equal importance in the history of the entire region, in the 1860's a sceptical Mormon church fined one of its members for what it thought was a false boast. The member had alleged in court that he had produced a wheat crop without irrigation. For this he was charged and convicted as a perjurer. But he had his revenge. When the church leaders got a second look at his flourishing wheat field, the sign that greeted them said "Perjury Farm." He had introduced "dry" farming to a region thought impossible for wheat.

In a drive for self-sufficiency, the central planning agency of the Mormon Church decided what "missions" should be launched: how many Welsh coal miners, for instance, needed conversion so as to develop Utah coal deposits; or how many men should be sent to "Dixie"—the southern Utah counties, to experiment in cotton planting. The planners thus kept the population in a constant state of ferment by "calling" men from one place to break new lands in a second place and then in a third. The internal discipline was strong and the external pressure was great. On being "called" men spat and swore and scratched their heads in wonderment, but in the end they generally went where they were told to go. Moreover, they were of a hardy breed whose talents are best illustrated in the story of Mrs. M. L. Ensign. In 1858 she had been left behind with but twenty pounds of flour while her husband was sent on a mission. What happend next is in Mrs. Ensign's words:

> After my husband left, an Indian came to me with a nice buffalo robe which he wanted to trade . . . for old clothes and a brass kettle. Soon thereafter, another Indian traded me a pony for the robe. I sold the pony for a yoke of small oxen and 300 pounds of flour. Immigrants soon came along and traded me a yoke of large oxen, which were very poor, for my oxen, which were fat. The poor oxen became fat on our meadows and I sold them for $110 in cash, thus . . . from a few old clothes and a brass kettle I soon realized $110 in cash and 300 pounds of flour.

Shrewdness was needed in other matters as well. A settlement had been made at Huntsville and to gain a temporary source of water, a ditch had been dug to the South Fork of the Ogden River. This displeased the Indians of the neighborhood and they ordered the settlers to leave the valley or there would be trouble. Captain Jefferson Hunt, the founder of the settlement, replied to the Indians that if they carried out their threats against his new community he'd burn all the water in the canyons. To prove that he could do this he plunged a dipper into a pail of colorless liquid—it must have been alcohol—and ignited it. The record reads: "The Indians resumed friendly relations."

Still other talents were found in Ogden. Here dwelt the son of Jonathan Browning, the mechanic and gunsmith whose shop in Nauvoo, Ill., built many of the wagons and manufactured many of the firearms the Mormons used when they crossed the plains. The son, John Moses Browning, had won local fame at the age of 19 for his skill in producing firearms from pieces of scrap metal. He went on from there to invent innumerable automatic weapons known throughout the world both to sportsmen in peacetime and to soldiers in war.

On the sweeter side of things, there was the formation in a Mormon setting of the Lehigh Sugar Factory, one of the first in the United States that successfully made sugar out of sugar beets. Since the beginning of the Utah settlement the search for a local means to make sugar had been carried on with great zeal for reasons best stated in a study in logistics and dietetics as the First Presidency of the church proclaimed it in 1850:

> Sugar is not only a beverage, a Luxery, but it is, in its nature and substance, one of the component parts of our animal structure; and a free use thereof is calculated to promote health; and could the Saints have a more abundant supply, they would need less meat. Should every person in Deseret [the name the territory gave itself] consume one-third of an ounce of sugar per day through the coming year, it would require about one hundred and twenty tons, more than has been or will be brought in by our merchants this season; and according to the best estimate we can make, three hundred tons would be consumed in this State the next year, if it could be obtained.

When the earliest ventures by capital provided mostly by a French convert to Mormonism led to bankruptcy, the Mormon Church by arrangement took over the sugar-factory machinery the convert had bought in France. If the sugar venture could be made to succeed, then the currency drained off to the East in payment for sugar bought there would remain at home. However, the Church did no better in managing the machinery for the processing of sugar. The reason was that the French companies who had with great charm sold the machinery less charmingly kept the facts of sugar chemistry and controls to themselves. But the hope for a factory continued, and were finally realized—thanks to the efforts of David Eccles, the father of Marriner Eccles who was to become the head of the Federal Reserve Board in 1935 and one of the "fathers" of modern public finance.

BALLOONS IN THE WIND

The penetration of the Great Plains brought the westward-moving immigrant into regions where there were no trees or where trees were scarce, and this in turn imposed sharp limitations on the construction of their first homes. In a second direction, it made the community facilities that sprang up—the "hotel"—the refuge and resting place of the immigrant until he could get settled. Hotel life might be derided for its seamy side, but it had its defenders who looked to it as the symbol of the fluidity of dynamic America, as a place where caste walls were broken, and where a sense of fellowship was invigorated.

Meanwhile, many of the first private dwellings on the great plains were made out of sod, and a few of these "soddies" still remain. The sod "blocks" were generally two feet long, 18 inches wide and four inches thick. They were cut out with a spade and laid in a wall much like bricks and held together with wooden stakes driven through two or more courses. For a roof, the pioneer generally had to content himself with a covering of turf or straw.

But even when a community took root the lack of traditional skills in wood construction and the shortage of wood itself led to a revolutionary change in the way of building houses. The great innovation—the balloon frame—is still known by the derisive name first given it, as if to contrast its flimsiness with the craft-hewn heaviness of the traditional house. It was, indeed, ridiculously light and respectable builders prophesied that the first strong wind would surely blow it away. Yet without the balloon frame it would have been impossible for so many villages and cities to spring up so suddenly where nothing had existed before.

The balloon frame first appeared in Chicago in 1833, and within twenty years prevailed in the American urban West. It was made possible by the revolutionary advances in nail manufacturing which had been accomplished mostly in New England before 1830. The old craft of making the head of each nail by hand had been replaced by an American system of manufacturing which, by mechanizing the process, produced nails quickly and cheaply. With this revolution in being, the balloon frame followed next. It was nothing more than the substitution of a light frame of two-by-fours held together by nails in place of the old foot-square beams joined by mortise, tenon and pegs. The wall plates, studs, floor joists and roof rafters were all made of thin-sawed timbers, nailed together in such a way that every strain went in the direction of the fiber of the wood. "Basket-frame" was the name sometimes given it, because the light timbers formed a simple basket-like cage to which any desired material could be applied inside and out. Usually light board or clapboard covered the outside.

One of the byproducts of this kind of construction—about two-thirds of the houses in the United States are built this way today—was that the balloon frame could easily be taken apart and put back together. Its light parts could be piled compactly and conveniently transported, and reconstructed on a new site. This was well suited to Americans on the move. They could either take their houses along or ship them ahead, or they could order by mail for shipment to farms and cities in the west, standardized prefabricated houses, churches and even hotels. By 1850 in New York alone some 5000 such prefabs had been made or were under contract to relieve the housing shortage in California. One concern there shipped 100 portable wooden houses to be carried on pack mules across the Isthmus of Panama, and another 175 went all the way by sea around the Horn. "To lay out and frame a building (of traditional design) so that all its parts would come together," observed a certain influential Chicago writer in 1855, "requires the skill of a master mechanic, and a host of men and a deal of hard work to lift the great sticks of timber into position. To erect a balloon-building requires about as much mechanical skill as it does to build a board fence."

MIXMASTER

The Civil War had sharply curtailed the inflow of immigrants to the United States. But then, after Appomattox, the historic process resumed its course at a seemingly geometric rate of increase.

One of the reasons stemmed from the great railroad-building boom throughout the West in the decades immediately after the war. People were needed to make the ventures profitable, so now, railroad agents went to work in Europe organizing mass migrations of settlers for lands near the railroads. The railroads had acquired vast tracts of land as a direct gift from the federal government, and these could now be resold for a small sum or given outright to the new settlers. Besides, under the Homestead Act passed during the Civil War—after the slave-owning South had previously opposed it (and this broke the historic tie between the South and the West)—sections of land could freely pass to settlers who undertook to bring the land under cultivation.

There were many abuses in the distribution of land by the railroad agents and the Homestead land agents. People were settled in places which should never have been brought under strip-crop cultivation, but should have remained as range territory for a livestock industry. Further, once on the land the settlers were subject to razor-edged financing, tight-fisted foreclosure systems, and cruel monopoly practices by the railroads in league with the owners of grain elevators and flour mills. Untold personal family and community tragedies marked the whole of the settlement effort on new lands, yet the influx of immigrants continued.

Then, thanks to the increasing number of Norwegians, Swedes and Danes, following the Germans, Irish and English in that order, the upper Mississippi Valley seemed about to become a new Scandinavia of industrious and thrifty farmers, law-abiding citizens and highly literate citizens. It was at this time, too, that the French-Canadians entered New England in force. Though fewer than the newcomers from Europe, these folk—actually more French than Canadian—thronged into the mill towns and augmented the Catholic character of what had once been a Puritan citadel.

Just as the railroad building boom had as its corollary the settlement of the upper Mississippi Valley by railroad and their allied shipping companies who prepaid the passage of European farmers to new regions, American industrialists who were putting together giant trusts needed laborers to work the new mines that were being opened, the new steel mills that were being built, and the new mass-production consumer industries that had come into being. So now the industrialists sent their own agents to Europe to gather together and to prepay the passage to the United States of a labor force that was ready to work for a pittance. Overcrowded conditions at home, the immobility of labor and the persecution of Poles, Czechs, Jews and other minorities for political or religious reasons provided the motive behind the move of the laborers themselves.

In consequence, the previous migration from northern Europe was overtaken by the rising flood from eastern and southern Europe. Many of the new expatriates, like the Irish before them, congregated in mining and mill towns or in the growing cities, where their biceps were in demand and they could dwell in colonies. Many an American metropolis thus became a city of cities—a Polish city, a Czech city, a Sicilian city, a Slovak city, a Lithuanian city, a Greek city, and because of Jews arriving from Eastern Europe, a Russian city. All lived cheek-to-jowl within themselves and with each of the other groups. Where the log cabin had been the symbol of the agricultural frontier, that ran parallel to the earth since the first discovery of America, the tenement house became the symbol of the vertical frontier of an industrialized and urban America. At the Pacific end of things, there was an analogue in the presence of the destitute strangers who since the mid-nineteenth century had been swarming across the Pacific from China. Immigration restrictions and exclusion acts were now in the wind, and though the outbreak of the first World War in 1914 of its own accord served to curtail immigration from abroad, the United States began to close its historic open-door policy that gave poignant meaning to the Statue of Liberty's brave invitation to the Old World:

> Give me your tired, your poor
> Your huddled masses yearning to be free.

A CONGREGATION OF TRADITIONS

Each turn in American history prior to 1914 had its own distinctive architectural style, expressed locally by the type of people who settled a particular region. There was, before the Revolutionary War, a Feudal Style and a Georgian Style. Then with the winning of independence, there was a Federal Style which predominated until the first decades of the nineteenth century. French styles of construction and design had been incorporated into the American building psyche with the acquisition of the Louisiana Territory. Spanish styles had been incorporated with the acquisition of the Floridas, and then, by remote control, the acquisition of Texas, California and the Southwest before and immediately after the Mexican War.

Cutting across this last, and leaving frontier experiences out of account, a "Greek revival" had set in around 1820. This was partly due to a new literary interest in ancient Greece and to the struggle of the contemporary Greeks for independence from Turkey. It was also due to the fact that the southern plantation owner was beginning to think of establishing a new-style "democracy" based on slavery but in imitation of the ancient Greek city-state of Athens.

Benjamin Henry Latrobe is generally credited with having begun the Greek revival in the United States among architects, and his designs were widely imitated in one or another way. To be sure, American builders knew little about classic Greek construction. But they nonetheless achieved classic forms by copying them from building handbooks which circulated widely. The results were temple-like structures of stone, brick and often of wood, all erected to serve as residences, churches and public buildings.

Latrobe, too, is sometimes credited with introducing into America not only the Greek revival but also the Gothic revival. Christ Church in Washington, D. C., done in the Gothic style was his work. So was St. Paul's Church at Alexandria, Virginia. The style reappeared in Trinity Church, the design of Richard M. Upjohn in New York City. So, too, in the case of St. Patrick's Cathedral and Grace Church by James Renwick in New York City.

But after the Civil War the "Gilded Age" which embraced a new class of financial and industrial barons seemed made to order for a "French Rennaissance" introduced to America by Richard Morris Hunt. Its distinctive architectural features, based on Hunt's study of French chateau architecture, was a building bristling with towers, turrets and mansard roofs. Another variant was introduced into America by Henry H. Richardson after he returned to Boston from a time of study in Paris. Using time-honored Romanesque monuments of southern France and northern Spain as models, he designed robust stone structures of picturesque mass and romantic interest.

Another "culture carrier" was Charles F. McKim who returned from study abroad to enter a three-year tenure in Richardson's office. In 1879 he joined with Stanford White to form the architectural firm of McKim, Meade and White. He rejected the popular Romanesque and practiced a variety of refined classic designs based on French versions of Roman grandeur. Through him, and the influence of the snow-white buildings of the Chicago World's Fair in 1893, the nation came to welcome designs of classic purity for its schools, courthouses, libraries and other public structures.

The architectural profession became unified nationally at this time and began to exert an important role in American culture. The profession, at the time, however, tended to place too much emphasis on style as such, rather than on the functional solution of a building's problem. Into this situation stepped Louis Sullivan in partnership with Dankmar Adler. Sullivan taught the philosophy that architectural form should follow function and he converted to this doctrine of architectural independence a group of brilliant young architects who had been attracted to Chicago by the rebuilding that was needed following the disastrous Chicago fire. It was a group that included Frank Lloyd Wright, Dwight Perkins, George Grant Elmslie, Irving K. Pond, Hugh Garden, George Maher, Max Dunning, Walter Griffin and other modernists known as "the Chicago school." Their distinctive style, known as the "prairie school," at first emphasized horizontal lines and wide overhangs.

The architects of several Chicago firms—among them William Holabird and Daniel H. Burnham—participated in the movement led by Sullivan and carried it into the sky. For at this time structural steel and the electric elevator became available to American designers. The combination opened up the possibility of the skyscraper, and architects like those just named led the exploratory process. Now the weight of the structure was carried not upon the walls, but upon a skeleton framework of I-beams and columns concealed within the walls. For some time, however, engineering and esthetics went their separate ways, and the early skyscrapers were sheathed in traditional raiment. It remained for Adler and Sullivan in the Wainwright building in St. Louis (1891) first to express adequately the structural frame of the building in its external lines. This was achieved by giving the vertical members, which carry the main loads, dominance over the horizontal members, which carry the loads of one floor only.

The city of skyscrapers was now around the corner.

Within the city of skyscrapers, and across the nation itself, what remained to be done was to make architecture and municipal forms a benediction on life itself.

What still remains to be done is to carry the best of the past in the marrow of our bones and as visual objects before our eyes and to go on from there in building, as Jefferson would say, an empire for liberty.

LANDMARKS OF BEAUTY AND HISTORY

Christopher Tunnard

Fortunately, the past never completely dies for man. Man may forget it,

but he always preserves it within him. For, take him at any epoch, and he is the product,

the epitome, of all the earlier epochs. Let him look into his own soul, and he can find

and distinguish these different epochs by what each of them has left within him.

Fustel de Coulanges, THE ANCIENT CITY

"WHAT DOES THE PAST HAVE TO OFFER?" THIS FAMILIAR question implies that history is capable of handing us something like a pudding on a plate, or that its contribution is somehow limited compared with that of the present.

Intellectually, we sometimes grasp at history for reassurance or help. Both are there, but one of the more important questions to ask is: "What can we offer in collaboration that may be of help to this and future generations? Can we, by learning from the past, enrich the life of contemporary culture?"

"By studying the works of the old masters," the American painter Washington Allston advised a student, "You will imbibe their spirit insensibly, otherwise you will as insensibly fall into the manner of your contemporaries." He observed a function of history. There is a need in every generation to study the past, to absorb its spirit, to preserve its messages. There is an enrichment of life to be found there which cannot be recreated artificially or by searching for it in our own world. It is a collaboration of ourselves and our ancestors, the result is deeper understanding for individuals and in consequence, a broader culture for the nation.

There are specific reasons for our need to be in physical contact with our past, as well as gaining the vicarious knowledge of history.

The early settlers established our own chance for the future. What they created has enabled us to develop our own institutions, and to expand our own economic and cultural surroundings. They gave us our basic freedoms: and over the continent they established varied patterns of settlement that are our heritage. A familiarity with the concepts and values of America in its emergent stages provides a viable intellectual background for future planning.

Not only structures, but also the artifacts of daily life—tools, implements, household utensils—reflect the meaning of living patterns which grow increasingly distant from ours, in both time and manner. From these we can learn the conditions of life close to nature and the soil, in which the individual is also the means of production. Yet very often in these archaic things we discover patterns—both esthetic and technic—which can be employed to enrich our own lives.

Approximately 54 per cent of all museums and preserved structures in America are historical in nature. This museum activity provides a process of education for the general public which also reveals, through their interest, the vitality the past has for the present.

History, as the complex of intellectual disciplines which it represents in the present century, is a relatively recent development of our culture, as opposed to chronicles, and mere tales. Yet no matter what theory of history one may hold, and no matter what particular field of history one may practice, the physical presence of artifacts from the past, particularly such large ones as structures is an invaluable adjunct to the pursuit of any historical discipline.

Landmarks, whether natural, such as hills, streams, woods or man-made in terms of familiar buildings, have a cultural use in geographic and psychological orientation. Just as the small child finds a sense of security in recognizing the building in which he lives, so do the mature and elderly derive pleasure and a sense of belonging from recognition of old or historic structures. As Karl Deutsch, the social scientist, suggests in his book *The Future Metropolis:*

> Ways will have to be found to let planners use the powers of the community to guide urban growth toward a clear and pleasing pattern of new and old landmarks, where people can once again feel well-oriented, exhilarated, and at home.

Many examples of architecture are true works of art. Not only great and famous buildings are in this category: many small towns possess residences, small public buildings and other structures of great artistic integrity and charm. The nineteenth-century French poet, Charles Baudelaire, was thinking of great works of art when he wrote: "You are immediately struck by that feeling of reverence which causes children to doff their hats and which catches at your soul in the way that the dust of vaults and tombs catches at your throat." Such a mixture of awe and admiration is aroused by truly great architecture, no matter what its size or function. It comes from a combination of proportion, design, workmanship and detail: the creation of a harmonious building, whether by an anonymous eighteenth-century master carpenter or by a famous architect of a later period.

The past is a challenge. Can we, with our facile technology, our ability to create virtually anything we wish, rival it in beauty, in workmanship, in perfection of detail? If we do not have existing examples of past craftsmanship, our theoretical comparisons will lose meaning.

Our preservation of the past is a responsibility to the future. The expansion of population, the increasing consumption of space by motor vehicles and economic pressures, are destroying our cultural heritage at a constantly-increasing speed. Whether our acts are in the form of mere intrusion, in which an incongruous structure abuts an architectural masterpiece, or something which blocks the view like a bulky new hotel on a colonial waterfront, or the greater evils of intensive alteration, calculated ruin and demolition, we shall be judged by the future for our treatment of the past. There is world-wide concern over this aspect of modern civilization, and if we are to match the efforts of the more progressive countries we must have cities and countrysides which reveal enhancement of our cultural heritage as a national responsibility, willingly undertaken.

THE NATURE OF HISTORIC PRESERVATION

In his Message to the Congress on Natural Beauty (Feb. 8, 1965), President Johnson did not forget the role played by historic preservation in enhancing the beauty of city and countryside. He said:

> In almost every part of the country citizens are rallying to save landmarks of beauty and history. The government must also do its share to assist these local efforts which have an important national purpose. We will encourage and support the National Trust for Historic Preservation in the United States, chartered by Congress in 1949. I shall propose legislation to authorize supplementary grants to help local authorities acquire, develop and manage private properties for such purposes.

The President correctly emphasized the importance of citizen participation in this movement. By its very nature—the fact that it deals with immovable objects which have a close relationship with the land—there is involved a strong element of local participation and pride.

A recent survey of preservation projects shows that the vast majority are in private hands, though the federal government, through the National Park Service, cares for our National Monuments, and many local governmental groups also have done significant work. We should never forget that it was the Mount Vernon Ladies' Association of the Union which preserved America's greatest historical attraction.

When, more than a hundred years ago, George Washington's home was offered to the Commonwealth of Virginia and to the federal government, both refused. Ann Pamela Cunningham created the Mount Vernon Ladies' Association, and succeeded where government had failed. In her last charge to the ladies Miss Cunningham formulated her credo: "Ladies, the home of Washington is in your charge—see to it that you keep it the home of Washington! Let no irreverent hand change it; let no vandal hand desecrate it with the fingers of progress."

The ladies of the Association have remained faithful to their trust, and the home of Washington today receives more than one million visitors yearly. However, the "vandal hand" still threatens its desecration. George Washington had written that "no estate in the United America is more pleasantly situated than this, on one of the finest Rivers in the world." He certainly included the view from the mansion in his assessment, and this view of the Maryland banks of the Potomac opposite *Mount Vernon,* has remained much as it was in 1750. By the early 1950's however, it became obvious that the view which Washington admired could not survive the great population change taking place in the metropolitan Washington area.

Another dedicated lady, the Honorable Frances P. Bolton, Vice-Regent of the Mount Vernon Ladies' Association and a Congresswoman from Ohio, recognizing the danger, took charge of the campaign to save the overlook. Under her leadership the Accokeek Foundation was chartered in 1957, and private effort began. This effort included the purchase of real estate, the evolution of plans and the securing of easements from private property owners in the area. When it was announced in 1961 that a sewage treatment plant was to be constructed on Mockley Point, opposite *Mount Vernon,* it became clear that other action was needed. In that same year Congress acted to preserve for all time, for all people of the nation, the view enjoyed by George Washington. Supplemental appropriations have still not been made however, and the overlook is still in jeopardy, though the Accokeek Foundation has purchased other parcels of land, and private land controlled by easements continues to be acquired. Meanwhile land initially offered for $900 has now risen in value to $2000, making the battle for appropriations even more difficult.

Requests for zoning changes to permit high-rise construction, and the construction of new highways giving access to the region have caused speculative land values, which make the area more expensive to preserve. Though the Foundation now owns the land on Mockley Point where the sewage treatment plant was to have been built, it will be built just outside the limits of the overview park, and the phosphates, nitrates and other fertilizers released into the river will cause further algae bloom and pollution.

In addition the Smithsonian Institution has proposed the creation of a National Armed Forces Museum at Fort Washington, within the overlook. This would include the anchoring of more than a mile of ships directly in the overview. It can hardly be argued that naval vessels constructed in the present century were visible from *Mount Vernon* in 1750.

We must not forget the thousands of owners of old houses who are keeping them in repair through love and respect for the past, often at financial loss to themselves. Sometimes they find an adaptive use which enables the building to survive rising real estate taxes and costs. A typical example is the Timothy Bishop house, built by the architect David Hoadley in 1816, in the heart of what is now the business district of New Haven, Conn. This great house of the federal period, with its attic ballroom and Palladian detail, is owned by a local business man who has carefully remodelled it into an office building, in spite of the fact that the site is worth far more than the revenues from the old mansion can provide.

The owner, who maintains the house because he likes it as a work of art, has consulted New Haven Preservation Trust, Inc., to retain its authenticity of detail. This operation which is entirely private, is a source of local admiration and pride.

The fact that many of our oldest buildings are near the centers of cities, towns and villages which are being swallowed up in development has brought about other preservation measures, adapted to American necessities. Instead of spending money to repair European castles, as some did in the 1920's, we are more likely at present to assist the "historic house" museum at home. In 1895 there were twenty of these in the entire country, while today there are nearly a thousand. State interest and activity in preservation has increased, the National Park Service has developed and administered hundreds of historic sites since 1935, while our National Trust for Historic Preservation has, since 1949, shown us that preserving a house here and a site there, was not the whole answer to our problem. The great increase in numbers of local preservation organizations is a definite indication of general public concern for a sensible program for historic preservation. At present more than 650 of these were guided in their organization by the Trust.

Frequently whole streets and neighborhoods of interesting buildings demand preservation. One method, used increasingly in the United States, is *historic district preservation.* Albert B. Wolfe describes its objectives: "Historic district architectural controls aim at preserving appearance without change in ownership or use; *where the setting is important as well as the buildings,* or the relationship to each other of a sufficient number of historic buildings creates a whole that is greater than the sum of its parts. . . ." Historic district legislation deals largely with the exterior appearance of buildings and not the uses going on inside them: The district will contain buildings and structures *not* of historic or architectural significance, although districts are chosen on the basis of having a majority of buildings constructed in the period of periods of architecture it is desired to preserve. The historic district in larger cities is an attempt "to keep alive the village within the city" as Harry E. White Jr. described it in the April 1963 *Columbia Law Review.* District boundaries are drawn and described, a Historic District Commission is set up, and the Commission issues a "certificate of appropriateness" upon submission of plans involving change in exterior architectural features. All Historic Districts imply a consideration of the setting as well as the individual buildings. The motive in obtaining the District may be purely esthetic or it may be to prevent a run-down part of the town from getting worse. It may be to preserve the architecture of a specific period or of all periods. It may even be monetary, since historic districts have proved to raise values within their own limits and in surrounding areas.

CHANGING ATTITUDES TO AMERICAN LANDMARKS

The spectrum of historic sites, buildings, monuments and landmarks is broad, and it is expanding further as we discover new areas of interest in the past.

For instance, the relics of our early industrial technology are beginning to be classified as landmarks—metal bridges, mines, foundries and furnaces. Examples from both private and governmental efforts are the Saugus Iron Works reconstructed by the First Iron Works Assoc., Inc.; and Hopewell Furnace, a remaining eighteenth-century furnace, restored, along with its complex of buildings, by the National Park Service. It is becoming increasingly important, also, to preserve buildings which may not accord with the taste of our own time. A Gothic City Hall of the 1860's with elaborate polychromy and zebra-striped stonework may still be considered grotesque by some, but it is likely to have an equal or greater number of defenders.

Similarly, buildings of quite recent periods are becoming candidates for preservation, if their architects or their structures are sufficiently important. The American Institute of Architects has for some years now been encouraging owners of Frank Lloyd Wright houses to put plaques on them. Some New Yorkers were surprised when their new Landmarks Commission designated the New York Stock Exchange, built in 1903, as a landmark. Few people have noticed that it has a glass non-supporting curtain wall rising four stories behind its Corinthian columns, probably the first use of this construction technique in the city. George B. Post, the architect who designed the Stock Exchange, also designed the State Capitol of Wisconsin, and in 1899 was one of the members of the American Institute of Architects who preserved The Octagon, in Washington, D.C. It is possible that the works of other forgotten architects of Post's era will receive belated recognition if they are not completely destroyed.

At present, industrial structures which are technically, if not always architecturally, important ought to be considered for preservation if they are historically significant. Possible candidates, if any still exist, would be a small nineteenth-century oil refinery, a small coal mine and breaker of the same period, an early electric furnace installation belonging to either abrasives manufacture, or the metallurgical industries. In this connection, the possibility of industry and crafts museums, housed in old buildings with authentic equipment, ought to be considered. The printing trades in America have a heritage going back farther than any industry, yet except for the preservation of old presses here and there, little has been done to dramatize it. The same is true of the clothing industry, in its shift from household to industrial production.

FUTURE CONCERNS

Contrary to general belief, once a historic house has been purchased it has not necessarily been saved. Rehabilitated buildings must have an environment in which it is possible to maintain their newly-acquired respectability. One device is the historic district. Other devices for up-grading an area of older building and for saving those which are important esthetically or historically, are to be found in recent urban renewal legislation. The Kennedy-Tower amendment to the Housing Act of 1965 provides for the first time that federal funds may be used for the moving and preparation of site and foundation for old historic buildings in urban renewal developments. Thus, in certain designated areas, distinguished buildings may be saved from the path of the bulldozer. Moving, of course, is a last resort when no other path can be found for the highway or for new building. Whenever possible, buildings should remain on the sites with which they are associated.

When redevelopment is not the issue, there are other measures to be taken. What can be done for instance to save a large area from blight and intrusions? In Newport, R.I., which we tend to regard in terms of the summer palaces of the very rich, there are dozens of individual buildings of historic importance scattered through the old colonial seaport. These are mostly the colonial and post-colonial wooden houses, recalled so understandingly by the novelist Henry James in *The American Scene*. These are still standing, threatened by a general decline in the downtown area and by the plans of the State Highway Department for a new four-lane highway cutting through the quaint old residential streets. A group called "Operation Clapboard" was formed in the interest of preservation to provide loans to people who would buy the houses, restore them and live in them. This plan has been fairly successful and many of the houses have been rehabilitated under the scheme.

Another approach has been taken by the city of Brooklyn Heights, the first residential suburb for ferry commuters to Manhattan, which contains 13,000 residences, many built in the aristocratic era of the mid-nineteenth century and 600 of them dating from before the Civil War. The present residents have requested the Landmarks Commission to designate as a historic district a 50-block area which has been investigated by architectural historian Clay Lancaster, who has published a detailed study of 619 houses in the old Brooklyn Heights area. Parts of Greenwich Village in Manhattan will also be designated as historic districts, and in lower Manhattan a section of Greene Street between Canal and Broome Streets will be preserved as the Cast Iron District.

It should be obvious by now that although the defined historic area has certain legal and administrative clarity, it cannot serve for all preservation purposes. It cannot cover the architecture of region or of types of community, like the ghost towns of Colorado, the early canal towns of Ohio or the watering places of Virginia.

In the future it would be desirable to extend the restoration principle to groups of communities in distressed areas, or those threatened by sudden change or slow deterioration. After the example of Wallace Nutting, the antiquarian who in 1915 established his "chain of houses" in New England, it should be possible nowadays to substitute a chain of white valley towns in Vermont (say Chelsea, Tunbridge and South Royalton) or some of the steamboat towns on the Ohio, Missouri and Mississippi Rivers, or gold mining towns in California. Some of these are already preserved as individual communities as in the case of Columbia, Calif., a gold rush town which is now in the State Park.

As President Johnson said in his Message "our concern is not with nature alone but the total relationship between man and the world around him." These regional towns and villages, which are not necessarily remarkable for the quality of their architecture, are nevertheless unique in character and plan. Those which are still inhabited and have no protection are prey to depredation by nationwide retail chain operations or single function public agencies like the state highway departments. The latter, in fact, can have a great role to play in the preservation of our urban heritage. They should consider the view of a village *from* the highway as well as the effect produced by a truck-load of trees and shrubs which they apply as cosmetics to the paved ribbon. They, too, should treat these older communities as precious reminders of a past not entirely forgotten.

As the *Fordham Law Review* commented in April 1961, "There is a certain amount of irony in the judicial reasoning which sustains historical zoning on economic grounds. Such reasoning suggests that zoning ordinances have been held valid because they tend to preserve the historic areas as tourist attractions and hence have a favorable effect upon business. Yet those who urged the preservation of historic areas will attest that the primary motive was quite the contrary. Objection was raised to the immolation of historic areas to the demands of burgeoning business. A desire existed to preserve the beauty of these areas quite apart from the incidental economic benefits resulting thereby. It is time that the courts recognize that the very preservation of historical monuments, the beauty of the settings in which they are placed and the beauty of our communities as a whole is an end in itself."

In 1962, UNESCO made recommendations on the schedule of extensive landscapes by zones. This was an attempt at total preservation, and the principle is more comprehensive than the "scenic corridor," which is based so largely on the automobile. The UNESCO report suggests that in many areas control should be exercised over whole river valleys or mountain regions. Realizing the values of earlier settlements which have used local materials in their construction, the reports recommend setting up standards of an esthetic order which would cover the use of materials, their color, height of buildings, prevention of removal of topsoil, regulation governing the cutting of trees and so on. Probably the most notable example of controls operating successfully over a wide region, but dating from an earlier period, is the Cotswold district of England. One can see how such an ecological approach might be used in areas lying outside the scope of the roadside easement but too near civilization to be included in great natural reservations. The recommendations of the International Commission on Monuments and Sites, which stress the importance of *using* historical buildings in the zone, preserving them *with their additions* rather than undertaking arbitrary restoration are a valid addition to the ecological concept. Application of such a total program might be started in inhabited beauty spots like the banks of the lower James River, San Francisco Peninsula and the Bayou country of Louisiana, to name only some obvious candidates which might be saved.

It is as important to prevent intrusions as wrecking and demolition. We all hear about the Storm King power plant and the damage it can do to the scenery of the Hudson River, but less is said about the lack of city planning which allows a skyscraper apartment to dwarf a beautiful sidestreet off an avenue in the metropolis, or a blank new office building to replace a distinguished hotel and thus ruin a square, as in the case of the Savoy Plaza in New York.

Truly, the *character* of an area has its effect on people, and those who tamper with it against the wishes of the public are not blameless in the whole matter of the city's decline.

As the New York *Times* put it so wisely and so sorrowfully, "Any city gets what it admires, will pay for, and, ultimately, deserves. Even when we had Penn Station we couldn't afford to keep it clean. We want and deserve tin-can architecture in a tin-horn culture. And we will probably be judged not by the monuments we build but by those we have destroyed."

It is easy enough to say that the past contains its quota of ugliness as well as the present.

But we are not so sure as we once were *what* is ugly or what our descendants will find to admire in our common heritage.

If a building has been created and admired, the fact should make us pause. For, as Geoffrey Scott once said so well, "Whatever has once genuinely pleased is likely again to be found pleasing; and all the enjoyment of art continues in the condemned paths undismayed."

"PROMOTED TO GLORY..."

The Origin of Preservation in the United States

Walter Muir Whitehill

IN DESCRIBING THE TEMPLE OF HERA AT OLYMPIA IN the second century A.D., the traveller Pausanias noted that the style of the temple was Doric and pillars ran all around it, and that in the back chamber one of the two pillars was of oak. Originally the columns of this ancient building had been of wood, but in the course of the seven centuries preceding Pausanias's visit, all save this one had been replaced with cut stone. Presumably this single oak column had been allowed to remain out of piety, as a visible symbol of the antiquity of the temple on this site.

In his life of Theseus, Plutarch observed that "the ship wherein Theseus and the youth of Athens returned [from their celebrated voyage to Crete] had thirty oars, and was preserved by the Athenians down even to the time of Demetrius Phalereus [317-307 B.C.], for they took away the old planks as they decayed, putting in new and stronger timber in their place, insomuch that the ship became a standing example among the philosophers, for the logical question as to things that grow; one side holding that the ship remained the same, and the other contending that it was not the same."

In the two instances just noted, the motives were different.

At Olympia a single pillar of oak was long preserved as evidence of the antiquity of a holy place that had over centuries been remodelled in a more up-to-date manner. At Athens an entire old ship was not only maintained, but piously renovated when necessary, because of its association with a hero of antiquity.

But despite these Greek instances that might be considered the beginnings of historic preservation, the ancient world, like ours, far oftener destroyed vestiges of the past in some effort towards present improvement. In the third century, for example, Roman Emperors dismantled ancient structures to gain materials to build new ones. The arch of Constantine, put up in 315, is largely an arch of Domitian, with most of its sculptures transferred from monuments of the time to Trajan, while the first St. Peter's was hastily built by Constantine in a part of Caligula's circus, with columns rounded up from other buildings in every part of the city. Edward Gibbon summed it all up in the sonorous sentences: "The spectator, who casts a mournful view over the ruins of ancient Rome, is tempted to accuse the memory of the Goths and Vandals, for the mischief which they had neither leisure, nor power, nor perhaps inclination, to perpetrate. The tempest of war might strike some lofty turrets to the ground; but the destruction which undermined the foundations of these massy fabrics, was prosecuted, slowly and silently, during a period of ten centuries; and the motives of interest, that afterwards operated without shame or control, were severely checked by the taste and spirit of the emperor Majorian."

This emperor's edict of 458 made clear that he was "determined to remedy the detestable process which has long been going on, whereby the face of the venerable city is disfigured." The restraining effect of this edict was only temporary. Throughout the dark ages that soon followed, whatever was built anew in Rome was at the cost, and from the materials of, the ancient city. Blocks of stone and columns were cannibalized for new construction; statues and inscriptions found their way into the kilns of the lime-burners.

Although the greatest city of the world suffered thus during the centuries of its decline and fall, many less monumental and utilitarian buildings throughout Europe continued in the use for which they were originally constructed for extended periods of time. When there were fewer people, and less money, in the world, a soundly constructed building normally remained in use until it collapsed of sheer old age or an enemy destroyed it in war. Thus Romanesque masonry chapels in Catalonia and stave churches in Norway have survived relatively unchanged for close to a millenium, for the simple reason that in various mountain villages of the Pyrenees, as in northern fjord settlements, people scraped together money enough in the early middle ages to build a respectable church, and at no time since had anyone seriously felt the need, or had the means, to think of changing it. Where men have farmed, or fished or raised cattle for centuries on end, as their grandfathers had before them, buildings continue to serve their purposes for long periods of time. They continue to be useful; consequently nobody thinks about them one way or the other. By contrast, wherever there is industrialization, or where great cities sprawl over the adjacent countryside, buildings seldom reach great age by the simple process of inertia.

Americans are a restless and wasteful people by comparison with the rest of the world. We make a dirty mess in one place and move on to despoil another. When there were fewer of us, it was easier to ignore this national bad habit. Today we have reached the point where, as the late President Kennedy observed in his introduction to Secretary Udall's *The Quiet Crisis,* a once beautiful nation is in danger of turning into an "ugly America."

In fifth-century Rome ancient buildings were imperiled by men who coveted their columns, marble blocks and sculptured decoration as building materials. In nineteenth- and twentieth-century America they have always been in danger from men who coveted the land upon which they stood. As Sir Shane Leslie observed thirty years ago in *American Wonderland:* "The American sign of civic progress is to tear down the familiar and erect the monstrous."

Between 1790 and the year 1818, when he moved to Washington to become Architect of the Capitol, Charles Bulfinch literally changed the face of Boston. By designing the State House, the Court House, the Boston Theatre, banks, insurance offices, hospitals and schools, in addition to numerous churches and many private houses, he made a handsome city out of an indifferent town. Yet before his death in 1844 some of his finest houses had already been destroyed, and within the next half-century the great majority of his other buildings in Boston disappeared in a haphazard and thoughtless manner. From pressure of immigration, the city was growing rapidly. Once-handsome areas were allowed to lapse into slums, while the former occupants moved off to new streets on newly made land. It was, as is normal in the United States, a restless and wasteful performance, in which the desire to turn a quick dollar by real estate maneuver or new construction took precedence over everything else. There were nineteenth-century Bostonians, who subordinated to their own profit the dignity and appearance of the city and the convenience and desires of their neighbors, quite as brazenly as did the fifth-century Romans who were the cause of the emperor Majorian's edict.

In 1808, when the First Church of Boston, during the pastorate of Ralph Waldo Emerson's father, sold its "Old Brick" meetinghouse of 1713 in Washington Street to move elsewhere, an indignant proto-preservationist complained in the *Independent Chronicle:* "If a proposition had been made in London, Paris or Amsterdam to the society owning the First Church of either of those respectable cities, to sell (on a principle of speculation) their ancient edifice, it would have been spurned with indignation—the trifling profit anticipated by the sale would never have led the proprietors to have razed a house of worship so well repaired as the Old Brick to gratify the rapacity of a few men who trouble society both in Church and State. After the demolition of the Old Brick, there is scarcely a vestige of antiquity in the town."

Nevertheless, the Old Brick came down, and sixty-eight years later the Old South Meeting House of 1729, a few blocks down Washington Street, narrowly missed doing so. But the Old South exists today as a respected historic monument because, in the years following 1850, a few devoted people had demonstrated that there were values in the historic past that transcended even the delights of a profitable real estate transaction.

The history of the historic preservation movement in the United States is a subject too vast for condensation into a few dozen pages. In the space alloted to me, I can only mention certain selected instances which indicate phases in the development of the concept. Indeed until last year anyone who wished to survey the development of the subject had no easy means of doing so. The record was to be found in scattered reports of organizations, ephemeral pamphlets, memoirs and the columns of newspapers, few of which could be found in proximity to one another in any single library. The publication in 1965 by Professor Charles B. Hosmer, Jr., of *Presence of the Past: A History of the Preservation Movement in the United States Before Williamsburg*, for the first time brought together in convenient form a readable and well-documented account of the beginnings of the effort. Originally prepared as a doctoral dissertation at Columbia, the book represents an expansion undertaken at the request of the National Trust for Historic Preservation. Although it deals with its subject only through the mid-nineteen-twenties, for the field that it treats, *Presence of the Past* is not only comprehensive but perceptive.

Dr. Hosmer makes it clear that until the early years of the twentieth century historic preservation in this country was chiefly concerned with buildings in which great men had lived or great events had taken place. In this "ship of Theseus" phase, buildings were chiefly esteemed for their associative value, rather than for their inherent architectural qualities or their relation to their surroundings. The main purpose of preservation was to convert them into museums that would supposedly provide inspiration to visitors.

The phrase "promoted to glory," by which the Salvation Army reports the deaths of its faithful officers, applied very literally to George Washington in the half-century following December 14, 1799. In his lifetime the head of armies and state, in his death he became the object of a cult that in its thoroughness and in the rapidity of its development rivaled the respect paid to a deified Roman emperor or a canonized Christian saint. The new federal capital was named in his honor while he was still living. In 1832 Horatio Greenough received a governmental commission to carve Washington as a half-naked

American equivalent of the Olympian Zeus to adorn the rotunda of the Capitol, while in the next decade was begun the great marble obelisk that dominates the city of Washington—higher than the pyramids of Egypt. With such veneration being paid to his memory, it is not surprising that the earliest successful ventures in historic preservation within the United States were concerned with the perpetuation of scenes which Washington had known in his lifetime.

WASHINGTON'S FIRST STABLE MEMORIAL

The first of these was a relatively modest effort—the purchase by the state of New York in 1850 of the Hasbrouck House in Newburgh, which had served as Washington's headquarters during the last two years of the Revolution. In his message to the legislature for that year, Governor Hamilton Fish had submitted "that there are associations connected with this venerable edifice which rise above considerations of dollars and cents," and pointed out that it was "perhaps the last relic within the boundaries of the State, under the control of the legislature, connected with the history of the illustrious" George Washington.

The legislative committee appointed to study the matter pulled out all the stops, including the tremolo, in support of the proposal. Its argument, somewhat abbreviated, was as follows: "If our love of country is excited when we read the biography of our revolutionary heroes, or the history of revolutionary events, how much more still the flames of patriotism burn in our bosoms when we tread the ground where was shed the blood of our fathers, or when we move among the stones where were conceived and consummated their noble achievements. . . . No traveler who touches upon the shores of Orange county will hesitate to make a pilgrimage to this beautiful spot . . . and if he have an American heart in his bosom, he will feel himself a better man; his patriotism will kindle with deeper emotion; his aspirations of his country's good will ascend from a more devout mind for having visited the 'Headquarters of Washington.'"

The preservation of the Hasbrouck house, involving only the legislative appropriation of $8391.02, was simple and inexpensive compared with the effort begun in 1853 by Miss Ann Pamela Cunningham of South Carolina to purchase *Mount Vernon* from its unwilling owner, John A. Washington, who had set the high price of $200,000 upon the house and the 200 acres of land that surrounded it. From 1846 petitions to Congress urging the purchase of *Mount Vernon* by the federal government had met with no response, and in the course of 1853 rumors circulated that a syndicate was eyeing the plantation for development as a hotel site. Obviously it would have been a good one, with Washington's tomb as a built-in tourist attraction, easily accessible by steamboat from the capital. Because of that threat, in the first week of December 1853 Miss Cunningham sent out an anonymous appeal to the women of the South to attempt the preservation of Washington's home. "Can you be still with closed souls and purses, while the world cries 'Shame upon America,' and suffer *Mount Vernon,* with all its sacred associations, to become, as is spoken of and probable, the seat of manufactures and manufactories? . . . Never! Forbid it, shades of the dead!" Within the week the Governor of Virginia sent a message to the legislature asking that some means be devised of achieving the same end. The legislature boggled over the price asked and declined to use public funds, but eventually, on March 17, 1856 chartered the Mount Vernon Ladies' Association of the Union, "carefully offering," as Dr. Hosmer puts it, "to accept the title without helping to raise the purchase money."

Miss Cunningham proved to have a genius for organization. By choosing energetic women in each state to supervise local efforts in fund raising, she eventually succeeded, where the governments of the United States and Virginia had failed, in saving Washington's home for the future. Moreover she set a precedent for accomplishing the seemingly impossible, which has been the inspiration of preservation efforts ever since. From Mount Vernon sprang the tradition of carefully organized private effort as the means of securing the funds for historic preservation.

In 1946 the Adams family gave to the United States the family house in Quincy, Mass., that had been the home of the second and sixth presidents, together with the furnishings, pictures and books that had accumulated there during four generations of occupancy. Thus another great house, full of associations with founders of the Republic, carefully preserved over decades by the family, became publicly accessible under the care of the National Park Service. This collective act of generosity represents an ideal that it is seldom possible to achieve. Inheritors of historic property do not always necessarily have a sense of public responsibility equal to that of the Adams family. Moreover they are even less frequently able freely to give away, even for the highest purposes, property that has very considerable financial value. With the passage of time, particularly in cities, land increases in value, and private owners—whether individuals or institutions—find temptingly large sums of money dangled under their noses by promoters and developers. Such considerations as these were dramatically involved in the close brush with destruction that the Old South Meeting House in Boston suffered in the eighteen-seventies.

This Third Church in Boston, founded in 1669 to serve the southern part of the town, was situated at the corner of Washington and Milk Streets. In its first meetinghouse Benjamin Franklin, born across Milk Street on January 6, 1706, had been baptized. In 1729 this original wooden building was replaced by a larger brick meetinghouse, with a graceful steeple that reflected in colonial terms the new Georgian style of England. In the decade preceding the outbreak of the American Revolution, the Old South Meeting House was the scene of numerous political public meetings, of which the most renowned were those leading up to the Boston Tea Party on the night of December 16, 1773. Here also were held the anniversary commemorations of the Boston Massacre. Thus the building acquired a series of resounding historical associations in no way connected with its official function as a Congregational church.

In 1729, when the Old South Meeting House was built, Boston—although the largest community in British North America—was a town of some 13,000 inhabitants. One hundred and forty years later it was a crowded city at least twelve times that size. Moreover the region surrounding the Old South had been almost completely given over to business, and the land owned by the church had acquired a commercial value that could never have been anticipated by the generous parishioners who had first given it in the last third of the seventeenth century. The congregation had moved away, and the meetinghouse was rapidly reaching the situation of the City churches of London in our time. In 1869 the society bought lots on the northwest corner of Dartmouth and Boylston Streets in the recently filled Back Bay and built upon them an Italian Gothic building, dedicated in 1875, which has since been known by the contradictory name of the New Old South Church. For the continued health of the religious body, this was unquestionably a rational move; moreover other churches of early foundation had already moved to the new and fashionable region, or were in the process of doing so. Yet a vigorous minority of the congregation, devoted to the historical associations of the old meetinghouse, wished at all costs to keep it.

The problem was essentially one of finances. The land on which the old meetinghouse stood was worth more than a third of a million dollars, its sale would cover the cost of the move and the new building. The congregation was entirely agreeable to the preservation of the historic building, as long as someone else footed the bill and they got their money. Their attitude was not unreasonable, for the memory of the American Revolution had very little to do with problems of individual salvation, which they considered their business. Thus in 1872 they attempted to sell the meetinghouse to the Massachusetts Historical Society, which had neither the funds to enter the competitive real estate market, nor, indeed the inclination to do so, inasmuch as its purposes were chiefly the acquisition and publication of manuscript sources of American history rather than the acquisition of historic property for exhibition. This effort having failed, the congregation now turned to the alternative of sale for commercial purposes. This was not as simple as it seemed at first sight, for the land had been given in 1669 by Mary, widow of the Reverend John Norton, for the erecting of a meetinghouse and parsonage "and for no other intent, use or purpose whatsoever." Nevertheless the Massachusetts courts eventually cleared this hurdle, and the congregation determined to tear the meetinghouse down in preparation for the sale of the land.

The building, exclusive of the cornerstone and tower clock, was sold at auction on June 8, 1876 for $1,350, subject to removal within 60 days. The workers were beginning their work when George W. Simmons, a dealer in ready-made clothing, stepped in on the 11th and bought a seven-day stay of demolition. A mass meeting was called in the building for the 14th, at which Wendell Phillips delivered a resounding address, in the florid style for which he was noted, in which he declared that "the saving of this landmark is the best monument you can erect to the men of the Revolution." The burden of the theme that night was, as Dr. Hosmer puts it, "that Bostonians must not permit the destruction of the one thing that set their city apart from all other American cities: the last visible reminders of a proud past." A committee was formed to solicit contributions, and several thousand dollars subscribed on the spot.

General popular clamor having achieved postponement of demolition, the committee turned to specific ways and means. This first positive step was the purchase of the building itself for $3,500 by twenty Boston ladies, thus assuring that, no matter what happened about the land, the meetinghouse could, if necessary, be moved to a new site. Finally on September 15, 1876 an agreement was reached by which the church undertook to sell the land for $400,000 in cash. The New England Mutual Life Insurance Company took a $225,000 mortgage, the citizens' committee paid over $75,000 that it had raised in the preceding weeks, and Mrs. Augustus Hemenway, by a dramatic contribution of the last $100,000, assured the success of the project.

THE OLD STATE HOUSE

Although the Massachusetts legislature incorporated the Old South Association in Boston to hold the meetinghouse as a historic site, it never appropriated any funds to assist in that purpose. The money required to amortize the mortgage was, over the years, obtained by a great variety of popular enterprises. Lectures, balls, fairs were held; Emerson, Holmes, Longfellow, Lowell and Whittier contributed poems to the cause; the young Thomas A. Edison exhibited his new phonograph. Thus was the Old South Meeting House preserved as the first instance in Boston where respect for the historical heritage of the city triumphed over considerations of profit, expediency, laziness and vulgar convenience. The sum of money involved was twice what John A. Washington had demanded for *Mount Vernon* a quarter of a century earlier. With the success of this effort, historic preservation moved into its urban phase.

Once saved, the Old South Meeting House was not only opened to visitors, with exhibitions of objects connected with the building and the Revolution, but with popular lectures and publications in American history. The appeal of the project, as with the sites connected with George Washington, was still associative and inspirational. Early in the campaign, President Charles W. Eliot of Harvard said of the building: "It is chiefly because we love it, I think, that we want to save it, and love is unreasoning, cannot be accounted for, has no logical processes. We love it because it has always been speaking to us of courage, uprightness, independence; we love it because of the memories of famous men which are associated with it; we love it because it is one of the familiar objects of our youth; we love it because it has always spoken to us that one emphatic word, which Thoreau, I believe, said was the whole speech of Bunker Hill monument, 'Here.' Here on this very spot, within these very walls, were words spoken which were heard round the world. Here, in this very place, our forefathers were wrought up to resist the fearful power of Great Britain; here they worshipped their stern God . . . I think we Americans particularly need to cultivate our historical sense, lest we lose the lessons of the past in this incessant whirl of the trivial present. . . . We need to recall our own past, to remember our fathers, to remember our heritage. In this present moment of political difficulty let us bear in mind what we owe to those who have gone before us; to the generations that were brought up in this old building —in the very Old South that we desire to preserve. We depend at this very moment upon the political sense and sober second-thought, the self-control and readiness in emergencies which in good measure we have inherited from the generations that have gone before us. Let us pay this debt by reverently preserving the shrines of those generations. If we have any faith in free speech, if we have any faith in freedom of public meeting, why, the Old South is the best shrine of that faith."

This neo-Roman expression of *pietas* by a singularly chilly and unemotional chemist is typical of the mood that saved the Old South. Esthetic considerations hardly entered in. Indeed James Russell Lowell, who worked hard in the campaign specifically denied that the Old South was a model of architecture in any esthetic sense. But in another sense he pronounced it a model on the ground that "it was the best thing that our fathers could do in their day, and they thought it beautiful." But taste is mutable, for today I would guess that the *appearance* of the Old South Meeting House is every bit as highly valued as its historical associations.

Although the preservation of the Old South Meeting House was accomplished entirely through private efforts, the interest that the campaign had generated in monuments of the past soon led the city of Boston to undertake much needed restoration of the nearby Old State House, two blocks east on Washington Street, at the head of State Street. This brick building, more precisely and properly called the Second Boston Town House, was constructed soon after a fire in 1711 had destroyed the wooden Town House that had stood on the site since 1657. Until the Revolution this second structure served the needs not only of town and county but of the royal government of the province of Massachusetts Bay. Consequently within its walls some of the fiery speeches of Samuel Adams and James Otis had been delivered; directly below its windows the Boston Massacre had taken place. It further served as the Massachusetts State House until 1798 when the present Bulfinch State House on Beacon Hill was ready for occupancy. For the next three decades, however, the Old State House was rented out for various less dignified purposes. Indeed in 1826 a group of Bostonians seeking a central site for the placing of Chantry's statue of George Washington, proposed that the Old State House be demolished to make way for a new building that would fittingly display this monument. This proposal caused such public complaint that the Old State House was, in 1830, refitted as a City Hall, in which capacity it served for more than three decades. With the completion of the present City Hall in School Street in 1862, the Old State House once more reverted to ignominious rental as private offices. By the mid-seventies it was plastered over with signs, and disfigured by a mansard roof. "So completely were the memories of the site forgotten, and so arrogant were the fancied demands of commerce," William H. Whitmore wrote, "that, in 1875, it was almost decided to pull down the building." The Old South campaign had its effect, for the associations of the Old State House were strikingly similar to those that had saved the meetinghouse. Thus in 1881 the City Council authorized a thorough restoration, which was completed at public expense the following year at a cost to the taxpayers of $35,000. The Bostonian Society, a new organization dedicated to the history of the city, was installed in the Old State House to maintain a local historic museum. Similarly in 1898 the city of Boston spent $103,000 in the renovation and fireproofing of Faneuil Hall, once again because of its Revolutionary associations.

IN PRAISE OF FAMOUS MEN

Through the early years of the twentieth century, enterprises in historic preservation sprang from a pious desire to preserve buildings associated with great men or great events with the avowed intent of the inspiration of those who visited them.

Thus Jamestown Island, Washington's headquarters at Morristown and Valley Forge, as well as at Newburgh, Independence Hall in Philadelphia, Andrew Jackson's *Hermitage,* the house in 10th Street in which Abraham Lincoln died, and the "White House of the Confederacy" in Richmond, were preserved by a variety of means, sometimes public, sometimes private. It was invariably assumed that some useful moral inspiration would accrue to visitors, who were expected to swarm in sufficient numbers to make the buildings self-supporting. That was not always the case. Often the sledding was difficult, for, as Dr. Hosmer points out: "Many preservation groups thought that they could imitate the work done by Miss Cunningham, but they all found that she had achieved something that was not likely to be repeated for years to come. Now, as then, far too few preservationists, overwhelmed by the importance of their particular projects, realize how many *other* buildings are supposed to be 'second only to *Mount Vernon.'* " Nevertheless many houses were in this period preserved through the efforts of local historical and patriotic societies, almost invariably because of veneration for some distinguished former occupant. The homes of authors as well as the scenes they described were commemorated in this way.

Fifty and more years ago my parents diligently took me not only to Paul Revere's house, the Old North Church, and Concord bridge, but to the Wayside Inn in Sudbury and to houses associated with Emerson, Longfellow, Hawthorne, the Alcotts and Whittier. So generally was it assumed that such buildings would be accessible to visitors that I remember my puzzlement that James Russell Lowell's *Elmwood* was still occupied by members of the Lowell family and hence visible only from the street. Where buildings no longer existed, it seemed to many local groups a pious idea to mark their sites by tablets, though nothing remained of the original appearance.

The first phase of historic preservation was concerned with the associative value of buildings; the second was quite as much concerned with their inherent architectural significance, irrespective of what had or had not taken place within their walls. This change of direction is explicit in William Sumner Appleton's statement of the purpose of the Society for the Preservation of New England Antiquities, which he organized in 1910, as "to save for future generations structures of the seventeenth and eighteenth centuries, and the early years of the nineteenth, *which are architecturally beautiful or unique,* or have special historical significance. Such buildings once destroyed can never be replaced."

Sumner Appleton's first venture in historic preservation occurred when he was 29 years old, five years before he, single-handed, founded the S.P.N.E.A., which has accomplished more for preservation with fewer people and less money than any organization that I know. In 1905 he joined with two older

Bostonians to raise money for the preservation "as a permanent patriotic memorial"—in the normal *Mount Vernon* tradition —of the house in North Square, Boston, which was the home of Paul Revere during the Revolution. Although the primary motive of the Paul Revere Memorial Association that was founded in consequence was associative and commemorative, emphasizing occupancy by a Revolutionary patriot, the building thus preserved was, incidentally, the oldest in the city of Boston. Built about 1680, and already old when Paul Revere occupied it, it is, indeed, the only surviving example of the type of wooden house, with an overhanging second story of English medieval inspiration, that predominated in seventeenth-century Boston. Having been much abused and altered during the two-and-a-quarter centuries that preceded its purchase by the association, it was in grave need of restoration. With such a building, there is always the problem of what one is trying to restore. If one chooses an intermediate period, interesting earlier work is likely to remain obscured. If one "restores back" to the earliest survivals, then many additions of later periods may well be sacrificed, and a great deal of hypothetical reconstruction along old lines substituted. Joseph Everett Chandler, who restored the house for the association in 1907-08, chose the latter course. Thus he removed most later additions and went back to its 1680 exterior appearance, treating the building as an architectural monument to such an extent that Paul Revere, were he to return to North Square, would not recognize it as the house in which he long lived.

VALIDITY OF ARCHITECTURAL BEAUTY

By the time he founded the Society for the Preservation of New England Antiquities in 1910, Sumner Appleton's motives had become more architectural than associative, so that he was chiefly concerned with *preserving* buildings, by any means possible, rather than exhibiting them for inspirational purposes. With increased population and prosperity, the New England scene was fast changing. Unless prompt action were taken, many significant buildings would soon disappear, for the existing activities of historical and patriotic societies, which were mostly concerned with single houses, coped with only a fraction of the threats. "The situation," Appleton stated in 1910, "requires aggressive action by a large and strong society, which shall cover the whole field and act instantly wherever needed to lead in the preservation of noteworthy buildings and historic sites. This is exactly what this Society has been formed to do. . . . It is proposed to preserve the most interesting of these buildings by obtaining control of them through gift, purchase or otherwise, and then to restore them, and *finally to let them to tenants* under wise restrictions, unless local conditions suggest some other treatment."

In both the above quotations from Sumner Appleton's statements, I have italicized the phrases that represent the significant characteristics of this second phase: the validity of architectural beauty or uniqueness, unrelated to historical association, as a criterion for preservation, and the idea of preserving buildings for continued use rather than for exhibition. This second notion, of keeping buildings in current use (with adequate safeguards against damaging change), as a part of continuing American life, rather than isolating them as objects of inspirational and antiquarian veneration and wonder has had far-reaching consequences in the development of historic preservation.

Sumner Appleton began his society with no resources beyond his own time, energy, and modest private income, yet by unremitting effort he achieved extraordinary results, entirely through private sources. In the fifty-five years that have elapsed since the foundation of the society, he and his successors have acquired through gift or purchase some fifty properties in five of the New England states, as well as investments for their maintenance with a current value of close to $3 million. Some of the properties are regularly open to visitors; others are preserved through private occupancy; the Smith Tavern in Weston, Mass., is used as town and community offices, but all are safeguarded for the future. Some of the houses were built or occupied by persons of historical or literary significance, but all of them have strong claim to survival on their architectural merits.

Although the Society for the Preservation of New England Antiquities owns three houses in Newbury, Mass., and two in Portsmouth, N.H., its efforts have been directed towards the rescue of significant single buildings rather than of such buildings in relation to others of their kind, or to the surroundings of the town or city in which they stand. A third phase in historic preservation—that of coping with a community as a whole, or a large area thereof—first sprang from the dream of the Reverend William A. R. Goodwin and the extraordinary generosity of John D. Rockefeller, Jr., at Williamsburg, Va., in the nineteen-twenties.

WILLIAMSBURG

Williamsburg had been the capital of Virginia from 1699 to 1780 as well as the seat of the College of William and Mary, the second to be founded in British North America. After the state government moved to Richmond, the importance of the place declined. The Governor's Palace burned in 1781, the Capitol in 1832, and the Raleigh Tavern in 1859. But although these buildings, which were the scene of so significant a part of Virginia's Revolutionary activity, had vanished, and the College of William and Mary had been sadly disfigured by tasteless rebuilding, Bruton Parish Church, the eighteenth-century Courthouse and Powder Magazine and a considerable number of private houses remained as reminders of the former dignity of the place. There had been many intrusions. The most prosperous public institution was the Eastern State Hospital, which grew over the years. Thirty irrelevant structures, ranging from a national bank to a pigsty had been crowded into the Market Square, and with the coming of automobiles, corrugated iron garages and filling stations began to occupy conspicuous positions on Duke of Gloucester Street. Nevertheless Williamsburg had the undoubted charm of a sleepy town that had seen better days and had kept respectable vestiges of them.

Dr. Goodwin, the Rector of Bruton Parish, had achieved a restoration of his own church in 1907 and had secured the adjacent ancient residence of George Wythe as a parish house. But he dreamed of nothing less than the preservation of the entire colonial capital. This aspiration would have remained simply a grandiose dream had he not had the good fortune to enlist the support of John D. Rockefeller, Jr., who visited Williamsburg in 1926 and caught the infection. The following year Mr. Rockefeller decided to carry out Dr. Goodwin's plan, which was defined as "an endeavor to restore accurately and to preserve for all time the most significant portions of an historic and important city of America's colonial period."

This was an undertaking of unprecedented magnitude, which required, first of all, the acquisition of key areas in the town before local speculative instincts had a chance to develop. Between May and November 1927, Dr. Goodwin succeeded in buying some 200 pieces of property, while keeping the identity of his backer as an essential secret. By June 1928, when the full scope of the plan was announced at a public meeting in Williamsburg, the Williamsburg Holding Corporation (now Williamsburg Restoration, Inc.) had been chartered, and the Boston firm of Perry, Shaw and Hepburn selected as the architects for the restoration, and Arthur A. Shurcliff, also of Boston, placed in charge of landscape restoration and city planning. Williamsburg Restoration, Inc., which was designed to cope with the multifarious business undertakings of the project, was, and is, a wholly-owned subsidiary of Colonial Williamsburg, Inc., the latter being a non-profit educational corporation.

The properties thus acquired were divided into two areas, one earmarked for immediate restoration, and the other regarded for the time being as a protective cushion. The region designated for restoration included the impressive Duke of Gloucester Street, the original College yards, the Palace Green, the Court House Green, the Market Square, the Capitol Square and the bordering properties. As the plan proposed to turn back the clock and return the town to its appearance as a colonial capital, some 600 nineteenth- and twentieth-century buildings were eventually torn down or moved outside the restoration area. Fortunately most of these were of types that never would be missed. As no precedent existed for an undertaking of this magnitude, it was necessary to develop a sizeable body of research workers to establish what should be done, as well as a force of specially trained craftsmen to execute the architects' interpretations of the evidence.

The *Official Guidebook & Map* provided today for visitors to Williamsburg makes a clear distinction between buildings that were *restored*—"which were still standing in whole form or in major part and needed only to be repaired and stripped of later additions"—and *reconstructed,* "which had fallen victim to fire or dismantling and had to be entirely rebuilt on their original sites." It further notes: "Eighty-five buildings that survived from the eighteenth century have been restored to their original appearance. Over half the major buildings, in fact, are original eighteenth-century structures." But as it was felt that a capital without its key public buildings would resemble the play *Hamlet* with Hamlet left out, the Capitol, the Governor's Palace and the Raleigh Tavern—three of the principal exhibition buildings open to visitors—were reconstructed. Otherwise reconstruction was chiefly confined to buildings deemed necessary for the completion of the setting, some of which are used for practical purposes. Many of these, like a number of the restored buildings, are occupied as residences by the staffs of the restoration, the college or townspeople, or as taverns for the victualing of visitors.

THE RECKONING

As the years have passed, and the gardens have matured, the scene has become increasingly homogeneous and unified. The remarkable furnishings of the exhibition buildings draw their specialized admirers of furniture, china, silver and glass; the gardens attract horticulturists and those who love to potter with plants; but these are only a fraction of the hundreds of thousands of visitors who flock to Williamsburg from less specialized motives. To accommodate this national incursion, Williamsburg Restoration, Inc., provided first an admirable Inn and Lodge, outside the restored area, then a great Information Center, Motor House and Cafeteria, and most recently a Conference Center, adjacent to the Lodge. Thus the attempt to return a small and sleepy town to its eighteenth-century appearance has required the creation of extensive twentieth-century supporting services, as well as constant and unremitting vigilance to prevent the commercialism of highway appurtenances, in the form of gas stations, motels, nut stands, waxworks and the like, from creeping objectionably close to the town.

The restoration of Williamsburg brought to historic preservation in the United States the ideal of saving buildings in relation to their neighbors, by attempting to rescue an entire town. Yet certain unusual circumstances made the effort atypical and of no general application as a pattern. It was, first of all a relatively small and isolated place, where time had all but stopped. Secondly, it had behind it the extraordinary generosity of Mr. Rockefeller who, before his death in 1960, had given some $68.5 million to the project. Today Williamsburg is a kind of museum piece, an eighteenth-century fantasy in which the more pleasing aspects of colonial life are meticulously evoked, with the omission of smells, flies, pigs, dirt and slave quarters, sheltered from the outside world (figuratively if not literally) by a vast glass case. But the atmosphere of *le temps perdu sous cloche* is hardly one in which Americans of the present day would willingly choose to live, unless their professions brought them there, or they were attached to the place by previous ties of family and habit. Armies of visitors make the normal life of any town or city disagreeable if not downright untenable without necessarily achieving the supposed economic benefits alleged by the promotionally minded. It is worth in this connection to observe the most recent financial reports of Williamsburg.

"During 1964, the gross income of Williamsburg Restoration, Inc., [the business corporation operating the hotels and other properties outside the historic area], was $10,059,616. After operating expenses of $9,278,197, a cash operating balance, before depreciation, of $781,519 resulted. Capital expenditures of $1,560,070 for hotel improvements, property purchases, and other projects were financed from this cash operating balance, from the sale of capital stock, and from long-term loans made to the corporation.

"Operating expenses incurred in presenting the Historic Area of Williamsburg to the public, in restoring, reconstructing and furnishing the historic buildings, and in conducting the educational program of the corporation, totalled $3,861,756 during 1964. Income produced by these operations amounted to $2,776,415, leaving an operating deficit of $1,085,344. This excess of operating expenses over operating income was provided from investment income of $2,705,673 on the endowment funds of the corporation, substantially all of which were made available to Colonial Williamsburg through the personal generosity of the late John D. Rockefeller, Jr."

The last sentence is the key to the high standards of Colonial Williamsburg. Without the presence of an endowment fund of some fifty millions, the situation would be untenable, for as Carlisle H. Humelsine, the president of Colonial Williamsburg, has observed: "The more successful we are, the more money we must spend to keep up our standards." Just as many organizations over the past century have dreamed of a "second

Mount Vernon," others have optimistically envisioned a "second Williamsburg." But unless some exact duplicates of John D. Rockefeller, Jr., unexpectedly materialize, this vision will be as chimerical as those of the enthusiasts who hoped to reproduce the achievement of Ann Pamela Cunningham.

A MODERN DREAM OF THE PAST

Although it is unlikely that second, third, fourth and fifth Williamsburgs will spring up, the practice of looking at a town as a whole, or certain large areas of a city, as appropriate fields for preservation, has become widespread during the past quarter of a century. Country towns, well isolated from industrial areas, present a more manageable problem than larger places. Of these the Connecticut valley frontier town of Deerfield, Mass., is a remarkable example. There, through the joint efforts of the Pocumtuck Valley Memorial Association, a historical society organized in 1870, Deerfield Academy, a boy's school of national reputation, and the Heritage Foundation, established by Henry N. Flynt of Greenwich, Conn., (the president of the association and a trustee of the academy) and his wife, Deerfield has unobtrusively become one of the most attractive towns in New England. It is a small country town, centered on a single long, tree-shaded main street. The object has been, not an antiquarian restoration to any particular period—for everything from the seventeenth to the twentieth century is to be found along this street—but the maintenance of a town in which people live, teach and learn, where the best of the past is enhanced by thoughtful improvements and additions. Half-a-dozen houses are open to visitors; the rest are occupied by the academy and townspeople. As Deerfield Academy has required new buildings, these have been designed to blend unobtrusively into the scene. The Heritage Foundation has bought a number of houses, and even brought some (threatened with destruction elsewhere) into the town. Some of these are admirably furnished as exhibits, while others are rented to provide living space and to help support the museum houses. The Pocumtuck Valley Memorial Association maintains the seventeenth-century Frary House and a museum in Memorial Hall. The trappings of the tourist trade are completely absent, for the Heritage Foundation recognizes that a venture of this kind can never be made self-supporting. The remarkable thing about Deerfield is that one can never tell at a glance what organization is responsible for a given agreeable feature, for individuals and institutions alike work together for Deerfield with uncommon skill, taste, generosity and reticence.

Williamsburg, one might say, is preserved for exhibition; Deerfield for continued daily life, yet both strive to recreate a past that is very different from the surrounding present. Professor John Coolidge has observed: "We oppose to the inevitable fluidity of the present, a dream-image of an immutable past. Much of the drive to preserve is the result of a desire to make this image concrete. We set up a Pioneer Village; we recreate Colonial Williamsburg" as, in effect, "a modern dream of the past made concrete." Yet in various American cities, where there could be no question of the dream obscuring reality, much has been accomplished in preserving noteworthy build-ings *for continued use,* sometimes for the purpose for which they were originally built, at others, for adaptations that are compatible with their architectural character. In this fourth phase of historic preservation, private initiative has often been augmented and strengthened by public legislation, particularly that creating historic districts.

THE RIGHT OF CITIES TO BE BEAUTIFUL

Walter Muir Whitehill

A 1954 UNITED STATES SUPREME COURT DECISION (Berman *vs* Parker) ruled that a city has as much right to be beautiful as it has to be safe and clean. Such an assumption is basic to the present wide acceptance of the preservation of historic districts by architectural control as a legitimate function of government. Architectural control is the device used to prevent the construction of incompatible new buildings, or alterations to existing ones, that would detract from the esthetic values of an area in which a large proportion of the buildings were constructed during a significant architectural period or have important associations with the history of the community, state or nation. It is designed to protect the harmonious exterior relationship of buildings to one another, without necessary regard to the practical use of their interiors.

While few areas in the United States can be compared for quality and harmony to the Place des Vosges, the Place Vendôme or the Place de la Concorde in Paris, there are many in which buildings dignify a community because of their pleasing relationship to one another. In Louisburg Square in Boston, no single one of the red brick houses of the second quarter of the nineteenth century is so remarkable as to warrant preservation apart from its surroundings, yet the whole is considerably greater than the sum of its parts. Yet were one of these houses to be replaced by a ten-story structure in yellow brick, concrete or plate glass with magenta plastic panels, the effect of Louisburg Square would be irretrievably ruined. It is areas such as this that have in recent years properly been cloaked in the protection of historic district legislation.

It by no means necessarily follows that every building standing in a historic district at the time of its creation is sacrosanct for all time. Oftentimes there are solecisms that are capable of improvement, provided due concern is given to form, color and materials. The whole purpose of architectural control is to assure that care is taken to avoid incongruities in alterations or in necessary new construction.

The earliest legislation in the United States creating a historic district dates from 1931 when the "Old and Historic District of Charleston" was established in South Carolina. Upon the recommendation of the landscape architect and city planner, Frederick Law Olmsted, Jr., the city undertook a survey of the economic and physical character of the city and its buildings.

A special committee organized under the leadership of Robert N. S. Whitelaw obtained grants from the Carnegie Corporation of New York, and later from the Rockefeller Foundation for an evaluative survey of Charleston's architecture.

Written and photographic reports on 1168 Charleston buildings were submitted to an expert jury, which classified them in five groups as Nationally Important, Valuable to City, Valuable, Notable, and Worthy of Mention. A graphic report of the committee's work was exhibited in the spring of 1941 at the Gibbs Art Gallery, and published in book form in 1944 under the title *This is Charleston,* in which 572 buildings were described and illustrated. This inventory indicated that, in spite of heavy concentration within the area already designated as "Old and Historic," a very great number of the buildings classified were scattered about the city in regions unprotected by architectural review. Therefore, in 1947 a Historic Charleston Foundation was incorporated to educate the public as to the worth of these fine buildings, and to assist in their preservation. Income derived from spring tours of historic houses was applied to various preservation projects, and in 1955 the Foundation raised the funds needed to purchase and restore the notable Nathaniel Russell House, which became its headquarters.

The Historic Charleston Foundation then set out to create a revolving loan fund to further its preservation objectives in terms of a *living community,* particularly by rescuing for residential use fine houses that lay outside the "Old and Historic Charleston District;" especially in the Ansonborough area which had fallen on evil days. The plan for the administration of the fund provided:

1) That historic areas rather than individual houses, be given preferential consideration for restoration. By partially restoring an area of architectural importance, now deteriorated, private funds would then be attracted to restore the remainder. This would enhance values and provide a two-fold return on the fund's investment.

2) That properties that should be saved could be purchased and developed into rental units such as apartments, offices, stores, etc., depending on the neighborhood. Exterior restoration rather than elaborate interior redecoration would be emphasized.

3) That worthy properties would be purchased for resale with restrictions concerning future alterations and use.

4) That both in purchases for resale and rental adjacent properties of little value may be bought and buildings torn down to create either gardens or well-designed open areas. This will improve neighborhoods by removal of unsightly structures.

5) That properties be purchased or accepted as gifts with life occupancy by existing tenants as is done by Colonial Williamsburg, Inc.

6) That the Foundation seek to have worthy properties willed or donated, with no restrictions as to their use, and that these properties may be sold to persons who will agree to maintain their architectural integrity.

In the course of four years' work in the six-block, mid-city areas of Ansonborough, the Historic Charleston Foundation bought 26 pieces of property, resold 11 which were renovated as residences, turned three into apartments which were held for rental income, and cleared five of sub-standard buildings. The remainder are awaiting renovation or sale.

When a new edition of *This is Charleston* was published in 1960 some fifty of the 572 buildings illustrated in it bore the depressing notation "Gone." That the number is no higher does great credit to the imagination and energy with which Charlestonians have applied themselves in the last quarter-century to devising means for returning fine buildings to dignified uses, even though they are not always the purposes envisioned by their builders.

In 1921 the Constitution of the State of Louisiana authorized the Commission Council of the city of New Orleans to create a Vieux Carré Commission. "In order that the quaint and distinctive character of the Vieux Carré may not be injuriously affected, and so that the value of those buildings having architectural and historical worth may not be impaired. . . ." In 1936 this Commission was created, its powers and duties outlined and the boundaries of the historic district defined. It has been amended in several additional sections since.

SOUTHERN BEGINNINGS

After these southern beginnings, little progress was made with historic district legislation until the end of World War II, when increasing change and vastly more automobiles began to threaten many cities. An ordinance was passed by Alexandria, Va., in 1946, Williamsburg in 1947, and by Winston-Salem, N.C., in 1948. In the convolutions of war-time Washington,

Georgetown was the only old section of the District of Columbia that showed positive signs of improvement rather than deterioration. To strengthen this trend, the Congress passed in 1950 a law for the preservation of "Old Georgetown." Natchez, Miss., and Annapolis, Md., followed with ordinances in 1951 and 1952, respectively, while in 1955 the Massachusetts legislature passed acts establishing historic districts on Beacon Hill in Boston and in Nantucket. The Beacon Hill district has subsequently been enlarged and extended, most recently in 1963. Furthermore, in 14 states, among them Massachusetts, Alabama, California, Illinois and New Mexico, the legislatures have passed historic district enabling acts, under which communities may by local ordinance establish architectural control for areas of particular significance. Of the remaining states not having such enabling legislation there are a number whose constitutions do not require it before their cities can adopt such legislation themselves.

In the past decade various imaginative and useful efforts have been made to further the cause of preservation for current use by combining private activity with governmental effort. In Rhode Island, for example, the Providence Preservation Society, organized in 1956 by a group of private citizens, sponsored jointly with the Providence City Plan Commission a study of the College Hill area, the society raising $18,500 by popular subscription, and the remaining two-thirds of the cost of $50,000 being contributed by the Urban Renewal Administration of the Federal Housing and Home Finance Agency for a pilot study. The federal government supported the College Hill Study as a demonstration of how rehabilitation and renewal can be accomplished in historic urban areas. Private enterprise in Providence has restored approximately 75 historic houses for occupancy in the area at a cost of nearly $1.5 million. Similarly, in Portsmouth, N.H., Strawbery Banke, Inc., has been utilizing the processes of urban renewal to secure land and fine but deteriorated buildings in the center of Portsmouth, not for demolition but for restoration. Such efforts as these presuppose that an important aspect of historic preservation is the rescuing of fine buildings for current and future use. The intention is not to make, in Professor Coolidge's phrase, "a modern dream of the past concrete," but to use beauty where you find it, in furtherance of the Supreme Court decision that "it is within the power of the legislature to determine that the community should be beautiful as well as healthy, spacious as well as clean, well-balanced as well as carefully patrolled."

Until very recent years historic preservation was undertaken on a highly individualistic basis, usually in response to some emergency that threatened a site. The rumor of destruction would mobilize friends, sometimes from very unexpected quarters, and through the enthusiasm generated by a crisis a goal would be achieved. By such means a great number of buildings and sites in all parts of the country have been preserved through the efforts of almost as great a variety of sponsors, private and public. Most projects represented somebody's very strong personal and emotional commitment, and love, as everyone knows, is irrational and capricious. Few men marry their wives as the result of an impartial survey of a wide choice of candidates, and, until recently, few buildings have been preserved as the result of a similar investigation. The 1940–41 survey that led to the publication of *This is Charleston* was a pioneering effort, for it carefully undertook to discover the surviving early buildings that remained in the city, and to appraise their relative merits. The accomplishments of the Historic Charleston Foundation in reclaiming the Ansonborough district would hardly have been possible without the judicious knowledge that had been acquired through the earlier survey.

HISTORIC DISTRICTS

Similar investigations have preceded the creation of historic districts, for one can hardly expect public authorities to agree to the imposition of architectural controls on any part of a community without careful and reasoned demonstration that there is something genuinely worth saving. The College Hill Study clearly demonstrated that there were elements worth preserving in that part of Providence. Thus in the last few years there has been increasing activity in many parts of the country in such surveying and recording, but there is still a long road to be traveled, for with surveying, as with actual preservation, much depends upon individual activity and commitment, which is by no means equitably distributed through all parts of the 50 states.

It therefore becomes necessary at this point to consider the role that the federal government has played in historic preservation. As the earliest attempts to buy *Mount Vernon* from John A. Washington through Congressional action and appropriation were without effect, the success of the Mount Vernon Ladies' Association set a precedent for private rather than public acquisition of historic sites. Nevertheless, during the Civil War the federal government stumbled, for irrelevant reasons, into the acquisition of two buildings that are now maintained as historic sites by the National Park Service.

General Robert E. Lee's house, *Arlington*, overlooking Washington from the Virginia bank of the Potomac, was occupied by federal troops in May 1861 soon after its owner had cast his lot with the Confederacy. Through the vindictive action of Secretary of War Stanton, who contrived to have a tax levied which could only be paid by the owner in person, the estate was sold at auction for taxes in 1864 and bought by the federal government, which, to make it permanently untenable as a private residence, regardless of the outcome of the war, established a national cemetery on the grounds in May of the same year. Post-war litigation led to the compensation of the Lee heirs for the seizure, and in 1883 the federal government acquired an undisputed title to the property, although *Arlington* for more than forty years thereafter stood vacant and desolate in the midst of the cemetery. Finally in 1924 Congress authorized the restoration of the house as a historic site as it had been at the time of the Lee family's occupancy. Similarly, Ford's Theatre, in which Lincoln was assassinated, was taken over by the War Department and converted for departmental offices, and only on the approaching centenary of the tragic event that occurred in it on April 14, 1865, was restored to its original appearance by the National Park Service.

At the time more than a century ago when the government took possession of *Arlington* and of Ford's Theatre, they were, of course, simply a house and a theater of current practical utility; the recognition of their historical and architectural interest developed after their acquisition, rather than being the cause of it. Preservation activities of the federal government were first concerned with natural rather than historic areas. Thus in 1872 more than two million acres of the world's greatest geyser area, chiefly in Wyoming, but with extensions into Montana and Idaho, were established as Yellowstone, the first national park. With this precedent it is not surprising that the first federal project in historic preservation was in the wild country of the southwestern United States, where archaeological ruins of Indian cliff dwellings and pueblos existed in great numbers. The last inhabitants of these had abandoned them suddenly, perhaps driven out by a 24-year drought which began late in the thirteenth century. Although later Indian arrivals and Spaniards had passed by these ruins without doing great damage, the story was different when Americans from the eastern states began to move into the Southwest in substantial numbers. Wholesale commercial looting by "pot hunters" had become such a peril that in 1882 Senator George F. Hoar of Massachusetts presented to Congress a petition of the New England Historic Genealogical Society requesting that steps be taken to protect these important archaeological sites. Seven years later Congress appropriated two thousand dollars for the protection of the Casa Grande ruin in Arizona, and authorized the President to reserve the land on which it stood. Thus by executive order of June 22, 1892, President Harrison reserved the site containing the ruined adobe tower built by Indians who farmed the Gila Valley six hundred and more years before.

In the last decade of the nineteenth century the scientific interests of the Bureau of American Ethnology of the Smithsonian Institution, the Archaeological Institute of America, and the Colorado Cliff Dwellers Association led to increased protests against the vandalizing of such sites. Various proposals for archaeological protection were introduced in Congress in the early years of this century, culminating in the so-called Lacey Act of 1906 for the preservation of antiquities. This provided penalties for destroying or injuring any historic or prehistoric ruin or monument on lands controlled by the United States and authorized the President by proclamation to set aside historic spots, landmarks and structures on government lands, and if on land privately claimed, the Secretary of the Interior was authorized to accept gifts of such lands. Thus on June 29, 1906 was established the Mesa Verde National Park in Colorado, whose fifty thousand acres contained some of the most notable and best preserved prehistoric cliff dwellings and other works of early man in the United States.

THE NATIONAL PARK SERVICE

In 1916, the National Park Service was created within the Department of the Interior. Under a series of able directors, beginning with Stephen T. Mather, it has in the course of fifty years acquired custody of more than 26 million acres of land, including not only the great chain of parks preserved for their natural beauty and value, but an extraordinary variety of historic buildings, monuments and sites that had, by one means and another, come into federal possession. The categories into which these areas are classified include 32 national parks, 10 historical parks, 77 monuments, 11 military parks, 1 memorial park, 5 battlefields, 3 battlefield parks, 3 battlefield sites, 22 historic sites, 15 memorials, 10 cemeteries, 5 seashores, 3 parkways, 1 capital park, 4 recreation areas and the White House.

Within the area of historic preservation are the homes of the Adams presidents, of Andrew Johnson and Franklin Delano Roosevelt, superb examples of military architecture ranging from the Spanish Castillo de San Marcos in St. Augustine to nineteenth-century fortifications, archaeological sites of a high order, as well as unnecessary synthetic birthplaces of George Washington and Theodore Roosevelt, reconstructed by private admirers and wished off onto the government. The finest achievements in historic preservation of the National Park Service lie in regions where buildings and sites extending over an area too extensive to be coped with by private resources have been brought together under governmental protection. The nine thousand acres of the Colonial National Historical Park in Virginia include not only most of Jamestown Island, the site of the first permanent English settlement in America, and Yorktown, the scene of the culminating battle of the American Revolution, but a 22-mile parkway of extraordinary beauty that links these with Colonial Williamsburg. Here are not only the foundations of the early settlement of Jamestown, carefully excavated and preserved, but a remarkable 5-mile roadway, constructed through the woods and swamps of the island, that permits the visitor to appreciate both the terrain chosen by the seventeenth-century settlers and the present-day flora and fauna. Here archaeology, history, nature, conservation and the handling of armies of visitors, have been blended with singular felicity.

In the Minute Man National Historical Park in Massachusetts, first established in 1959, the National Park Service strives to preserve, in a region of creeping urbanization, what can be rescued of the natural setting of the battle road from Lexington to Concord, which marked the opening of the American Revolution.

More specifically focused upon buildings are urban projects of the National Park Service in Salem, Mass., and Philadelphia. The Salem Maritime National Historic Site, designated in 1938, preserves Derby Wharf, the Old Custom House at its head in which Nathaniel Hawthorne once worked, and the adjacent Derby and Hawkes houses, thus ensuring the protection of a portion of the now disused Salem waterfront, and preserving buildings associated with the maritime, literary and architectural history of New England. The Independence National Historical Park, authorized in 1948 and established in 1956, was conceived to safeguard various structures in the center of Philadelphia, intimately associated with the American Revolution and the founding and growth of the United States.

Going far beyond the properties owned by the federal government are certain projects of the National Park Service concentrated upon the recording of historic buildings. The need for such activity had been recognized as far back as 1869, when at a national meeting of the American Institute of Architects, its president and founder, Richard Upjohn, proposed an investigation of early American architecture. Dr. Hosmer notes the activities of McKim, Mead and White in 1876 and of Arthur Little in 1878 of drawing and recording examples of New England colonial architecture. Systematic work on a national scale only began, however, in 1933 with the inauguration of the Historic American Buildings Survey by the National Park Service, in collaboration with the American Institute of Architects and the Library of Congress.

THE NATIONAL TRUST

In 1947 a National Council for Historic Sites and Buildings was organized through a discussion that originated with David E. Finley, Director of the National Gallery, Ronald F. Lee, a National Park Service historian, Christopher Crittenden of the North Carolina Department of Archives and History, and George McAneny of the American Scenic and Historic Preservation Society (a New York group organized in 1895) toward the creation of an organization along the lines of the National Trust in England. From this origin developed Congressional action establishing the National Trust for Historic Preservation. On October 26, 1949 President Truman signed the bill, which provided that the Trust should facilitate public participation in the preservation of sites, buildings and objects of national significance or interest; and empowering it to receive donations of sites, buildings and objects significant in American history and culture to administer them for public benefit. It was also empowered to administer gifts of money, securities or other property for the carrying out of a preservation program.

A detailed account of its development has recently been set forth by David E. Finley, now its Chairman Emeritus, in his *History of the National Trust for Historic Preservation*. Thus it is sufficient to observe here that, although the National Trust has received by gift or bequest various significant properties— including the Decatur and Woodrow Wilson houses in Washington, *Woodlawn Plantation* in Virginia, *Lyndhurst* at Tarrytown-on-the-Hudson, and *The Shadows on the Bayou Teche*— its greatest usefulness has been in the dissemination and exchange of information between organizations and individuals engaged in projects of historic preservation throughout the United States. Through its meetings, its publications and the personal energies of its staff, it has provided accurate and scholarly information, guidance and encouragement in many quarters.

The National Trust, alas, has never had funds to give or lend in support of individual projects, but it has supplied invaluable information on techniques and methods that have assisted many groups locally organized to cope with crises in preservation. Through its Congressional charter and its location in Washington, it has been in a position to serve as a link between the activities of the National Park Service and many private groups, and most recently to investigate some of the possibilities that are constantly coming into being for linking federal assistance and private undertakings in support of historic sites and buildings.

As the population grows and urban sprawl increases, preservationists are becoming acutely aware of the need for space and proper surroundings. It is not enough to preserve a building if its environs are completely out of context. A few years ago in Athens a small Byzantine church was completely engulfed by the construction of a high-rise office building a few blocks from Constitution Square. The church still exists, unchanged, in the middle of a high two-story pedestrian arcade with shop fronts, but any esthetic significance that it had was irretrievably lost by the ridiculous incongruity of its situation. Such exaggerated instances are a constant reminder of the need of thinking beyond the monument itself to its environment. Consequently, the tie between the interests of historic preservation, urban planning and the conservation of natural resources grows steadily more important. To save a building or a site out of context is not enough; one must relate it to broader public action on behalf of the community as a whole. Sometimes one cannot accomplish anything without imaginative combinations that would have seemed impossible to earlier antiquarians and preservationists.

The Inter-Agency Archaeological Salvage Program, conducted since 1946, is a case in point. "Inter-Agency" is no exaggeration, for this enterprise involves the National Park Service, the Smithsonian Institution, five federal agencies, 14 state bodies or universities inside the Missouri Basin and 40 outside that region. The problem is "the salvage, preservation and interpretation of the archaeological, historical, and palaeontological remains that are threatened with destruction by the tremendous program of dam and reservoir construction throughout the United States." In short, the innumerable dams and water-control projects altering stream valleys of the United States will shortly flood various valley floors for miles, thus obliterating the archaeological evidence of Indian life and white frontiersmen's activity as completely as the Aswan Dam will inundate Egyptian monuments in the path of the heightened Nile. But great challenges sometimes evoke great responses. The coordinated archaeological activity of 56 public and private agencies in consequence of this one gives hope that preservationists concerned with the historic period of the United States will prove as flexible in their responses to emergencies as have their prehistoric colleagues in the Inter-Agency Archaeological Salvage Program.

CRITERIA

The decentralized and individualistic pattern of historic preservation in the United States has resulted in widely varying standards. The National Park Service and the National Trust for Historic Preservation have both, in their criteria for preservation, strongly emphasized *integrity* of structure as a prerequisite. "There should be no doubt," the National Park Service states, "as to whether it is the original site or structure, and in the case of a structure, that it represents original materials and workmanship."

Once this is determined, there is now common agreement that it is "better to preserve than repair, better to repair than restore, better to restore than reconstruct." But as the National Trust points out in a 1964 *Report on Principles and Guidelines for Historic Preservation in the United States:* "A worthy building deserves careful and sympathetic maintenance to keep out the weather and to guard against deteriorating features. When parts wear out they should be promptly replaced in kind, thus preserving architectural character." And, parenthetically, any-

one who tries to keep up his own house knows that parts *do* wear out. "But," the report continues, "few buildings are so favored. When their design goes out of fashion and equipment becomes worn or obsolete they usually fall into a state of neglect or even abandonment. If fortunate, they may be able to remain standing until the cycle of taste again allows them to be recognized as assets. When maintenance has failed—or some other misfortune has caused the loss of original parts—the process of restoration must be invoked to recapture the character with which the building was formerly endowed. At that time it is usually necessary to strengthen the old fabric, and to add such conveniences as may be needed for modern use."

The report further points out that "it is also well, before initiating a project, to consider carefully the possibility that once started it may lead to 'creeping reconstruction'—the tendency for repair to lead to restoration and for restoration to become, by degrees, total reconstruction." This is what happened to the ship of Theseus in Athens.

Some old buildings, chiefly churches and dwelling houses, are still used on their same sites for the purposes for which they were originally designed, yet even these have their share of new timber. The White House, even though on its original site and in use for its original purposes, is, after being burned in the War of 1812, redecorated through the nineteenth century, and thoroughly reconstructed both at the beginning and middle of this century, is clearly not the same building that President John Adams first occupied, and never can be, no matter what is done to it. But there are other houses, and some churches, that have suffered less extreme changes, and these unquestionably hold first place in the categories of historic preservation.

In the next category come those buildings that are preserved on their original sites, through public or private piety, as memorials to distinguished occupants—like *Mount Vernon,* the Adams Mansion in Quincy, and *Monticello*—or as examples of architecture. Throughout the country there are hundreds of less widely-known buildings in this category, open regularly to visitors, through the activities of a myriad of historical societies and public agencies.

NEW WINE IN OLD BOTTLES

Moving through the spectrum, one enters the area where houses remaining on their original sites have been converted to new uses; where, in their transformation to apartments, schools, clubs, funeral homes or offices, the exteriors, and sometimes a number of the interior features, have remained unchanged. This is indeed the situation in much of the Beacon Hill Historic District in Boston. On Beacon Street, between the State House and Charles Street, there remain only two houses that are still occupied by single families in the manner that as late as the nineteen-thirties prevailed throughout the area. Yet the majority of the facades remain unchanged; the appearance of the street from Boston Common is little altered, even though behind these facades are clubs, publishing houses, apartments, charitable organizations, schools and offices.

With Williamsburg one enters the fourth category, for there examples of the previous three are combined with a totally new element, that of the reconstruction of what has been destroyed. Bruton Parish Church has always continued in its original use. George Wythe's house, looking as he would have enjoyed seeing it, both inside and out, is exhibited to visitors rather than occupied as a dwelling, while other eighteenth-century buildings, not open to visitors, have been converted within to wholly new and practical purposes. But, as has been noted previously, the Capitol, the Governor's Palace and the Raleigh Tavern, having perished completely, have been rebuilt upon the original foundations, after meticulous investigation.

Many buildings have survived at the cost of being trundled off to new sites. A recent instance, on a major scale, is that of *Boscobel,* a great manor house in the Adam style, built in 1804 at Crugers in Westchester County, New York. Demolished in 1955 after being sold to a housewrecker for $35, the building has been reassembled on a new site overlooking the river fifteen miles away at Garrison-on-Hudson at a reported cost of $1.25 million. The rescue of this great house was chiefly due to the Reader's Digest Foundation, headed by Mr. and Mrs. DeWitt Wallace. Other more modest ancient buildings, displaced by parking lots, housing developments or new highways, have found shelter in the lee of friendly institutions. Early in this century the Essex Institute in Salem began gathering architectural flotsam in its back garden; recently the Crowninshield-Bentley House of 1727 has found a new home on a corner of the Institute's grounds.

Many smaller buildings hitherto unrelated to one another, have been transported to new surroundings and resettled in a manner inspired by the open-air folk museums of Scandinavia. It should be remembered that the prototype of these institutions, Skansen in Stockholm, was founded by Artur Hazelius at a moment in the 1880's when Sweden was rapidly being industrialized, and numerous artists and writers were consoling themselves by reviving the memory of a simpler agricultural world in which none of these nasty things existed. As Dr. Ingvar Anderson has remarked, "They harked back to a world of fantasy that bore no relation to Sweden." Thus Hazelius, in addition to founding the Nordiska Museet of Ethnology, created nearby at Skansen a scene in which various ancient farmhouses and rural buildings were reestablished, in the midst of what amounted to a tasteful amusement park. Here again, in Professor Coolidge's phrase, was opposed "to the inevitable fluidity of the present, a dream-image of an immutable past." On holidays, workers could get away from their machines, drink beer in pleasant surroundings, and have a good time while imagining they were farmers as their grandfathers had been.

A similar form of this self-deception inspired Henry Ford to purchase the Wayside Inn in Sudbury, Mass., in the 1920's, to take up square-dancing, promote the "McGuffey type" education of children (in air-conditioned log cabins with indirect electric cove lighting), and to transport to the Edison Institute Museum and Greenfield Village in Dearborn, Mich., an incredible quantity of artifacts and buildings, unrelated in any mind save his own. Thus among other things he hauled to Dearborn a miscellany of structures that included the brick shed in which he built the first Ford car, a Cape Cod windmill, a courthouse where Lincoln once practiced law, the early laboratories of his hero-crony Thomas A. Edison, and much else besides.

Henry Ford collected omnivorously. He was fascinated by the mechanic and domestic arts, and now that the collections have been sorted and selectively displayed by a highly skilled corps of museum experts they reveal an amazing breadth and quality. The tip of the iceberg that now shows includes some of the finest examples of the decorative arts in china, silver, pewter, pottery and textiles. Not to be underestimated are the homely items of domestic use which other collectors of his era ignored and which can never be acquired again. For example, the stoves range from the elaborate early eighteenth-century tile stoves of German and Dutch origin to iron fantasies in the form of Grecian urns or Gothic pinnacles; and the same applies to the collections of farm implements, vehicles and the whole impedimenta of an American domestic life.

Another great collection is that established at Wilmington, Del., by Henry Francis du Pont at the Winterthur Museum. It has been described as "the largest and most distinguished collection of American decorative arts of the period 1640-1850 ever brought together. Displayed against a background of 185 period rooms it provides a commentary on tides of taste as exemplified by the finest examples of American artists and craftsmen." In cooperation with the University of Delaware it is used for teaching museum work and connoisseurship.

OPEN-AIR MUSEUMS

A strong element of the "dream-image of an immutable past" has been present in the development of most open-air museums in the United States during the past quarter-century. At Cooperstown the New York State Historical Association has collected from various localities a school, church, country store, tavern and small offices and shops to form a "Village Crossroads" as an adjunct to its imaginative and beautifully installed Farmers' Museum. At Mystic, Conn., the Marine Historical

Association, Inc., has assembled ships, smaller craft and buildings to create a synthetic seaport of the nineteenth century, of equally nostalgic intent. Two other assemblies of old buildings in New England have become institutions from the enthusiastic acquisitiveness of private collectors. Old Sturbridge Village in Sturbridge, Mass., sprang from the antique collecting of Albert B. and J. Cheney Wells of Southbridge; the Shelburne Museum in Vermont from the omnivourous accummulations of the late Mrs. J. Watson Webb. Old Sturbridge Village presents a pleasing illusion of an actual New England community; at Shelburne the impression is simply of a fine field in which buildings from various parts of New England have been reassembled after moving, to house Mrs. Webb's miscellaneous collections.

Only incidentally do such villages serve the cause of historic preservation, for, although they have doubtless rescued from destruction some buildings by moving, their primary purpose is the creation of a well-walled illusion, within which the visitor may enjoy a synthetic "past," that relieves the ugliness and monotony of the tedium in which he spends most of his life. "There is," in addition, as Carl Feiss has pointed out, "a curious contradiction in the great popularity of the simulated villages used as museums, while real villages, one after the other, are subject to the deterioration and misuse caused by the automobile age. In fact, villages on the way to Sturbridge and several other historic museums, which in their own right had at one time great beauty and artistic value, are being destroyed by those very tourists who are looking for quaintness and culture at the museums. In just the same way that the flower market, the Place Verte in Brussels, has been converted to a parking lot, so have village green after village green in New England."

Passing further in the spectrum of historic preservation, from the ship that remains the same to the one that does not, one leaves restoration and crosses the Styx to reconstruction. Here again there are degrees and variations, depending upon the amount of data available, the care given to research, and the skill of architect and craftsman. But even the finest reconstruction is quite another matter from an actual building that has simply been repaired and stripped of later additions. When Governor William Tryon's palace in New Bern, N.C., burned in 1798, only the separate west wing survived. Yet nearly a century and a half later, through the personal generosity of the late Mrs. James Edwin Latham and appropriations from the state of North Carolina, the palace has been recreated at a cost of just under $3 million.

Fortunately, in addition to the foundations and the west wing, John Hawks' elevation and plan of the building survived in the Public Record Office in London; and the architects, Perry, Shaw, Hepburn and Dean, had had a wealth of experience from their work at Williamsburg. Here again, however,

is not preservation but "a modern dream of the past made concrete."

One may well echo Professor Coolidge's question about reconstructed palaces. "These millions could have preserved a Newcastle, Del., a Marblehead, a Portsmouth, or a Newburyport forever. They would have saved permanently a hundred historic houses. Which is more important, a genuine old building saved, or a modern dream of the past made concrete?" The same question applies with equal pertinence to the First Iron Works Association, Inc., at Saugus, Mass., where, in addition to preserving a fine seventeenth-century ironmaster's house, $2.3 million provided by the American Iron and Steel Institute of New York, were spent on a full-scale reconstruction of the seventeenth-century hammersmith works, complete with buildings, waterwheels and machinery.

Tryon Palace and the Saugus Ironworks, like many less ambitious ventures in reconstruction, have the merit of standing upon the actual sites of the buildings they recreate. There is, however, still another category to be considered: out-and-out reconstructions of early buildings, for which there is only fragmentary evidence, built for commemorative celebrations or for supposedly "educational" purposes in public parks or upon other sites than those occupied by the structures whose memory they attempt to evoke. Sometimes they are designed by learned men after careful research; at others they are pure fantasies of invention. Even so, they are so far from their originals that even the most contentious of the Greek philosophers would hardly argue that they were the same ship in which Theseus journeyed to Crete. In short, whatever they may be, they are no part of historic preservation. Their existence simply confuses and beclouds the issue, in addition to diverting large sums of money that might have been used for better purposes.

The Pioneers' Village in Forest River Park, Salem, Mass., was built to mark the Massachusetts Bay Tercentenary of 1930. It was a serious attempt to reconstruct, in a public park, examples of the rude huts, dugouts, wigwams and houses that sheltered the first settlers. The village was planned by George Francis Dow, a knowledgeable antiquarian; the planting arranged by Harlan P. Kelsey, a historically-minded nurseryman. At the time of the Tercentenary, it stimulated the popular imagination, and for the succeeding 35 years it has been decently maintained by the Salem Park Commissioners. The thatch is getting thin; here and there plaster has fallen away from a chimney, revealing wire lath; trees and shrubs have grown so as to obscure the original pattern. In retrospect it seems somewhat futile, but as commemorative efforts go, it deserves a better mark than most.

At Plymouth, Mass., the modern town is built on the site of the original settlement. Consequently, the Pilgrim Village of 1627 and the Fort Meetinghouse reconstruction undertaken since World War II by Plimoth Plantation—a nonprofit educational organization formed, according to its circular of information, "to tell the story of the Pilgrims"—are on an entirely unrelated site at Eel River, two miles south. On the Plymouth waterfront is exhibited *Mayflower II,* the replica of the Pilgrim vessel designed by the American naval architect William A. Baker, built in England and sailed across the Atlantic in 1957, under command of Captain Alan Villiers. The aim of the reconstruction is to have Plimoth Plantation "look as much like the original Plantation as historical and archaeological research can make it." The research has been careful, yet the reconstruction that results has much of the unconvincing impermanence of pageantry about it.

DREAM IMAGES OF AN IMMUTABLE PAST

Throughout the United States there are numerous reconstructions of one thing and another, some of which are nothing more than tourist traps. But even those, like the Pioneers' Village and Plimoth Plantation which are based upon careful research, are in essence expensive life-size toys, manufactured for children of all ages who have forgotten how to read. They may be effective instruments of education, amusement, propaganda or some kind of special pleading, but they have precious little to do with history, and absolutely nothing to do with historic preservation.

An unfortunate aspect of our tendency to isolate the past in institutions, and particularly in museum-villages and towns, is the fakery and nonsense that results from the inappropriate application of decorative elements from this romaticized past to modern buildings of a utilitarian sort. In Andover, Mass., settled in 1645, I had my teeth filled for several years in a respectable yellow clapboarded house of the late nineteenth century on Main Street. In the course of time, my dentist died. A developer bought his, and a similar adjacent house; completely enclosed the two in red brick, added an imitation of the portico of *Mount Vernon,* and, for good measure, named the resulting shopping arcade "Olde Andover Village." Although Andover is still rich in fine ancient buildings, it had not previously seemed necessary to the inhabitants to advertise it as "old," particularly with a redundant "e." Yet fakery of this kind is contagious. What one huckster does, others will shortly emulate.

We used to hear of buildings with a "Queen Anne front and a Mary Ann behind," but even in our era of self-proclaimed functionalism, many utilitarian buildings have a similarly split personality. A supermarket remains a supermarket, even if frosted with an adobe or a supposedly-Georgian facade, and nothing can redeem the sea of asphalt that surrounds it. Houses disfigured by cheap approximations of the portico of *Mount Vernon,* which are almost as numerous as children named George Washington, have done little to elevate the quality of American life. No mass-produced developer's house will ever be mistaken for George Wythe's or Thomas Jefferson's, even if built of red brick with small window panes.

Red brick with certain pseudo-Georgian flourishes is almost joining motherhood as an article of national belief. In too many instances we let the automobile ruin our towns and cities. We then go in our automobiles to one of the isolated and seductive "dream-images of an immutable past," and return to perpetrate parodies of what we have seen. There is much food for thought in Daniel J. Boorstin's *The Image, or What Happened to The American Dream,* in which he analyzes the "pseudo-events" that loom so large in our lives. In treating the "lost art of travel," he remarks: "In order to satisfy the exaggerated expectations of tour agents and tourists, people everywhere obligingly become dishonest mimics of themselves." Thus in too many historic sites, attendants disguise themselves in fancy dress, which is seldom convincing and often ridiculous. Because of this in many American towns the growing of whiskers and the wearing of hoop skirts have been essential elements in any historical observance.

I was startled a few years ago to find that the plantation *Tara,* the set created for the filming of *Gone with the Wind,* was piously preserved as a tourist attraction, but downright dismayed to find that someone had built a copy of *Tara* to live in (in New Orleans, of all places). This is like the restaurant-keeper who decorates his dining room with a mass-produced copy of a *Chinoiserie* wallpaper, thus using a twentieth-century reproduction of an eighteenth-century western fantasy of the East to prove that he *is* Chinese.

With this kind of fakery going on, people often fail to recognize the significance and value of genuine survivals of a later period that surround them. The disease is spreading, but it received a descriptive name only recently when a Maine postmistress, hearing that a summer resident had a Boston painter spattering the floors of a local farmhouse, remarked that Mr. So-and-so was "anticking-up" the old place. It should be clearly understood that "anticking-up," like reconstruction, has nothing whatsoever to do with historic preservation. Nor for that matter does the pseudo-pious repetition of that much-overworked word "heritage."

Just as there are many degrees of authenticity in historic preservation, so there are varied opinions on what is worthy of preservation, particularly where architectural and artistic tastes are involved.

Most people think poorly of their parents' wedding presents, and some even turn up their noses at their grandparents' notions of interior decoration, but when buildings or objects are three or more generations away, they begin to be treated with respect. Thus buildings less than a century old, in styles currently unfashionable, often are victims of neglect, if not of downright antagonism.

The Back Bay in Boston, handsomely conceived as to plan and harmoniously built up, chiefly between the years 1860 and 1900, is in every sense as admirable an example of American architecture of the *second* half of the nineteenth century as the adjacent Beacon Hill Historic District is of the first half. I doubt if any other city in the United States has retained so many fine blocks of brick and stone town houses of this period. Many architects and historians firmly believe that the Back Bay should be subjected to the architectural control of a historic district before irretrievable inroads are made in its present unity of style and height. José Luis Sert, Dean of the Harvard Graduate School of Design, wrote last year: "Boston has many magnificent man-made sites as well as natural ones. Their scale, too, should be maintained. Beacon Hill is quite obviously more than buildings. There is a scale about the whole which should be maintained. I feel the same way about the Back Bay and Harvard. We must keep these as entities rather than isolated monuments. As they are relatively small areas, plenty of room remains for tearing down and building up, but we always seem to want to tamper with what is good. Commonwealth Avenue is one of the most beautiful avenues of the world and everything should be done to keep it that way. It is lively. Although the architecture is not great, it has character and harmony." Yet there is still a battle to convince many Bostonians, who should know better, that this is so.

In some cities residents seem to develop positive glee at the prospect of obliterating their nineteenth-century past. St. Louis today has its share of such people, who are as determined to destroy the old Post Office as a vigorous group of preservationists, with national support, are to save it. It is ironical that in Philadelphia in the 1950's during the creation of Independence National Historical Park a number of nineteenth-century buildings esteemed by architectural historians were demolished under the banner of historic preservation in the course of supposed enhancement of their eighteenth-century predecessors. In removing everything that had not been there in the eighteenth century, from various blocks near Independence Hall, the surviving buildings, which had been built for a crowded urban setting, were left in unaccustomed and irremediable nakedness. Carpenters' Hall, designed to stand in the middle of a block, at the end of an alley, is now left exposed, incongruously out of scale in great open space, and defenceless from the unrelated structures outside the historic area against which it is silhouetted. Tasteful brick-walled beds of ivy and lines of trees never will put poor Carpenters' Hall down an alley again. To many visitors Independence Hall is as damaged by the grandiose malls that approach it, as was Bernini's Piazza San Pietro when Mussolini swept away the Borgo and created the ridiculous Via della Conciliazione, which spoils, by giving away the surprise too soon, the once-dramatic approach to the most breath-taking open space in Christendom. A desire to enshrine any building out of context is bound to fail. It also hopelessly mucks up normal life in the environs, leaving a vacuum to be filled by busloads of tourists. As in the parable recorded in Matthew xii 43–45, "the last state of that man is worse than the first."

PRINCIPLES AND GUIDELINES

Hopefully we are getting beyond the point where people will attempt to "restore back" an area or building to a given period of time when it involves the destruction of creditable work of a later period. The previously cited National Trust 1964 *Report on Principles and Guidelines* well observes: "It is ordinarily better to retain genuine old work of several periods, rather than arbitrarily to 'restore' the whole, by new work, to its aspect at a single period. This applies to work of periods later than those now admired, provided it represents a genuine creative effort, or is a part of the life history of a building. In no case should our own artistic preferences or prejudices lead us to modify, on esthetic grounds, work of a bygone period representing other artistic tastes. Truth is not only stranger than fiction, but more varied and more interesting." This applies to towns and cities quite as much as to individual buildings. The circumstance of the National Trust for Historic Preservation moving the Pope-Leighey house, a Frank Lloyd Wright building, to *Woodlawn Plantation* when highway construction threatened its destruction on its original site in Falls Church, Va., should make it abundantly clear that no building of architectural merit is too recent to be considered for historic preservation if it otherwise meets the necessary standards.

If most preservationists were honest, they would admit that they seek to preserve ancient buildings and sites because these add to the variety and beauty of a life that is daily more mechanized and stereotyped. Yet too often conscience enters in and makes them feel that they must scrabble about and discover some high purpose that will justify their preoccupation. John D. Rockefeller, Jr., once wrote: "The restoration of Williamsburg offered an opportunity to restore a complete area and free it entirely from alien and inharmonious surroundings, as well as to preserve the beauty and charm of the old buildings and gardens of the city and its historic significance. Thus, it made *a unique and irresistible appeal.*" So far, so good, but then enters conscience, for Mr. Rockefeller continued: "As the work has progressed, I have come to feel that perhaps an even greater value is the lesson that it teaches of the patriotism, high purpose and unselfish devotion of our forefathers to the common good." This second thought is understandable in a man of his generation and religious background, but let us hope that future preservationists will be as little moved by such considerations as they will be by the earlier quoted resolve of the 1850 New York legislative committee concerning the Hasbrouck House, or President Eliot's rhapsody on the emotional values of the Old South Meeting House.

We already have on exhibition more historic houses and museums than we need, or are good for us as a nation. Indeed, they multiply so fast that some form of institutional contraception must soon be invented. And some of these deal out, in the sacred name of "education," some pretty dubious nostalgia, disguised as "history." Meanwhile, we urgently need to improve the quality of our lives and of our surroundings. Therefore let us save what we have around us that is good, not for exhibition, not for "education," but for practical use as places to live in and to work in. Preservationists should try to keep America Beautiful, rather than to create little paradises of nostalgia in an ocean of superhighways and loudspeakers, billboards, neon signs, parking lots, used-car dumps, and hot dog stands.

It is heartening to see that the President of the United States and Mrs. Johson, like the Emperior Majorian a millenium and a half ago, are "determined to remedy the detestable process which has long been going on, whereby the face of the venerable city [and in this case, of the entire country] is being disfigured." But now as then the public edifices are still too frequently "being pulled to pieces at the suggestion of the city officials," not on the old "pretense that the stones are wanted for the public works," but on the new one that the space is required for something more up-to-the-minute. At some levels of American life the sign of civic progress is still "to tear down the familiar and erect the monstrous." The great duty of preservationists at the present moment is to see that the ideal of beauty and order that is now not only respected but enjoined at the highest level of the United States government be brought home in unmistakable terms to state and local officials and to private citizens everywhere throughout the United States. For this task it is fortunate that historic preservation has traditionally been in this country a widely diffused local responsibility, carried on by energetic persons in many walks of life. Only by such a widespread effort will vestiges of America's past remain on their original sites to lend dignity, continuity, grace and variety to the course of American life.

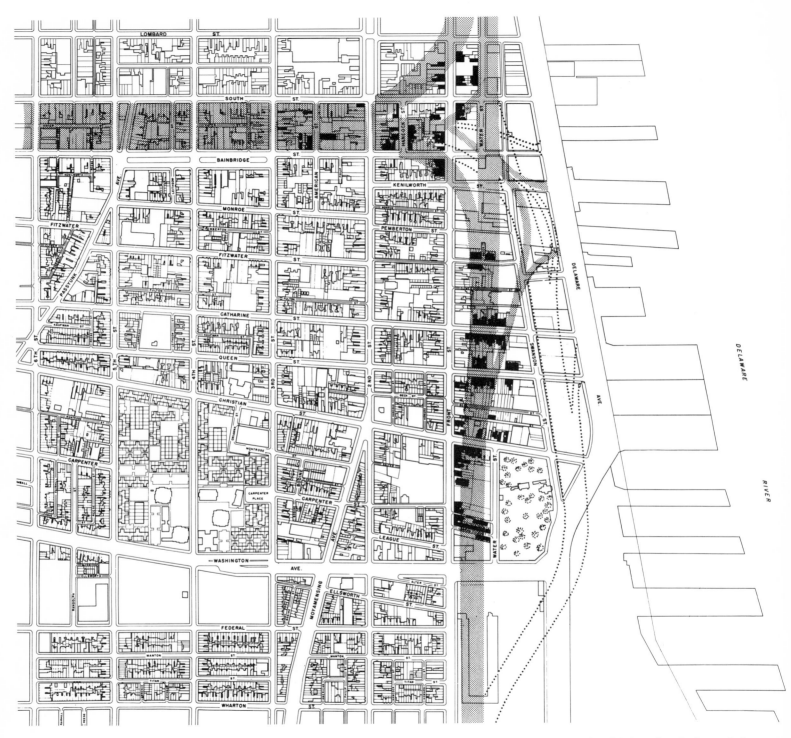

Often, planning for alternates can avert the ruin of historic areas. In the above map of Southwark, Philadelphia, the shadow of destruction, shown in grey, marks the proposed Delaware Expressway, in whose path 182 buildings, which have been certified by the Philadelphia Historical Commission as being of merit, are to be destroyed. By rerouting the highway, through the old warehouse district indicated by the dotted lines on the map, 135 of these buildings could be saved from demolition.

56

WINDOW TO THE PAST

George Zabriskie

Not since the war of 1812 has the united states suffered any serious loss of its buildings through foreign military action. Yet in the second half of the twentieth century we suffer an attrition of distinguished structures which has the aspect of a catastrophe when the human use of our architectural resources is considered. For the true loss is in the measure of how well or meanly we and our descendants are to live: not in the terms of historical sentimentality or preservation for preservation's sake. The real value of any building to the community lies in its being a delight to the eye and in its susceptibility to human use. Where true historical value exists, it is enriched by the possibility of continued use of the building, as in the case of many government buildings, rather than by lifeless embalmment as a museum. Unhappily, in this decade we are losing many buildings which meet the criteria of beauty and usefulness. Many buildings less than a century, or even half a century old, and still suitable for their tenants' purposes, are demolished for reasons of financial gain rather than those of obsolescence or unfitness for use.

In every large city new office buildings are rising at a pace which often exceeds that of actual space demands. Their architects are faced with the need to deliver the maximum amount of rentable floor space at the minimum cost. Under such circumstances they are forced to neglect many of the purely human considerations permitted their predecessors. A street of such buildings at night has its own impersonal impressiveness, but where an older building has been allowed to stand, breaking the blank facade we are reminded with a shock that the older architecture added much to the sheer joy of living.

The impact of the mechanized and more or less standardized impersonal buildings—Le Corbusier's "machine for living" come true in a way he did not intend—has made an increasing number of Americans aware of the value inherent in many older structures: not that they are old, but that they contain so much of ourselves. This awareness of human values, whether conscious or hidden behind the expression of other motivations, plays a real part in the growing movement for preservation of older structures. People wish to save those things which are familiar to them and which they love. This seemingly simple platitude has had an ever increasing force in American life, and in the present decade has become an important factor in politics. More than one candidate for state or local office has been forced to take a stand on either particular or general issues of preservation and conservation. Unhappily, all candidates do not live up to their campaign promises after election: but the mere fact that they have been driven to make such promises is significant in itself.

Politicians with good will, preservationists, trained or untrained, and increasing popular support are not enough unless united in purposeful action. Each week some American city loses a part of its past which might be retained, or an entire area may be threatened with extinction. So rapidly do things change that as this book has been written some buildings and areas have been given a reprieve for a time at least, and others despite efforts to save them, have perished.

Some structures, such as the Kelley Mansion in Columbus, Ohio, a Greek revival house at Rochester, N.Y., and the Firehouse belonging to the Society of Oldest Inhabitants of the District of Columbia have been dismantled for preservation and the pieces stored awaiting a promised future resurrection. In the 19th century John Brown's Enginehouse at Harpers Ferry suffered similar treatment. It was dismantled, exhibited at the Chicago World's Fair, stored in pieces, reassembled temporarily on a farm outside of Harpers Ferry, dismantled again, and reassembled on the campus of Storer College. At present the National Park Service hopes to dismantle it for the last time and rebuild it on its original site. While such preservation is better than total loss, it leaves much to be desired.

In Saint Louis, Missouri, the Old Post Office Building, at Eighth and Olive Streets, is threatened with destruction, although local citizens have formed a workable and interesting plan for its future use—if they can save it. The General Services Administration is authorized to use the land for a modern, 30 story federal office building which would house other federal offices in addition to the post office. The new building would occupy only one third of the land area used by the present structure, freeing the other two thirds for a proposed open square to be developed as a park. The old building itself was designed by Alfred Mullet, the first architect to breach the neo-classical tradition in government buildings, and who designed the old State, War and Navy (now the Executive) Building in Washington, D.C., and the San Francisco Mint. Although a park in the area has long been needed, Mullet's Saint Louis post office is *surely* worth preserving. The dilemma admits no easy solution, since the problem is to find equivalent land in the area for Federal and park use. If the Post Office can be preserved, the building may be transformed into a civic center, with provision for shops, offices, and an air conditioned interior esplanade.

In Cleveland, Ohio, The Euclid Arcade, built in 1890, is threatened by the harsh facts of its present economics. Designed by John Eisemann and George H. Smith, it is a light, airy structure of iron and glass built on the bed of a prehistoric lake. Among its early stockholders were Stephen V. Harkness, known as a philanthropist to Harvard, Columbia, and Yale Universities, Charles F. Brush, the early manufacturer of arc lamps and electrical machinery, and John D. Rockefeller. With its glass roof soaring one hundred feet above the central wall four hundred feet long, it is a still functional and handsome prototype for the modern enclosed pedestrian oriented shopping centers. Except for air conditioning, Eisemann and Smith accomplished many of the features found in contemporary construction of shopping plazas, and which the St. Louis group hope to include in remodeling the Old Post Office. Basically sound in design, the Arcade might be refurbished and saved as a continuing example of controlled environment.

In the past two decades Chicago has lost many fine buildings from its era of great architecture. Buildings by Adler and Sullivan, Richardson, Holabird and Roche and other great architectural firms have been demolished in the face of rising land values. In terms of vigorous approaches to design, no city in America has as rich an architectural heritage as Chicago, and each building it loses is a nation-wide, even an international loss. Yet when the Glessner Mansion, the last remaining example of Richardson's work in that city, was offered to the city or any non-profit group in return for maintenance, there were no takers. Philip Johnson, a New York architect, purchased an option on the building seeking to save it; but found, to his disappointment, that no group was willing to undertake its continued operation and preservation, even though it was being offered for use and not for museum purposes.

The Glessner House is an official architectural landmark of the city of Chicago. Mayor Daley has reportedly promised Johnson that it will not be sacrificed. The city has no power to save it, however, because legislation empowering it to preserve landmark buildings lies buried at present in a city council committee.

In Buffalo, N.Y., two famous buildings, Louis Sullivan's Prudential Building, and Richard Upjohn's St. Paul's Cathedral are threatened with isolation by the conversion of a flanking street into a limited access highway. The Prudential Building has already suffered some defacement by the dubious "modernization" of its ground floor, long respected for its integrity of design. One of the youngest of Sullivan's great buildings, there are rumors that the owners of the Prudential may destroy it within the next year or so.

Not all the important buildings threatened with demolition are in cities, or are victims of rising land values. *Hyde Hall*, designed by Philip Hooker, architect of the original State Capitol at Albany, stands in a state park at the north end of Otsego Lake, near Cooperstown, New York. A stately manorial house of dressed stone, with two formal rooms each 30 by 40 feet with 18 foot ceilings, *Hyde Hall* built in 1833, is indeed worth preserving, for architectural and historical value and for possible use in conjunction with varied projects. At present, it is scheduled for demolition sometime within the next two years, since there are no funds available for its rehabilitation and continued maintenance.

Yet urban problems of preservation are the most pressing and the most complex. A variety of conflicting interests: economic, automotive, human, political, private and governmental are encountered, and striking a just balance may appear insuperable. In many cities it is difficult to identify the degree of jeopardy of important historic areas, since it may change with such shifting circumstances as popular support and political administrations. As examples, the complex problems of Savannah, Ga., and New Orleans, La., may be cited briefly. The old central portion of Savannah and the Vieux Carré in New Orleans are both in serious trouble because neither community has found a happy way of integrating history and historic architecture with the solution of problems in the central city. The architectural character and the ground plans of these areas are totally different, and the preservation efforts in the two cities are also dissimilar.

In the case of Savannah, the unique town plan, with its twenty one squares and the Trust Lots which create a special street pattern, provides the city with assets of open spaces which most of the citizens take for granted. At considerable cost other cities are creating or trying to create open spaces where none have existed before. But many citizens of Savannah tend to consider the open squares and Trust Lots as nuisances or an exploitable opportunity for more parking lots. Old houses and commercial structures around the squares and along the boulevards have been disappearing one by one over a long period. Many are in jeopardy at present, and the number of threatened structures is likely to increase. The situation in Savannah is further complicated by the fact that there are no local historic zoning provisions, like those in Charleston and New Orleans. Fortunately, under the active leadership of Leopold Adler II, the Historic Savannah Foundation which has already acquired and restored the fine Davenport House, has established a revolving fund for the acquisition and preservation of numerous other Savannah buildings by a system similar to that used by the Historic Charleston Foundation in Charleston's Ansonborough District. In Savannah there is also a rapidly growing group of prominent citizens who have been acquiring and restoring for lease and sale fine old buildings in widely scattered holdings throughout the old city area. The Troop Trust Urban Renewal project, sponsored by the city with the Historic Savannah Foundation acting as developer, is a significant step ahead in the conversion of fine buildings in a small slum area into good residences. Through the combination of these efforts, substantial gains have been made during the past five years, and many squares are again becoming attractive and habitable. At the same time, several other sections of the old town are threatened with demolition and a portion of Factor's Row along the river front has recently been considered as an expendable site for a civic center. There is no overall plan for downtown Savannah which makes the necessary adjustments between the old and the new; and while there has been an inventory made of old and intrinsically valuable buildings, it has not yet been published, and cannot in itself constitute an adequate brake on destruction. It is impossible to predict the outcome of such a fluid situation.

In New Orleans, despite the excellent work of the Vieux Carré Commission and the far seeing laws within which it operates, the proximity of the Vieux Carré to Canal Street and to the pressures of the rapidly growing downtown business area has created a situation similar to that in Savannah. The rate of building loss appears to be less here than in Savannah, but the threats are continuous, particularly at the edges of the historic district. Heavy through traffic congests the streets and shakes the buildings. A major debate is in progress on the location and design of an eight lane expressway and its connections which would impinge on the area. New motels and hotels are rapidly changing the character of the Quarter.

Preservation, in New Orleans, is a hot and current battle. Hopeful indications exist. The Urban Renewal Administration of the Department of Housing and Urban Development in Washington is financing a demonstration grant study from which a plan for the preservation of the Vieux Carré will be developed, and Tulane University has been actively participating in a major inventory involving some 4,000 properties in the Vieux Carré along with highway studies.

In both cities there is an indication that in the search for reasonable adjustment there is much unnecessary blood letting, largely because of a lack of agreement on objectives and a false *a priori* attitude frequently held by both sides that the opposing positions are mutually incompatible.

Elsewhere in the South, there have been occasional chance preservations. One in Columbia, S.C. seems almost miraculous. The bulldozers were at work on the grounds and demolition crews were working in the cellar of Ainsley Hall Mansion, one of the last two remaining masonry houses by Robert Mills when a visiting architect noticed them, just before quitting time. He spread notice of the impending destruction to local civic leaders, who formed the Historic Columbia Foundation overnight, and found funds before morning to stop the destruction. The house was purchased from the ecclesiastical institution which had owned it and was preparing to sell it for a parking lot. By the next evening, a temporary fence had been built around the property to secure it from further damage. Today several community organizations are busy restoring the house and gardens as part of a historic area plan related to a historic zoning program. The kind of vigilance demonstrated in Columbia in this instance is cited in many other sections of the book, and is not unlike the story of England's St. Paul's Cathedral, within a peacetime context.

The West Coast too, has had its dramas of preservation, and one of the most important of these took place in Los Angeles. At stake were not historic buildings, nor parklands but idiosyncratic structures in a depressed area: human artifacts with no function but expression of purely human meanings, Watts Towers. The steep open structures loom from a flat and colorless neighborhood. They are constructions of steel rods, mesh and mortar, in a maze of forms which soar to a hundred foot height. The weblike members are covered with a glittering incrustation of broken tiles, dishes, bottles and seashells. Woven together by overhead arches around the spires are fountains, pavilions and labyrinths. The magic walled garden is covered too, with multicolored mosaic, or with imprints of tools, hands, corncobs, and baskets, interwoven here and there with the initials of the builder, Simon Rodia, who created the towers without aid, in 33 creative years.

James D. Van Trump has written of them:

> Watts webbed towers are an intensely private dream: the first is Renaissance-Classical, the heir of gods and kings, and the other, if it can be classified, may be Gothic, spun from the heart and hands of a simple workman. The one is founded in the City Beautiful, the other lies in the City Desolate, but both enormously transcend their surroundings, and they rise superior to all mundane considerations, Perhaps only this fabulous southwest land could have produced them both.

Barbara Jones obviously agreed. In her book, *Follies and Grottoes,* published in London in 1949, she wrote that "concentric towers or cones of spirals so beautiful, on so gigantic a scale for one man's work, that it . . . be held superior to all but

the finest work of the eighteenth century here. Rodia is a genius."

After the death of Simon Rodia, in 1959 the towers were condemned. Carl Sandburg and other internationally known writers, architects and scientists championed their preservation. The Museum of Modern Art in New York City wired "Urge public and private agencies to unite to save these works of great beauty and imagination which are a part of our cultural heritage." Delegates of 15 countries attending the 11th Assembly of the International Association of Art Critics adopted a resolution reading in part "We hope every measure will be taken for preservation and upkeep of the structure, a unique combination of sculpture and architecture and a paramount achievement of twentieth century folk art in the United States".

During five weeks of deadlocked hearings before the Buildings and Safety Department, the Committee for the Simon Rodia Towers in Watts fought valiantly for their preservation. When structural tests were applied to satisfy critics of their safety, a 10,000 pound horizontal load applied to the tallest tower at one third of its height from the base, resulted in a deflection of only 3/16 inch, with permanent deformation of only ⅛ inch.

The ultimate fate of the towers still rests however, on their being continued in use, and under present plans for the Watts area they will become part of a cultural center complex.

Throughout the West, there is an increasing interest in preservation of old structures and entire towns. At many mining and lumbering sites, isolation makes rehabilitation easier; at others, damage by fire, floods and vandalism has made it impossible.

Jacksonville, Oregon has been preserved—not as a museum ghost town, but as a living city, using its historic places for dwelling and working. At Central City, Colorado, along with other buildings, the old Opera House has been restored and is used for summer performances. In Arizona, the town of Tombstone has been largely rebuilt through the efforts of its citizens, and Bumblebee has been restored by its owner, Charles A. Penn, a former publisher.

In Annapolis, the capital of Maryland and also the site of The United States Naval Academy and St. John's College, Historic Annapolis Inc. is engaged in a determined fight to preserve the character of the older buildings and the waterfront. Since 1952 it has been fending off encroachments on the historic residential and harbor areas by the Naval Academy and by developers. The greatest present threat is the construction of high rise office buildings, motels and apartments in the old maritime area. The city council, local bankers and other commercial interests have failed to realize that once the waterfront has been taken over, Annapolis will lose most of its tourist trade, its marine business, and its appeal as an old residential city. The outside builders seeking to erect high rises are in the ironic position of expecting to profit from the very thing they will destroy: the historic character of the city. At present, Historic Annapolis Inc. owns three buildings and has engaged in three lawsuits to preserve historic areas. In Annapolis, as in other cities, the solution must be found through a comprehensive plan to preserve the charm of an expanding city by strong historic zoning and creative use of existing structures.

Area restorations, whether entire towns or complete sections of cities, are more rewarding than preserving a single structure in a hostile or indifferent environment. One of the earlier restorations of a historic area is Georgetown, in the District of Columbia. Once a slum, its successful rehabilitation, which began shortly before World War I, has been a continual struggle against a variety of adverse forces. Today, even though protected by the Historic Georgetown Act, its inhabitants know that they must still battle to keep their gains.

In Columbus, Ohio, more recent efforts have been successful in preserving German Village, a section of downtown Columbus settled in the middle of the 19th century by German immigrants near a string of breweries. Most of the village's 1700 houses are neat brick structures with wooden shutters, slate roofs, wrought iron fences and gates, tall chimneys and small gardens, set along narrow stone block streets, or on brick streets with brick sidewalks.

By 1959, the area seemed headed for destruction in the Columbus Urban Renewal program and many houses had already been condemned. In that year, a single restoration by Mr. and Mrs. Frank Fetch which was opened to the public and widely publicized helped turn the tide. A German Village Society was formed, and by 1963 its members and other property owners in the 40 block area had already spent more than $1 million for alterations and rehabilitation. By May 1965 more than 200 houses had been rehabilitated.

Frank Fetch, who heads the German Village Society, is proud of the work being done in the area. "This just shows what communities can do by themselves, without Federal or state monies" he says. "We have proved this type of thing will work". Today, protected by historic district area zoning, with new construction and rehabilitation policed by an official commission, German Village is an attractive area, offering small town living at moderate costs, within walking distance of downtown stores and offices. Its example is spreading to other parts of Columbus, since it has shown that restoration, of basically sound structures in a homogenous area, when intelligently directed can be an economically successful revitalizing force.

The little town of Cape May, New Jersey began as a seventeenth century whaling port. As early as the eighteenth century, it became a seaside resort, and through the nineteenth century it was a mecca where the elegant and wealthy built large Victorian establishments which they described as cottages. With the coming of the railroad, a number of handsome large hotels were built to accommodate visitors. Unlike Atlantic City, Cape May was always a rather quiet resort, and during the depression of the 1930's, it almost faded away. In that decade, railroad service died away, and relatively few people cared to drive the additional distance from Philadelphia when Atlantic City and other resorts were nearer. During World War II. Cape May was the site of a Naval Air Station. After the war the town slumped. Although it was able to attract some industry, there were limits to its industrial expansion, and other sources of revenue were needed.

In 1964 the ferry service between Cape May and Lewes, Delaware was reopened with ships from the Chesapeake Bay service. This renewed traffic made the tourist and resort business a possible source of revenues.

By good fortune, most of Cape May's Victorian buildings were intact, and it became obvious to the town that its appeal to tourists lay in its nineteenth century charm. The local newspaper carried a series of articles on the town's history, open town meetings were held to develop a program, and pamphlets issued for publicity. Funds were obtained from the Housing and Home Finance Agency's Urban Renewal Administration for studies and such improvements as a new sea wall and sewer and water mains. Roads have been improved, gas streetlights restored, and a museum has been created.

In Richmond, Virginia, Church Hill, the area around Saint John's Chuch, built in 1741, where Patrick Henry defied the British Crown with his speech of "Give me liberty or give me death" has undergone a renaissance in the past decade.

The Historic Richmond Foundation was organized in 1956 to insure the preservation and retention in use of historic or otherwise interesting structures in Richmond. Church Hill, which had 70 pre-Civil War houses still standing in various stages of decay, was selected as a pilot area.

More than $100,000 was collected in a drive for funds to purchase and restore historic houses which would be sold or leased to suitable tenants. The Historic Richmond Foundation also worked to secure the passage of a historic district ordinance, which established the Church Hill Historic District and made exterior architectural changes subject to approval by a board of review.

The Foundation worked toward revitalization of the neighborhood, returning buildings to their original use wherever possible. When such complete restoration was impossible, adaptive uses, not incompatible with the structure were followed. The Historic Richmond Foundation now owns 14 houses, has options on three more and has influenced local property owners to restore their own properties and purchase others for restoration.

Church Hill, a slum in 1950, is one of the nation's prime examples of selective urban conservation, in which sound old structures have been restored to constructive utilization through the help of private funds.

Although the success of any preservation activity gives the deceptive feeling that the process is simple, more factors work against preservation than for it. There are still millions of Americans who believe as a matter of principle that anything new is better by the sole virtue of novelty. Their attitude is attended by the equally naive belief that the passage of time brings progress, which is a continuous amelioration of the human condition: therefore, all change is for the better. Such people are not easily persuaded that any existing structure is better than a new parking lot, although they may be persuaded that a new structure is better than an old parking lot.

In many cities sound older structures, built to last as long as they might be useful, are being replaced by buildings with an estimated economic and physical life of twenty to twenty-five years. Tax laws, at federal, state and local levels have encouraged such construction. Some of these laws pertain to depreciation, others to the cost of maintenance or improvement versus replacement. In most cities, local laws favoring parking lot operations make it more profitable to maintain property as a black-topped open space than in use for human purposes. As long as we have a society in which the profit motive is operable, we cannot condemn property owners for wishing to profit from their holdings. We can, however, study tax laws at all levels, with the hope of adjusting them to permit profitable remodeling and retention of sound buildings of architectural and historic importance.

Museum properties are, of course, generally tax exempt. But blanket exemptions work a hardship on the community, and do not encourage preservation of structures for use. Moreover, many architecturally valuable office buildings and other commercial structures are too large and too expensive to be preserved as museums. They can be saved only by continued use, generally after rehabilitation. In too many cases, the cost of air conditioning, new elevators, and interior redecoration defeat the owners, who sell the property for another new building or other uses rather than face the outlay for modernization. Yet as the Landmark Building, formerly the People's Life Insurance Building of Washington, D.C. shows, rehabilitation can both rescue the building and be profitable. A twelve story office building, designed by Milbourn, Heister and Company in 1912-13, it was remodeled in 1961, leaving the exterior appearance unaltered. Inside, high speed elevators, central air conditioning and other improvements were installed. Unlike most of the newer office structures, the Landmark has no win-dowless interior rooms, and its ceilings are a foot and a half higher than those in modern buildings.

Rehabilitation in this instance has yielded a higher income to its owners, and a higher tax return to the community, while retaining an esthetically pleasing structure.

In the 1950's, urban redevelopment, then preceeded by a process of total demolition, was responsible for the destruction of many buildings which under the more enlightened policies prevailing today would have been saved. The new Department of Housing and Urban Development has shown an interest in both historic preservation and maintaining a balance of new and old structures wherever feasible.

The record for highway construction has been much the same. Since 1960, the Bureau of Public Roads in the Department of Commerce has pursued an increasingly enlightened policy toward historic structures and valuable architectural features. Beginning in July 1965, highway plans in urban areas of over 50,000 persons must be based on a cooperative, comprehensive transportation planning process, which will insure that all preservation plans will be given consideration. Unfortunately, the Bureau of Public Roads is dependent upon the state highway departments and local officials for both plans and information. The quality of the data supplied varies from state to state. Although all of it must meet certain minimum requirements to be acceptable, there is often a wide gulf between the ideals of the Bureau of Public Roads and the performances of some of the state departments. Furthermore, in a number of controversial cases, state highway departments and local officials have met the legal requirements for federal construction funds despite opposition in the community. If the interests of area preservation and even the preservation of isolated structures are to be served, the issues must be met at the local and state levels before highway plans are submitted to the Bureau of Public Roads. However, the Bureau of Public Roads should and can insist on evidence which justifies clearly the destruction of historic values directly or indirectly.

Not least among the indignities suffered by older buildings is tampering with the design. Such tampering has a long and often honorable history in American architecture. The Maine sea captain who built a framework of carpenter gothic around his square New England house was to be surpassed later by the conversion of Federal style Hudson River Valley mansions into French mansards and other architectural whimseys of the owners. Some of these early rebuildings were done with care and taste: others were grotesque at best, and the passing of time has done nothing to improve them. In our time, tampering has become more than a desire to change the basic style. The grocery store stuck into the side of a historic mansion, a facade interrupted by freakish fenestration, buildings of all shapes and conditions botched by conversions which could have been accomplished without destroying the integrity of design are familiar to all of us. Sometimes zoning laws or boards of review can prevent these monstrosities, but more often they should have been prevented by the taste of the owner. Although there have been a few cases of rescue, such tampering usually results in the ultimate demolition of the building. In the 1920's it was common to see blocks of stores cut into or surrounding a historic building, usually an old hotel. Today, most of these abominations have disappeared. The usual sequence was for fire to destroy the historic building, then later the stores would be replaced with a more substantial commercial structure. It is not always possible to continue the original use of structures worth preserving: country schools and small ecclesiastical structures are outstanding examples, yet many of these have been converted to residences with little loss of architectural integrity.

Merely because the owners of an area or building have managed to overcome the economic social and political difficulties in the way of rehabilitation does not mean that all has been settled. Short of ownership by the federal government and preservation as a National Monument there is no certain way of maintaining the status of old buildings. The consequences of state and municipal ownership are too often neglect or demolition when a highway project puts forward its claims. The sad fate of New York's beloved Battery Park and Aquarium are reminders of what can happen anywhere.

To privately owned or developed projects, such as German Village and Richmond's Church Hill, zoning laws often seem to give a comfortable measure of protection. Yet zoning laws protect against neither highway construction nor urban redevelopment, although generally an area which is sufficiently well managed is proof against the latter. Furthermore, zoning laws in most areas are subject to review and change by local governing bodies which are not always above political pressure. One of the less attractive forms of present day real estate speculation is the construction of high rise apartments and office buildings in areas where they are out of place and character. Historic Annapolis Inc. is faced with a constant battle to keep such unwanted structures from the historic community. Permission to build one such high rise in a community generally means the end of the community structure if it is granted. To many older suburbs, such as Roland Park, and Garrett Park, Md., or Lewellyn Park, and Essex Fells, N.J., ability to control the zoning laws is the key to continued existence.

In urban or semi urban restoration projects, many of the threats are peripheral. They include commercial enterprises in adjacent unregulated locations, successful pleas for zoning variations which open the door to flagrant violations, and the erection of structures out of character. Yet the effort to keep in character can be equally absurd, as in the case of demolishing an authentic victorian house in sound condition to erect a phony colonial building in its place. The ersatz past is no less displeasing than the incongruous present. By now, there are sufficient examples of distinguished modern architecture existing in an environment of older buildings to demonstrate that quality of design, not period is the determining factor in a harmonious neighborhood. A "colonial" gas station with strings of plastic pennants flapping in the breeze is not more congruous with a row of early 19th century town-houses than a gas station of modern architecture which serves its function unobtrusively. Certainly an unobtrusive service station is not too much to hope for in a country which hopes to send a man to the moon.

As valuable as our past is to us, it must exist as we do, in the world of present realities. Many compromises are desirable: we do not expect the tenants of 19th century houses to use gaslight or oil lamps, coal stoves for heating or cooking, and iceboxes or a hole in the cellar floor for refrigeration. Similarly, even though automobiles may be a wasteful and inconvenient method of transportation we are compelled to rely on them and must have some ways of coming to terms with them in our restored communities. When the area is not too large, we can utilize an idea from Charles Goodman's River Park Community (1963) and keep them outside the living area, although to do so may involve rearrangement of 19th century street planning ideas.

The essential task of retaining the architectural past in the second half of the twentieth century is to keep it in the form of living and functioning entities as far as possible. It is true that certain aspects such as old iron furnaces and plantation houses can exist only as museums; but there are many other kinds of structures—the vast majority—which can again be brought into our daily lives in familiar and useful ways. Even without air conditioning, the luxury of an office in a converted downtown mansion is far greater than that of a windowless room in the interior of a new building. Perhaps if we use the past to introduce windows into our lives again, it will have served no little purpose.

With sufficient wisdom and inventiveness on our part we can indeed use the past for a window into better ways of living. Its values of spaciousness, light and privacy can still be enjoyed in older buildings while they exist, and by reconsidering our uses of land values we can, if we wish, reintroduce them in future construction. The past need not be merely the neglected prelude to the present: it can be used as part of a richer future. The obstacles to such wise use are many, as this and other papers testify. The past has already paid its debt to us: it is now our responsibility to keep alive the best of it to pay our debt to the future.

IMAGES OF TRADITION

*Without some relics the total past becomes less
than a myth: neither useful nor believable, but
only a sense of unknown loss of knowledge which might
exist—a vanished world left for conjecture of
imagined cities in the sun.*

      *Of some buildings
we are glad to have a foundation stone. A lintel
fallen, or vestigial traceries of villages, excite us.
What will we leave our descendants, we
who level things completely, obliterating
every trace of buildings except in the
fallible shadows of human memory?*

*The drawing in our history books, the sentimentalized
saltbox house of our Christmas cards was livable,
so some have lasted. English in design, tradition
binds them to this continent, where earlier forms
of other builders were already deserted
when the white men came. Of this silent world
we have a potsherd knowledge—*

3

—while the lone
church surrounded by traffic and tiered offices
endures as a literary monument, although the town
around it has fallen away.

By the waters of rivers
we build our mills, their images mirrored in still
surfaces to remind us in double vision of our lives
imaged in machiney and of our voices and the
changeable voices of the river drowned by the
cataracts of noise in which we make our lives.

*Against these automatons the voiceless claims of books
in the old libraries, or a place for worship and
meditation—the landscape of variation from
the simple inn to the ornate elegance of Boston's
threatened avenues and trees—*

5

6

— the sturdy cowbarn,
the covered bridge, the Moravian Academy are the
past we cherish in our minds, yet need as standing
emblems of human ways which, seemingly lost, continue
in changed forms among our habits.

9

10

11

12

How can we judge?
May not the humble horse-turned bale press mean more
than the decorous church, the preserved mansion with
the family silver intact, and the impersonal ancestors?

*There are many pasts in the skeletal intricacies
of time gone: summers on porches of resort hotels or
tidy memories of some Greek Revival house which might
be anywhere—wintry New York, old Ohio or Indiana towns.*

15

16

So past supports the past—history rooms in Mill's
first fireproof—the cotton exchange is shut
yet Factor's Row echoes its dead king's memories

19

*Through bleak and plenteous seasons, the old
grain mill keeps going, tied to the present
by a three-phase umbilical, and transformers by the wall.*

*The cast iron traceries weave their thin delicate
patterns in shadows on southern balconies, filigrees
woven into fitful dreams—borne from the sea and
the sea's forts, their battles over, remaining
in memorial repose, waves stilling their silent guns.*

The Spaniards knew the west: their missions lasted
after aureate Eldorado and the argent floods
dwindled to nothing. One in silence, the opera,
and the gold-town church in Atlantic City named
by some land-locked lover of ocean remind us
of the mythos which began at the Mississippi, ended
at Golden Gate, based on cattle, silver, gold,
an effulgent westland, its splendor caught
by the old cathedral in the variable sun.

Spiders are geometers. But a spider never made a parabola of catenaries, to bridge a river, where in autumn spiders and webs fly suddenly in the air above the water. Like the flying spiders, the past flees

27

before a changing wind, and, as for them,
its survival hangs on chance irrationals.
—like the existence of Latrobe's Cathedral and

28

the castellated megalith of the old hospital.
Fortune has saved the bronze turtles ever climbing
toward the fountain's illusion, and the Florida
Mizener masterpiece with its stone ship ever
stormproof and never to leave its harbor.

31

32

*Miracles are not wholly gigantic: the Gothic
cottage, with wooden tendrils echoing life
came from a planbook, though it might have grown
by enchantment from an early novel.*

                    *Fictive, too
the combination of Moorish windows with the stolid
functional squareness of plain stone.*

                    *Yet real
in its lacy elaboration of tropical lushness, the
plantation house built sensibly for a warm wet land
grew from its landscape: even the water tanks
might plausibly have mushroomed on a rainy night.*

*So the northern city hall took form from
septentrional thought of castles and baronies:
even in summer it rises in an ice-encrusted vision.*

*Under the rolling sky, the peninsula hotel is
a remnant of idle days, the crisp smells
of the lake and the Michigan woods float about it
like clouds, and guests make sounds
like migratory birds.*

Looming from the flat land, the court house and its justice are human artifacts, not abstract as designs, but springing verticals against the downward thrust of a too-heavy sky and a world which might with desperation oppress us all.

Like those abstractions, enmeshed in history,
which rose from this Doric building by the river
and like the flooded river, trapped in violence
the helpless and the innocent until, ebbing and
dying away, only the knowledge of misery was left.

38

The Spaniards knew the west: yet the Indians
got there first. They changed the mission's style
and left inexplicable heads, posing
unanswered questions in an old, old land.

39

Explorers, trappers, fur traders plundered the woods;
those who got there late lumbered them over,
leaving brick hotels and wooden banks behind while
the trees again grew tall on the hills. Now on quiet
summer afternoons only the food stores stir.

41

In upper Mexico, the new customs house
was scarcely busy till the Yankees came.
The old Mexican building, a forthright
structure, remains to remind us
of other times, and other ways.

Planner of liberty, Thomas Paine had also plans
for iron bridges and buildings. Other people
built them later. We always expect frock-
coated men, and women with bustles to emerge
from them, yet in their viability they are
inhabited only by ourselves, enjoying the light within.

*Renwick's old Corcoran may have a third life,
restored to its original purposes. Across
the avenue, in newly cleaned splendor,
Mullet's monumental pile remains an ornament
to its time and ours. The steel apparition,
with a red brick integument, won't infringe
on the majesty of its neighbors.*

44

There's no return to ancestral houses gone beyond repair:
the cracked capital, the lost base, the sagging architrave
betray Greece and Rome in a final ruin up which the trumpet
vine climbs slowly to flame on the weathered wood. Who now
can halt the final desolation, when ruin works to its end;
a crumbled chimney, random remains fallen into the cellar,
the encircled wreck held captive by the vines?

Universal in our time, the rotting waterfront
can be anywhere. A stinking river
laps dully at rotting dolphins,
chewed anchorages. The dead end
of the cities' dead ends. Nothing
to do. No place to be.

46

Gaily they danced here, gaily.
Light. The house was ablaze with it.
More light. More music. Gaily, more everything.
All gone now. Vandals have stripped the place.
Mad. Blind. Toothless.
Glassless windows gape at the sun.

That noon is past and gone and yet that noon
is always shadowed on the convent clock.
And no bells toll the time, for there are none,
and none to toll them, now that nuns have gone.
Shuttered and darkened, the building waits its time
told by the sun, in shadows across the stone.

If the language were different, I. Cordova might be
a name in part of a song sung to a guitar in Spain.
But Cordova, whoever he was, left behind a fine
metal front with dented stone and a few lost pieces.
His small alcazar decays under the hot desert sun.

49

A thing alive, or about to spring
into a verdant newness, form in
perpetual growth from the sheer
logical exuberance of design!
The virtuosity of ornament,
the bold and decisive verticals,
the finality of the cornice—
words which are static when
the visual man moves in.
This building's death could only be
desolation to the eye,
desecration to the mind.

The humble customs house, its duty done,
but not its use, in its modest austerity
may have no future but an ignominious end.
In parking lots, cold-flecked with chrome,
the empty badlands of the cities grow.

With wide romantic lawns, by the elms and the willows,
the gentle Gothic dream of time that's past evokes
the curate for tea, the daughter in the tower, reading
deliciously, a novel by Mrs. Radcliffe.

52

*To be replaced
by aisles of detergents, cold cuts containing
anti-oxidants and artificial flavors, a roof like an
archaic aeroplane hangar, and ourselves as insects
swarming on asphalt, to find our cars.*

*In squalid latitudes of the trade winds, plain statement
of honest buildings turns to fraud, with phony stone,
sheet metal, glass, sinking behind a Sargasso of signs.*

53

The Roman temple defiled, the architrave shedding
its plaster above the abused doorway are becalmed
by our times. For defacement, we have classic analogies.

54

*We live in a time of planning our obsolescence, or tearing down
the walls about our ears: the manufacture of ruins which look
bombed-out is profitable and quick. Here was an indoor space
soaring to assert human importance, the glory of our enterprise.
We value ourselves as deserving less than these vaulted spaces,
living in cubicles, watched and watching by electronic eyes.*

56

57

*Home was. The rich no longer have
what the poor lost long ago.
The crane devours the house with high ceilings.
There's no address here:
none left for forwarding.*

*These are the ruins at Philadelphia.
trefoil columns distinguish them
from the ruins at Rome.
memento mori.
follow them
into nothing.*

58

High-stepping, the Black Diamond *paused here,*
the coal drags rumbled through: weekends
the long excursion trains brought multitudes
to ride the famed Gravity Railroad, exclaiming
—Ah! Mount Pisgah! O! The glorious view!—
The passengers are gone: the ticket window
slammed shut for the last time. Even the
wreckers have finished. Only the photograph remains.

We can never believe that the firm's masterpiece,
the house shown in the illustrated textbooks
for its symmetry and simplicity
was torn down.
We might have considered fire:
but the days of demolition are at hand.

59

60

Nothing can restore that totally lost:
the symbols of civic virtue were bodily
dumped into a lake, and the building site
paved for the non-human ends
of automotive insolence.

61

62

Benefit Street was a crummy neighborhood, not bad, by the quality of its inhabitants, but sinking into the indifference of slums. Benefit Street was saved by common efforts and the happy help of some outside money. Benefit Street lived up to its name. People can do lots when they bother to try.

All rivers once were clean and living places, sparking through meadows, or by tall trees shadowed. We who have dishonored them can also save—miracles are possible— and the living waters made to flow clean, the pleasant banks revived even in cities, for our own delight.

64

The church at Williamsburg, the ancient patio
in Puerto Rico were restored by the chance
of money and a discerning eye. Luck's
one way to preserve history: discernment
is helpless without the facts of cash.

65

Who could guess that our first World's Fair
might leave a monument behind? The old
Palace of Art, where Rosa Bonheur's work
hung in its glory, became a museum:
The one with the coal mine. *The kids beam happily.*

Everyone wants to save colonial houses:
truck them long distances, put them in preserves.
They serve everyman's nostalgia
for a life he really would not care to live.

In the center of town, it's another matter:
the land could be used for more income.
Some old houses stay alive as much by love
than by any seeming certainty.

*Nobody wants to remember Mount Vernon
as a half-kept rural slum. At least
the grass was mowed, or winter gave
the illusion of a lawn.*
                    *The government
didn't want it then,
            the decay increased.*

When women wore hoop skirts, were generally
flattered and despised as the weaker sex,
they showed their strength:
> *Washington's house*
is ours, because they made it theirs.

The city has grown, so only one side now
of Sullivan's building can be seen properly.
He wrote "form follows function," and
applied his ideas to the auditorium.
It deserves a continual photographic unfolding
of all its details, for only sight can praise
the visual fabric. Yet the ear is captured
by his acoustics, and touch is honored everywhere.
All that survives of his work glows with wonder.
His thoughts became traditions in our minds.

74

Like prairies, it spreads and seems to grow
in horizontal distances of earth.
A monumental stubbornness increasing
in strength from its relation to the land.
And meets our human needs with its restraint,
keeps storm without and warmth within
as did the cave, but no cave ever bore
so well a living human testament

to hold out hope that men may live
in dignity and freedom—that their homes
be worthy of the individual, who
because he is ourselves must bear
man's common heritage and cherish it
denying the beast in the wild world's wood.

OUR LOST INHERITANCE

Carl Feiss

In HISTORIC PRESERVATION ANTIQUITY IS RELATIVE. The coastal settlements of the early history of our country are nationally important but are of primary importance to the people who live with them day after day. To the people who live in the vicinity of the later settlements of the Midwest and of the West, the relics of the immediate historic past with which they live have exactly the same kind of value. The gold-rush towns of Colorado, Nevada and California not only have attached to them the golden aura of those exciting days and the romance which they recall but also they are the source of direct attachment to those who live in the areas and who have heard personal stories directly from their grandparents, which are still warm in their memories. And since antiquity is relative and gets more antique day by day even our newest communities are fascinated by the history of their settlement and the people who built it.

We find historical research under-way in the new cities in Florida and California. Our libraries are becoming filled with stimulating reports about what happened in the 1870's and 1890's. The work that is being done in the archaeology and the history of recent times is being handled with the sincerity and depth of the work done by historians and archaeologists in Jamestown or New Orleans.

Throughout the years we have lost much of the record of historical past and much is in jeopardy. We have succeeded in saving much. However, since this antiquity time differential involves also a psychological and emotional differential from one part of the country to the other, what may seem important losses and jeopardies to one may seem trivial to another. Midwestern communities and western communities, while they may have grown directly from colonial settlements of the East and the south coast, have little to show in the way of direct influence after the Mississippi is crossed. But the great Victorian architecture of the last century constitutes the major record of midwestern and western urban settlement. Its preservation has become of vital interest in those areas on which the classical architecture of the earlier history of the country made little imprint. To many an Easterner and Southerner who also finds around him similar Victorian architecture, these relics of the mid and later nineteenth century appear expendable.

Therefore, if we discuss the losses and the jeopardies and the gains on a national basis, we are considering the balances that the differentials in local history require. There are no fixed criteria of judgment. No matter how we approach the preservation of the architecture and the places and the objects of the past, our judgment must be subjective based on the interests and affections of the people.

In 1961, Dr. Walter Havighurst of Miami University, Ohio, made an eloquent plea to save the Alfred Kelley house which at that time was standing in the heart of Columbus. This was one of the great houses of the 1830's and played a vital part in the history of Ohio. It was also a building of fine architecture. Dr. Havighurst's plea speaks for all of us:

> The past is not the property of historians; it is a public possession. It belongs to anyone who is aware of it, and it grows by being shared. It sustains the whole society, which always needs the identity that only the past can give.
>
> In *The Grapes of Wrath* John Steinbeck pictures a group of Oklahoma farm wives loading their goods into an old truck for the long trip to California. They did not have many possessions, but there was not room for what they had. So "the women sat among the doomed things, turning them over and looking past them and back. 'This book, my father had it. He liked a book. *Pilgrim's Progress*. Used to read it. Got his name in it, right here. Why, here's his pipe—it still smells rank. And this picture—an angel. I looked at it before the first three children came—didn't seem to do much good. Think we could get this china dog in? Aunt Sadie brought it from the St. Louis fair. See—it says right on it. No, I guess we can't take that. Here's a letter my brother wrote the day before he died. Here's an old-time hat. These feathers— I never got to use them. No, there isn't room. . . . How can we live without our lives? How will we know it's us without our past?"
>
> These are not members of a historical society. They had never seen a museum or a memorial. They were just people, asking a poignant and universal question: "How will we know it's us without our past?" We do not choose between the past and the future; they are inseparable parts of the same river.

THE LOSSES

There is little to be gained in crying over spilled milk, but there is much to be gained from learning how to prevent spilling it

again. Therefore, we have to look at what has happened recently in the way of destruction of historic buildings and sites and consider this destruction as illustrative of what should be good prevention in the future where it is humanly possible. For instance, there is no point in our continuing to weep over the losses of the Civil War, of the Chicago fire or the San Francisco earthquake. What is of concern to us is what has been happening recently, and here and now. From any point of view these losses are appalling.

Because of our lack of thorough knowledge and lack of a national inventory it is impossible to document what has happened state by state. All we can do is to select or list at random examples which illustrate the kind of thing that has been happening and hope that these illustrations will be of sufficient and compelling interest to convince those interested in improving the national preservation programs to do something and do it quickly. It is not the purpose of this section of this book to discuss the philsophy of preservation, the financing of preservation, and the many other complex problems which face the country in the vital task of preservation of its culture against the inroads of a contemporary society which up to now has been indifferent or even hostile to the finite relics of its development.

As we shift from a rural society; as we shift handicraft to the machine; in our hurry and impatience and in many instances in our greed for land and for its increased value, we have pushed our historic culture aside or dumped it down the drain. When land value skyrockets in central cities and forces the market to discard all the old balances, much that should be saved cannot be saved for a great variety of apparently unrelated reasons. Perhaps the most spectacular recent example of this problem and one which has had nationwide attention is the demolition in 1965 of the Pennsylvania Railroad Station in New York City, a building unmatched in grandeur by any in the country and one for which there was a very real attachment on the part of thousands of citizens. The economics of land value, the economics of the transportation industry and the speed with which decisions had to be made all militated against finding a workable solution to saving this building. It is impossible to say whether any solution could have been found but it is important to note that similar situations can and will occur in the near future.

It is interesting to note that Madison Square Garden, which will in part replace the old Pennsylvania Station, has been rebuilt three times since the destruction of Stanford White's great Madison Square Garden on Madison Square in the 1920's. The original Garden, designed in 1889 "as the center of the city's pleasures," was a building of great exterior beauty; its successors have had mere anonymous facades enclosing vast covered arenas for commercialized sport.

There are many ways in which losses occur. They break into

two major categories: those losses which are accidental and unavoidable, and those manmade ones which are due to neglect, indifference or are deliberately planned.

It is quite extraordinary how many historic buildings in the United States have been destroyed by fire during the course of the last twenty years. Of course, it is true that many old buildings have been neglected, have been over-used or misused and are therefore fire-prone.

In the countryside, the house lying empty in a field of weeds seems to attract lightning. The isolated plantation house in the Mississippi Delta country by its very construction, its elaboration of stairs and great halls and provision for circulation of air, has a built-in fire hazard to which many such magnificent architectural monuments have succumbed in the past few years, including *Belle Grove* (1857) by architect Henry Howard near WhiteCastle, one of the largest of Louisiana's plantation houses; the Cottage (1824) near Baton Rouge; *Afton Villa*, a superb Gothic Revival house in St. Francisville; *Greenwood* in West Feliciana Parish, the 1830 Greek Revival Mansion designed by James H. Coulter; and in Mississippi the Calhoun House (1850) in Palmetto Community.

The fact is that most of our fire losses occur in urban areas. A building left unoccupied in a city, even for the briefest of periods, is picked apart by vandals and looters and more often than not, set afire by derelicts who take up quarters in them, or by the vandals who have ripped out plumbing, radiators and saleable items.

Just as there has been an incredible amount of "demolition by neglect" in areas where demolition is controlled by protective zoning ordinance, an amazing number of fires "of unknown or suspected incendiary origin" have occurred in similar areas. Large institutional structures whose future was being hotly contested by those who wanted the site and those who were attached to the Old Female Seminary, the venerable Courthouse, or the original church are particularly flammable.

Many historic buildings literally go out in a blaze of glory, having been purchased for demolition for various purposes. After having been stripped by predators, both official and unofficial, they are deliberately set on fire and before the admiring throngs which usually gather at such spectacles, volunteer firemen perfect their techniques. It is to be hoped they learn methods of control for historic structures by this practice. One great mansion that served this purpose was the Montgomery Blair Mansion at Silver Spring, Md., where the Montgomery County Fire Department practiced while clearing the site for a shopping center.

It was a strategic fire that ended the controversy for restoring the Old Howard Theatre in Boston and returning it to the eminence it had enjoyed for more than a century. The National Trust memorialized its loss in a traveling show on "Preserva-tion: Heritage of Progress," that has appeared in many cities throughout the nation in the past three years:

The first theater on the site was a wooden tabernacle erected by a sect of Millerites who retreated into it in 1844 to await the end of the world. When this failed to materialize on schedule, they sold it to a group of businessmen who, with some casual modifications, made it into a theater. It opened on October 13, 1845, with Sheridan's *School for Scandal* and an after-piece, *Day after the Wedding*—both decorous plays which could be viewed by the proper Bostonians. It burned in 1846, ten minutes after an audience filed out, in a fire that threatened the mansions of Somerset Street.

The second theater was designed by Isaiah Rogers who built the Gothic theater in Scollay Square in 1856 of massive Quincy granite, and its interior was handsomely embellished. It contained 1700 seats with tiers of stage boxes and a stage which raked or tilted toward the audience.

From the opening performance of Sheridan's *The Rivals* with William Warren, a Boston favorite as leading man, the theater saw the best of the nation's actors and actresses for almost half-a-century. This was followed by an era of vaudeville; and then it became, as Elliot Norton described it, "a bastion of burlesque."

Even in this field it outstripped most of its rivals. So frequently, in fact, that it was routinely closed by Boston police for "voluptuous dancing and profane dialogue." This was the era when the Harvard students who wished to be Bohemian ventured to Scollay Square; or they might merely have been following the sage advice of their great Shakespearean professor the eminent "Kitty," who averred that the humor of the pit had never changed and was to be found in its purest form in burlesque.

The house was finally darkened in 1953, and since then had been sagging into decay in a blighted neighborhood. The gold leaf had been symbolically peeling from the gilded figures adorning the elegant proscenium arch, and the theater was scheduled for demolition. Plans for a new government center to be constructed in the area as a joint federal-city project included renewal of the area. Although the center was not scheduled for erection on the Old Howard site, the building was slated for demolition.

Friends, led by Dean L. Gitter, theatrical producer and president of Repertory Boston, promptly organized a committee to raise funds to restore the building to its former architectural and theatrical grandeur. Ann Corio, a former burlesque queen, who once remarked that her performance was part of every Harvard student's education, offered her help and that of theatrical friends in New York to raise funds. Leading Bostonians interested in the arts and in preservation were marshalling forces when fire in June, 1961 seriously damaged the building. Gitter reported that damage to the basic structure, as designed by Rogers, was not too extensive to prevent reconstruction and the group continued to seek funds until the forces of complete demolition prevailed.

Many fine old buildings in urban areas have been neglected for years and have become slum structures, occupied by many more people than they were planned to accommodate. Electric wiring is primitive, frequently installed without the services of trained electricians. Building inspections in nearly all of our cities are years behind, and over and over again we find the newspaper account of a building loss—sometimes also with loss of life—due to "defective wiring" or defective heating or cooking equipment. The slumlord, willfully or unwillfully, is frequent a culprit.

Many buildings and whole areas of cities just wear out. They have been over-used too long by too many people and in the wrong way. Their state of repair becomes so precarious that they must be destroyed. It is extraordinary how many of these are still to be found in our urban areas and frequently they have had historic and architectural merit. These are the buildings, and sections of cities, to which history has been unkind. The sad derelicts we pass in our cars as we go downtown to work, are witness to a long national indifference to social and physical problems and to the appearance of our cities.

Large-scale demolition by neglect has occurred in nearly every city of the country. Once-noble sections of cities have been swallowed up either in parking areas or absorbed by scattered new growth. Famous areas like the lakefront "Gold Coast" in Milwaukee, and Euclid Avenue in Cleveland, two of the Midwest's most magnificent streets a few years ago, have disappeared by attrition, building by building, month by month, year by year. It is hard to tell when the process began, now that there is little or no evidence left that there ever was anything worthwhile there.

These events are still in process in several remaining great streets and areas of our cities. We can cite, for example, East Avenue in Rochester, N. Y., once a street lined with great federal and Victorian houses, with the Eastman museum more or less in the middle. One by one these houses have been disappearing to be replaced by modern apartments and institutional structures.

Despite the successes of Beacon Hill, Boston, Church Hill, Richmond, and Georgetown, D. C., preservation programming in substantial sections of the same cities is being neglected. Sections of equivalent merit such as Commonwealth Avenue in the Back Bay area of Boston, and portions of Massachusetts Avenue and the Capitol Hill area in the District of Columbia are in serious jeopardy. Monument Place in Baltimore is a sad vestige of a recently fine area. Annapolis and Savannah are hanging on with their teeth.

Despite valiant preservation efforts in the Vieux Carré in New Orleans, the edges have been whittled away and business blocks, filling stations, motels and other contemporary structures have chewed into the area little by little. In Savannah, perhaps the greatest loss is due to the speculative price on old Savannah gray brick, a material which has become a prestige item selling for a dollar a brick. Fine old buildings are being torn down for their bricks which are being used in the various parts of the city for the construction of motels, filling stations and contemporary houses. This is probably the only city in the United States in which historic structures are mined as the Roman Forum was up to the last century.

This is not to say that historic structures are not being mined all over the country. They are. The flocks of vultures looking for carved mantels, paneling and wainscotting, cornices and cantilevers, stair rails, pilasters and columns, and fancy plaster work, are stripping the interiors of any old houses they can get their beaks into. Once this happens, it is only in rare instances that the house or building survives more than a few years.

In the past, not the least of the malefactors in this operation by extraction have been the museums themselves. There is no question but that the process has saved much material which might otherwise have disappeared. Today the practice is frowned upon by the museum people themselves except in emergency situations where buildings cannot be saved.

However, there is a very big business among the antique dealers and the less respectable building-strippers which make the cold-hearted rape of old buildings still a lucrative practice. There are warehouses full of old barn timbers, fireplaces and all the other objects cited above, and there are still people advertising for such material to be used to give "validity" to modern "colonial." This same universal problem exists not only in the United States but throughout Europe, and must be recognized for what it is—frequently an essential rescue on the one hand and a destructive process on the other. It is doubtful that without adequate public education, the proper balance can be achieved.

Demolition by willful neglect is an extraordinary weapon; it is almost impossible to detect during the process. It is to be found almost everywhere. A property owner possessing a historic house or groups of them may simply lock the doors and leave the structures empty. Before long the windows are broken, the roof begins to leak and the building department orders the building boarded up or torn down. If it is boarded up, the boards are ripped off. Further vandalism occurs and ultimately the building comes down anyway. In one case the owner of a building ordered to be preserved by a local government agency arranged with the managers of an adjacent parking lot to have the side-wall of the building rammed by parking attendants and truck drivers until the side of the house was completely undermined and the building had to be destroyed on behalf of public safety!

Another form of destruction occurs which might be termed destruction by substitution. A house or church or public building is acquired and completely remodeled—so much so that almost nothing is left of the original facade. Additions are built in front or around the original structure and it finally disappears—lost somewhere behind new rooms and new exteriors.

In our central city areas, the major loss occurring over and over is the replacing of old buildings by parking lots. These instances are too numerous to count. It just happens that most of our fine old buildings in urban areas are in the downtown or its vicinity. Obsolete street plans and inadequate parking facilities force these old structures to become victims of sheer necessity, or at least of what appears to be necessity. Some buildings are salvaged and moved to other areas for safekeeping, but for the most part they come down.

At the present moment, there is loud public clamor in the preservation field against highway programs and urban renewal. They are the selected whipping boys in a situation in which a lot more people who should know better ought also to be whipped. This is not to say that they have been blameless. There is no question that throughout the country, state and municipal highway departments have been indifferent on their part. In a country that is now becoming self-conscious about beautification as a result of President Johnson's major campaign, destruction of the landscape must be considered in the same light as destruction of historic values by highway construction. The indifference of the highway engineer is neither greater nor less than that of men in many other sectors of our society, and it must not be forgotten that in many instances they were not informed of what they were doing until it was too late.

In the case of urban renewal, a similar situation exists. Historic buildings destroyed by urban renewal in blighted areas involve similar problems. Urban renewal is based on local plans locally determined. In city after city, we find that the local public agency charged with renewal and the local planning agency which must certify the urban renewal plans have not done their homework. They are unaware of or indifferent to the fine old buildings in project areas, and therefore these do not appear on project plans. When they do not appear on project plans, they usually disappear entirely. The Urban Renewal Administration has published excellent documents on historic preservation, emphasizing its interest and support. But the Administration itself cannot know how local decisions are made and what those decisions are.

The renewal process itself has, as a prime objective, the destruction of slums and blighted areas, and the feasible rehabilitation of buildings. The prime effort is to houseclean this nation's worst urban, social and physical problem areas. Since many of our historic structures lie in those areas, they are invariably involved in the renewal process.

Feasibility of their rehabilitation depends upon two things: The first is the kind of land-use called for in the plan for re-building the area. Frequently buildings that have been residential in character, and perhaps remained residential through the centuries, may not be usable for such within the plan. If they cannot be properly converted to a new use acceptable within the plan, they are either moved to another site or destroyed. In such instances the buildings must be considered as unadaptable to up-to-date requirements in a city.

The second problem lies in the financial feasibility of rehabilitation. In particular it is the economic feasibility of restoration, repair and reconditioning. Frequently, the cost of improvements to older structures is much greater than the appraised value of the structure. Thus its rehabilitation is hopeless. We are well aware of the fact that a truly historic building such as the White House can be rebuilt and restored using millions of dollars because of popular consent. We can house a Lincoln log cabin of dubious origins in a marble sarcophagus. We have limitless numbers of examples of restoration and rehabilitation where the dollar has been only a small consideration. There is no better example than Williamsburg, itself.

But within the average renewal area when the cost of fixing up a building is greater than its value, even computed in relation to its new surroundings, then feasibility itself ceases to be determinable by conservation motives—unless philanthropy pays the difference between the market price and the true historic value once restored. Since few local historical organizations and other special interest groups are adequately financed to undertake paying for this difference, our losses continue to mount.

These facts cannot be blamed on the renewal process which, in many instances, has given a new lease on life to older areas and buildings by refurbishing the areas in which they lie. It should be remembered that older buildings lying in slum areas are doomed invariably unless they are either removed to a better location or are capable of being returned to usefulness.

Not all the rascals are ruthless public agents. Some of our worst offenders are municipalities, colleges, universities and churches. They not only destroy their own property but they also destroy things around them. For instance, Brown university, which should know better, destroyed four eighteenth-century houses in the College Hill area. Of course, Brown University needs room on the Hill but it should have tried other solutions.

Princeton will not tear down Nassau Hall, and Harvard will not tear down King's Chapel, yet academic losses continue. Stevens Institute of Technology destroyed one of the great landmarks of New York harbor, Castle Stevens, built by the founder of the Institute and replaced by a faculty institute center. Syracuse University demolished in 1954 Yates Castle, built in 1860, designed by James Renwick, the architect of

St. Patrick's Cathedral in New York and the old Smithsonian building in Washington, D. C. The list is a long one and growing longer day-by-day despite supposed sentimental attachments to "Old Main."

Churches and ecclesiastical institutions are equally to blame. There is hardly a denomination that doesn't have a black mark against it in one part of the country or another. Frequently, ecclesiastical institutions, like educational institutions, are tempted to sell out. Considering the fact that many congregations have moved out of the center of the cities, this is not to be wondered at but it is to be regretted.

We can't afford to lose a building like the Church of the Unity in Springfield, Mass., built by Henry H. Richardson in 1872 and razed in 1961; or Christ Church in Cincinnati, Ohio, a 137-year-old building razed in 1954 for a modern Gothic church; or the Orphans' Chapel, Charleston, S. C., destroyed in 1953 to be replaced by a large store and parking lot. This chapel was built in 1802 by Charleston's most noted architect, Gabriel Manigault. In an architectural survey of Charleston, listing over 1,000 properties, the Orphans' Chapel was listed as one of 26 of national importance, its site added parking space for five additional cars to an already large parking lot.

It is to be hoped that as the preservation movement gains its momentum, academic and ecclesiastical intellectuals will join the fight. A great many have, as will be discussed later, but recent losses have been serious and can never be replaced. It is true that churches and old university buildings have a bad habit of burning down—they seem especially fire-prone. But what cannot be excused is the callous indifference on the part of the trustees of educational and ecclesiastical institutions to the very values to which they are purportedly adhering, the spiritual and cultural values on which any civilized society is based. If we are not to count on leadership from these sources, the preservation movement will be badly handicapped.

THE ROSTER OF THE DEAD

Those buildings which are gone but not forgotten are legion. Those portions of older cities, waterfronts, fine residential areas, handsome early office buildings, old mills, great churches and all the other storied places of our past that now form a roster of our architectural dead, form a formidable and heart-breaking list, too long to be recounted. But we should mention a few of our recent honorable dead. In order to make a convincing story it should be evident by this time that the roster cannot be completed and will never be complete and that quantatively it is impossible to assess the loss in dollar value regardless of what may have been on the tax assessor's books.

The destruction of any object of art, any valued manuscript, any great building no matter how many times it had been reproduced or documented, is a loss for which no one has been able to establish a monetary value. The Poles succeeded in rebuilding Warsaw not only because they had the facts about what had been destroyed but because they had the conviction that by restoring what had been lost they themselves could maintain the essential continuity of their own history. It would have been less expensive for the Poles and more efficient to build a new city, but we cannot be critical of the motives which made them decide to resecure their past before embarking on their future.

The British could easily have rebuilt Coventry Cathedral. Here there was a reverse statement to be made. It was better to leave the old ruins and build a new building. The impact is equally great in the Warsaw reconstruction. Each is a studied solution to the results of destruction. In this country we are just learning to design with history and only seldom in our cities have we found either the planning ingenuity, the desired skills or the political persuasion required to offset the fast and relentless forces of destruction.

The roster of the dead is now increasing at great speed as we add the names of the minor buildings and places of history. The personality of any city is not just dependent on its great buildings and great places but is created by the total complex of large and small, important and minor, the individual and the mass.

The character of a city like Philadelphia was established by its tradition of row houses a century ago. The same can be said of St. Louis, San Francisco and New Orleans, among many others. Minor buildings, in the aggregate, create the major urban scene. They are the body of any city. The body is being rapidly carved up bit by bit and sometimes in whole chunks. The process has been so drastic in some cities that absolutely nothing is left. History is dead in such a city just as though it had never existed, although there is still perhaps a bone or two lying around bleaching.

Cleveland, the "famous forest city," can barely contain a tree let alone a forest, and Buffalo, Detroit, Columbus, Baltimore, Minneapolis, Milwaukee and a limitless host of places selected at random are no better. Where good minor historic buildings—sometimes called "anonymous" buildings—still exist, as in Boston, Philadelphia, Washington, New Orleans, San Francisco and others, the loss of the aggregate in small or in large combinations, is serious. It is doubly so when they form a supporting cast for a square or an important historic building.

Over the years, the National Trust has been recording such destruction. A few examples are cited here which represent major losses, battles which often engaged the majority of the citizens in the area, backed by informed preservation groups throughout the country, in many cases groups who not only protested certain types of official vandalism but also were prepared to raise funds to rescue the threatened site or building.

Such a case was that of the Harral-Wheeler House in Bridgeport, Conn. In its "Requiem for a House," the New York *Times* on July 5, 1958 summed up the issue:

> Destruction of the Harral-Wheeler House, one of the notable examples of the Gothic Revival in the United States, is a tragedy that reaches beyond Bridgeport, where this historic mansion has stood for more than a century. Because it involves another irreparable loss in America's architectural heritage, its elimination in the careless name of "progress" is a responsibility in which each of us has a share.
>
> What does it matter that the Harral-Wheeler House was built in 1846 in the full flowering of the Gothic style by one of our country's great architects, Alexander Jackson Davis? What does it matter that Archer C. Wheeler, industrialist and philanthropist who lived in that house for 83 years until his death in 1956, willed it to the city for a library or museum? Or that Samuel J. Tedesco was elected Mayor of Bridgeport last fall on a platform that included as a major plank the preservation of this mansion which is now being sacrificed to create a conveniently located new city hall?
>
> It all matters a great deal, because it shows once more the loss of responsibility which we as a people sometimes show when we are faced with the alternative of gaining an immediate material benefit or preserving a priceless part of our cultural and historic tradition. Demolition of the Harral-Wheeler House is a symbol of one thing that is wrong with our society and civilization. No one, least of all a nation, can afford to live in the past; but no one, least of all a nation, can afford to reject the history, the tradition, the culture on which the present and the future are built.

The editorial does not fully recount the irony and the tragedy. The Bridgeport Historical Society, led by its president Ernest J. Hillman, raised $157,000 in pledges and contributions to endow the mansion if the City Council would stop the demolition. Of this, $17,000 was pledged locally and $140,000 from outside the state, the largest portion being the offer of a foundation.

The Smithsonian Institution salvaged some of the magnificent architectural detail, doors and windows, decorative arches and furniture, but eager wreckers had demolished much that could have found an honorable resting place in other museums. The new city hall was *not* built on the site, but with the help of an interior designer it contains a memorial to Bridgeport's philanthropist and benefactor, Archer Wheeler.

It took the designer seven months to sort the bits and pieces of the fine Gothic woodwork and the furnishings of the 17-room mansion for the single *Archer C. Wheeler Museum Room*. The resulting pastiche has some of the choice items including a Gothic bed, a dining room table, a mantle from one room, two chandeliers from two different rooms, walnut dressers and gilded parlor sofas. Much time was devoted to selecting "paintings, bric-a-brac and sculpture for their historical, as well as decorative value." The window hangings are of satin and lace, heavily festooned over the blank wall space of the new courthouse. Brooding symbolically over the whole is a mid-eighteenth century sculpture in Carrara marble of Pandora. It is indeed a box that she must regret seeing opened.

The site of this depredation is desolate, and a thrifty city gave testimony of its further appreciation during a recent holiday season, by cutting down a great hemlock and lugging it away for a brief moment of glory as Bridgeport's city Christmas tree.

The lack of inventories which rate both major and minor historical buildings is so prevalent that death by attrition of the lesser structures goes completely unsung unless there is a special circumstance such as the present threatened loss of 182 pre-1820 certified houses in the Society Hill area of Philadelphia doomed by a superhighway scheme. There is probably not a building in the group that by itself would be considered a great piece of architecture and there may be only a few in which are to be found historic associations.

However, in the aggregate when blocks of similar buildings of good character are destroyed, the loss is to be considered a major one. The Philadelphia circumstance is a complete entity, but the gradual attrition, the scattered destruction which takes place in most such areas over a period of years, is difficult if not impossible to recognize until the gaps become greater than the number of buildings and such areas take on a bombed-out look.

It is difficult not to be cynical and discouraged. At the same time it is obviously very important that the forces of action take into account the forces of destruction and clarify national policy, so that plans for destruction from many sources and for many purposes, can be scrutinized within sufficient time to give opportunity to find alternatives to killing a building.

There are still all kinds of heartbreaking losses, unnecessary and completely irrational. For instance, in Baltimore, the *Wyman Villa,* erected in 1853 on the campus of Johns Hopkins University, was razed in 1955 for a parking lot, despite the fact that money had been raised by local interests to save the house. There are several examples of this kind.

In Kentucky the Henderson County Courthouse, one of the best examples of Greek revival architecture in the state, and fought for and lost by the state's historical society and the local chapter of the American Institute of Architects, was demolished in 1964 for a standard type of new courthouse.

While we acknowledge the need for greater engineering schools, it is hard to understand how Yale University permitted Sheffield House, build in 1837, to be destroyed for a new engineering library in a school bearing the Sheffield name.

Perhaps one of the strangest of recent demolitions was that of three fine eighteenth-century townhouses on Monument Avenue in Baltimore which are important not only in themselves but as part of an ensemble of buildings around an important square. The demolition was made by the Maryland Historical Society for headquarters expansion.

The Oregon House in Bucyrus, Ohio, built in 1829, was the first inn on the overland stage route. Ironically, it was razed in 1956 for a restaurant site—one could rationalize that the tradition is still there.

One of the prime examples of robbing old buildings which might be considered a historic disaster was the loss of the Sparhawk Mansion in Kittery, Maine, in 1953. This was a great Georgian house built in 1742 by Sir William Pepperell. It was literally sold room by room and only a weather-beaten shell remains. The Lady Pepperell House still survives. Ladies frequently win out.

Despite the fact that New England is considered by many to be the most historically conscious area in the Union, the list of losses there, city by city, town by town, village by village, over the past 15 years is shocking. Boston allowed its old opera house to be destroyed in 1957, along with the superb India Wharf building designed by Bulfinch, one of America's great architects, around 1805. It was torn down in 1962. Lesser buildings are currently disappearing in this city and in many other parts of Massachusetts. This writer finds distressing the discussion of the widening of Boston's downtown streets, not only for the buildings that will be lost thereby, but because of the distinctly individual flavor of the crooked, narrow streets and many-sided blocks that have made the city unique.

We do not have records of all the destructions, but where the losses have become more and more visually apparent during the last several years is in the New England villages, particularly the villages with greens and fine buildings around them. Only a few are following the example of Ipswich, Mass., and are setting up a historic trust or establishing controlled districts.

The country town at the crossroads still may retain its white-spired church and its columned meetinghouse, but the filling station and supermarket and all of the other appurtenances of the highway age creep in, building by building, and even in some places usurp the village green. The loss of one of America's great community design contributions, a totally original concept, is incalculable. While the vista from a distance may seem to be intact, the closeup is dreadful.

This same situation is to be found throughout New York state, in particular up the great valleys. In many instances the superhighways have come too late, and the destruction by the automobile age has taken place prior to the great bypasses and turnpikes. In some instances, new restoration may be feasible, but it is quite unlikely. The Hudson River Valley and the Mohawk and Genesee villages still retain some flavor, but there is no assurance that it will remain.

In Pennsylvania, the Pennsylvania German villages have suffered the same fate. Although there still are to be found clutches of these neat and precise red-brick villages in the heart of the rural areas, there is no statewide program for their preservation.

In Virginia, there are several dozen fine small courthouse complexes, some of which have been well preserved but others completely destroyed.

Unfortunately, much of the special character of Gloucester Courthouse has been spoiled by the intrusion of a fake Williamsburg building within the walls of the complex and the construction of cheap and ugly buildings surrounding the courthouse center.

It is comforting to note that there are still groups to be found in the open country as at Prince William Courthouse. Goochland and Palmyra appear to be safe and well taken care of. What has happened at Warsaw and Fairfax, among several others, is greatly to be regretted.

In Georgia a great many of the small towns still retain their fine streets of Greek revival architecture. Happily, there is a conscious effort to mobilize forces to save some of them. But there is a long way to go and more losses can be expected until excellent groups working on a statewide program have mustered substantial support.

Throughout the Midwest the same problem prevails. Ohio has lost many lovely villages and will lose more. So will Indiana, Michigan, Illinois, Kentucky—the states lining both sides of the Mississippi River. The small town of Galena, Ill., (home of General Grant) is fighting for its life against serious economic odds, as are many other Mississippi and tributary river towns which are the relics of the great steamboat era. Hannibal, Mo., is being loved to death, and has become a kind of "Mark-Twainland" in a souped-up version of Tom Sawyer.

Comforting exceptions are the Mormon villages in Utah and Arizona. These remain neat, well preserved and a fine testimony both to the quality of their original settlers and to their descendants. As one stands on the cliffs of Bryce Canyon and looks down 1,000 feet at the little Mormon village of Tropic, or as one drives through St. George with its superb Mormon Tabernacle, one realizes that good taste can still hold out when it is conscientiously applied.

In East Texas serious losses have occurred in the early German settlements, although finally there is a courageous major effort centered around Fredericksburg to save the remaining villages and buildings. In San Antonio, the highway attack is a serious one, and there have been serious losses in fine early stone and adobe buildings throughout the city during the past 25 years, despite efforts of the local AIA chapter and citizens' historic groups. The highly successful development of the San Antonio River and the lovely restoration of La Villita do not give witness to the battles fought and lost in recent years by the San Antonio Conservation Society that has been as heroic in its own way as Travis and his followers were at the Alamo.

The losses in the ghost towns of the Rockies have been surprisingly recouped in recent years. There is hardly a Rocky Mountain state in which places on the way out have not been brought back. One of the most tragic recent losses was the very handsome library donated by Senator Tom Walsh to Ouray, Colo., where he "struck it rich." This majestic village, in perhaps one of the most spectacular Alpine settings in the United States, has been invaded by motels and has lost much of its excellent original flavor. Central City and Georgetown, Colo., and many other mountain mining towns, originally contained handsome buildings. Some have been saved but many have been lost, and the losses are frequently quite recent.

The same thing is also true in the West Coast states. The losses in San Francisco which are mentioned elsewhere cannot be passed without reference. Certainly as much has been destroyed since the earthquake as during it.

It was said at the beginning of this chapter that there is no point in crying over spilt milk. Even so, we have been crying over some of the cream.

Many safeguards have been achieved and much progress has been made in conservation, but it remains a portentious task to stave off a continuation of one of our worst traditions—the heedless destruction of the remains of our past.

SUPPORT OF PRESERVATION PROGRAMS BY STATES

State	Formal Program(a) State	Formal Program(a) Private	Years in Effect, as of 1964	Public Funds Used, %	Power of Acquisition Eminent Domain	Gift	Purchase	Types of Sites Public Building	Military Works	Monuments	Private Homes	Costs Met by Admission Fee	Appropriation	Other	Sites Defined by Law	Historic Sites Stimulate Tourist Trade
Alabama		*	10+	0(b)	*	*	*	*	*		*	*	*			
Alaska	*(N)	.		100(b)	*	*	*						*			
Arizona	*		17+	50+(b)	*	*	*	*	*	*	*	*	*		*	
Arkansas	*	*	28+	90	*	*	*	*	*			*	*			
California	*	*	25+	50+(b)	*	*	*	*	*	*	*	*	*		*	*
Colorado	*	*	83	(b)	*	*	*	*	*	*	*		*			*
Connecticut		*	1	0												
Delaware	*		31	100				*	*	*	*		*		*	*
Florida	*		5													
Georgia	*	*	13					*	*	*	*				*	
Hawaii	*(N)		5													
Idaho	(c)	*	7										*			
Illinois	(d)		3					*	*	*	*		*			
Indiana	(d)	(d)	35	20				*	*	*	*	*	*			
Iowa		*		(b)	*	*	*	*	*	*	*		*			
Kansas	*		30	100				*	*	*	*		*			
Kentucky		*														
Louisiana	*	*	4												*	*
Maine	(c)		10						*	*		*	*		*	
Maryland	*	*	3	(b)		*	*	*	*	*		*	*		*	*
Massachusetts	*		4	(b)				*	*	*	*		*	*		
Michigan	*		16+	(b)	*	*	*	*	*	*	*	*	*	*		*
Minnesota	*	*	23	(b)		*	*	*	*	*	*	*	*		*	
Mississippi	*	*	22+	(b)		*	*	*	*	*	*	*				
Missouri	*	*	8+	(b)	*	*	*	*	*	*	*		*		*	
Montana	*	*	25+		*	*	*	*	*	*	*		*	*		
Nebraska	*	*	7+	(b)		*	*	*	*	*	*		*			
Nevada		*														
New Hampshire	*	*	5						*		*	*	*			
New Jersey	*	*	45	(b)	*	*	*	*	*	*	*					
New Mexico	*	*	20+					*	*	*	*	*	*			
New York	*		7	100(b)	*	*	*	*	*	*	*				*	
North Carolina	*	*	31	e(b)	*	*	*	*	*		*	*	*	*	*	*
North Dakota	*	*	59	75(b)	*	*	*	*	*	*	*		*		*	
Ohio	*	*	65	100(b)	*	*	*	*	*	*	*	*	*	*	*	
Oklahoma	*	*	7		*	*	*	*	*	*	*	*			*	
Oregon	*			(b)				*	*	*	*		*			
Pennsylvania	*		20+	100(b)		*	*	*	*	*	*		*		*	*
Rhode Island	*		1906-13	.(b)						*	*		*			
So. Carolina				(b)												
So. Dakota	*	*	60	50(b)		*	*		*	*	*	(f)				*
Tennessee	*		15	100(b)		*	*	*	*	*	*	*	*			*
Texas	*	*	7					*	*	*	*		*	*		*
Utah	*		47	100(b)	*	*	*	*	*	*	*		*	*	*	
Vermont	*	*	17	(b)		*	*	*	*	*	*	*	*	*	*	*
Virginia	*	*	37	(b)		*	*	*	*	*	*	*	*	*		*
Washington	(c)		15					*	*	*	*					
West Virginia	(c)		3	100				*	*	*	*	*	*			
Wisconsin	*	*	10	10(b)	*	*	*	*	*	*	*	*	*	*		
Wyoming	*	*	50	(b)	*	*	*	*	*	*			*			
Puerto Rico	*	*	15	(b)	*	*	*	*	*	*	*		*	*	*	
Guam	*		4	(b)		*	*						*	*		

a. Includes historical markers except where designated by N.
b. Local Government Participation.
c. State marker program exists.
d. Special legislation.
e. $400,000 per year.
f. Locally regulated.

DEATH MASK OR LIVING IMAGE?

The Role of the Archives of American Architecture

Helen Duprey Bullock

T HE HISTORIC AMERICAN BUILDINGS SURVEY WAS CON-ceived in the depression and dedicated to the proposition that unemployed architects should be gainfully employed in recording the history of the nation's architecture.

In November 1933, a memorandum from Charles E. Peterson to Arthur E. Demaray outlined a project for employing a thousand men for six months to prepare a collection of measured drawings augmented by photographs and other data. This was in the opening period of Roosevelt's New Deal, and the memorandum won quick approval from Director Arno B. Cammerer of the National Park Service, Secretary of the Interior Harold L. Ickes and Federal Civil Works Administrator Harry L. Hopkins. Mr. Peterson recruited the first staff for the project, directed the work of the St. Louis field team in 1940, and from 1957 to 1962 directed the Historic American Buildings Survey for eastern United States from the Philadelphia office of the Park Service.

An agreement with the American Institute of Architects, the Library of Congress and the National Park Service was formally signed in July 1934. So successful were the initial returns from the first six-months project that it continued actively until it came to a long halt in 1941 with the ominous threat of World War II. By that time more than 23,765 sheets of measured drawings, and 25,357 photographic negatives of some 6,389 structures had been recorded.

The Historic Sites Act of 1935 had clearly specified that the continuance of the Survey was to be part of the regular duty of the federal government. World War II and the Korean War diverted manpower and resources from all National Park Service projects, and by the middle 'fifties, as the nation returned to normalcy, the Park Service faced the problem of rehabilitating its neglected parks and sites, and a bold program "Mission 66" was inaugurated in 1957. Also under this program HABS was revived and given more funds; and was also given a broad new direction.

Three factors greatly influenced the new direction after its eight years of pioneering effort and its revival. The Society of Architectural Historians was founded in 1940, and the National

Trust in 1947. Appreciation of the nation's architecture, and the shock of its rapid obliteration in the postwar building boom for an exploding population, became widespread. The HABS in the Library of Congress had provided efficient and economical copies of its survey records to all requesting the service, and annual reports of the Librarian of Congress are testimony that it is the most active collection in that entire national treasure house.

Throughout the nation framed certificates attesting that a building had been included in the HABS were hung with pride in mansions and modest dwellings. American taste and appreciation were coming of age. In evaluating this great archive, especially in its formative years, one must refer back to the philosophy which directed its beginnings, because, by a happy bit of serendipity, it has become the basis for whatever exists of a needed national register of our architectural heritage.

In selecting buildings for recording, for example, emphasis was placed upon those in danger. Ironically, many of the buildings regarded as eminently secure were not recorded and have disappeared. Emphasis, too, has been placed on buildings of the colonial and federal periods, partly because few historians had studied nineteenth-or early twentieth-century buildings and their architects. Good architecture had not died with the Age of Jackson, it had just been ignored.

In the depression funding of the first HABS, travel money was a precious luxury. Areas chosen for the survey were those having the largest number of unemployed architects, or which could provide matching funds for their services. This meant work in or near the largest cities, to the almost total neglect of small old towns and villages, and rural areas; thus large regions were omitted entirely.

HISTORIC AMERICAN BUILDINGS SURVEY INVENTORY

The new program stressed the importance of national coverage, and a broad base of selection. To increase the coverage, a program known as HABSI (Historic American Buildings Survey Inventory) was initiated. On a one-page form is entered a concise record, with photographs and supporting documents which afford an opportunity for recording less-and-less about more-and-more, but serves as a ready record to determine whether, if the building is in jeopardy, a full record and investigation should not be made. This has been a primary concern of Earl H. Reed, FAIA, of Chicago, and an able roster of preservation officers in the various chapters of the American Institute of Architects.

This has resulted in the brief recording of some 5,381 structures. Of this total more than 3,000 were from the Commonwealth of Virginia. It is simple to account for this disproportion because funds for the two-year program were contributed by the Old Dominion and Avalon Foundations for this purpose.

As Dr. Whitehill has said, in commenting on funds needed for such surveys, "The Survey, like everything else connected with historic preservation, suffers from short-handedness and lack of funds. It welcomes gifts of information that can be integrated into its archives. Many organizations and individuals, particularly architectural and preservation bodies, have photographs and data that should be submitted to the Survey, but lack the hands to transfer it to the forms on which it must be recorded. The Survey lacks the staff to gather in these sheaves; their possessors, however well disposed, are usually overburdened with problems and crises of their own. Cutting a foot off the top of a blanket to sew it on the bottom has never made a bed any warmer. In this, as in many other aspects of preservation, the needs far outrun the resources."

Nevertheless there has been a rich return for every dollar spent on this program. It ranges from the product of the ultimate in recording technique—architectural photogrammetry—introduced to this country by Perry E. Borchers, professor at Ohio State University; to the limited but useful one-page HABSI entry. Charles E. Peterson, FAIA (who was given the Louise duPont Crowinshield Award of the National Trust in 1965 for his lifelong dedication and contribution to this cause and other related scholarly work), sums up a heartwarming success story in an article "Thirty Years of HABS" in the November 1963 issue of the *Journal* of the American Institute of Architects, which the Trust keeps available in reprint form on its publications list.

Uneven as it was, the HABS was the first conscious attempt to record our American architecture on a national scale. It was added to the magnificent resources of the Library of Congress which included such other records as: The Archive of Early American Architecture (some 10,000 architectural photographs); the Detroit Photographic records, 1900-1920, of views of cities and famous sites and buildings of the eastern half of the United States which were produced for the picture postcard trade before the massive changes and destruction that ensued after World War I; the 30,000 stereoscopic views which were copyrighted in a pre-television America; the Mathew B. Brady Civil War photographs (some 10,000); and a large miscellaneous collection of prints, lithographs, engravings and photographs acquired by gift, purchase and copyright deposit.

In its own unique category are the more than 5,000 excellent photographs by the incomparable Frances Benjamin Johnston, pioneer of women photographers. On a Carnegie grant she photographed not only the great houses and gardens of the southeastern United States, but such picturesque and now vanished elements of the American scene as a mule-powered cotton-press, old slave quarters and covered bridges.

In a review of the architectural landmarks recorded in HABS and HABSI some unhappy statistics emerge. It is safe to say that in general many of them survive as a death mask of "This was America," an item in a preserved record. In fact, from 25 per cent to 40 per cent are in this category.

To cite specific examples: Charles S. Pope, AIA, of the Western Office of Design and Construction of the National Park Service, a veteran of HABS, reports from San Francisco that of 145 outstanding buildings recorded, only 23 survive; 95 having been destroyed, and 27 hopelessly mutilated. The losses include such major monuments as the beloved "Monkey Block," as the building was known to generations of San Franciscans.

The Montgomery Block was erected by Henry W. Halleck, later Lincoln's chief of staff. The rugged folk of the shanty seaport scoffed at the plan, "He's a dreamer—or a drinker." But in 1859 with champagne and fireworks, the first four-story building west of Chicago became a reality. It floated on a massive layer of redwood logs and had two-foot brick walls as a shock absorber. It was the Bohemian center of the West, the home of artists and writers—Frank and Kathleen Norris, Bret Harte, Sam Clemens, Charles Dobie, cartoonist Billy De Beck, sculptor James King. Here was first produced Pisco Punch; and here Sun-Yat-Sen and Wom Sam Arch plotted the overthrow of the Manchu dynasty. It rode out the devastation of the earthquake of 1906, but succumbed in 1960 to a voracious demand for parking space. Its great historic neighbor, the San Francisco Mint, of even greater architectural and historic merit, lives on, on borrowed time.

In New Jersey where the concentration of unemployed architects was great, one of the most comprehensive of the state surveys was achieved. The New Jersey Historical Society contributed a detailed report on the present state of buildings listed to date by the HABS for New Jersey. Its director, Robert M. Lunny, his assistant Howard W. Wiseman, and more than one hundred volunteers, made a building-by-building check especially for this study in December of 1965 of those worthy of recording.

Of the 735 buildings surveyed 20 per cent are destroyed. There are a number listed as boarded up, badly mutilated and in bad shape, covered with aluminum siding, or otherwise so severely altered or defaced as to be "lost" as objects of historic or architectural value. Plans are being considered to publish the results of this recheck of the HABS listings to show in detail the causes of the losses.

Many worthy buildings have been lost to freeways without record, and in the city of Newark about 80 acres were cleared for urban renewal with no evaluation having been made. They were in the older part of the city and included downgraded once-fine mansions, and some proper Victorian houses of good design and some historic association.

Perhaps one of the most wanton losses was that of the burying ground around the First Presbyterian Church (founded in 1666)—a present building dates from 1790. The graveyard contained the remains of the settlers and founders of Newark, many having been transferred to the "new Church" from a burial ground off Broad Street. For 75 years there had been no burials in the churchyard and the gravestones of those "waiting for the resurrection of the Just" were an expensive nuisance for a downtown city church to maintain. Maintenance of the church building alone was a drain on local resources.

No direct descendants could be traced to oppose a proposal from the Trustees of the Church to the Superior Court to place all the bones in a common trench and lay the headstones in the earth to become a foundation under material which could provide a parking lot surface. Despite protests from citizens, learned institutions (including Yale University), the National Trust and New Jersey preservationists, the parking lot triumphed in 1962. It still yields some income, but is not often filled, as public parking facilities now provide the needed spaces.

New York City, thanks to the Municipal Art Society, inaugurated a survey of its historic structures in 1951. Basing its survey on a list made in 1941 by Talbot Hamlin, FAIA, of structures built before 1850, it extended the area and period of coverage and requested nominations from architects and architectural historians. Of the 250 carefully selected and accredited buildings which resulted from a highly professional and selective survey, more than 20 per cent were either razed or drastically altered between the inception and completion of the survey.

Alan Burnham, AIA, Executive Director of the Landmarks Preservation Commission of New York City, reported in November of 1965 that in the past 15 years, fifteen of the most notable buildings in New York have been razed or damaged beyond redemption. To name Pennsylvania Station at the head of the list is to provide a clue to the magnitude and character of this destruction. It also includes the Brokaw residence at 79th and Fifth Avenue, the Stuyvesant Apartments at 142 East 18th, and the Studio Building at 55 West 10th Street; Mark Twain's house, designed in 1840 by James Renwick; The Studios built in the 1830's and turned into a studio for Richard Watson Gilder; and the Van Pelt Manor House (1686).

More significant, however, is the ominous note that accompanies the report. Of 11 major notable architectural monuments that are in jeopardy, are included: The New York Stock Exchange, The Friends Meetinghouse, The Astor Library, The Manhattan Club (Jerome Residence); and on Staten

Island the magnificent complex of buildings at Sailors Snug Harbor.

Chicago, a city which had recorded 295 of its architecturally significant buildings, reports that 57 have been destroyed or so materially altered as to have no validity. Many outstanding buildings of the Chicago and Prairie school were demolished and among the notable losses were the Cable Building on Wabash Avenue and Jackson Boulevard and Adler & Sullivan's Garrick Theatre (1891-1892). When the latter was razed in 1961 a Garrick Salvage Fund donated to the Chicago Historic American Buildings Survey fund by the Chicago AIA Chapter Foundation, was used to salvage its magnificent ornamentation and place it in museums throughout the nation.

The city of New Orleans, under a grant to Tulane University from the Schleider Foundation, has just completed an intensive study of the buildings in the Vieux Carré. Title to each building has been completely traced and its architectural character fully recorded. However, this great survey exists in only a single copy and the vast amount of historical and architectural data is too voluminous for publication.

VIRGINIA COMMONWEALTH

Virginia, at the outbreak of the Revolution was the largest, wealthiest and most populous of the 13 original colonies. This was reflected in its surviving architectural monuments as recorded in the HABS before 1941. On a grant from the Old Dominion and Avalon Foundations the National Trust undertook an inventory of surviving ante-bellum buildings. Of the less than 100 Virginia counties which existed about the time of the second survey (four having been absorbed in their entirety by independent cities), no records had been made in 36. An inventory in these counties was initiated. An effort was made to check back on all those previously recorded, and many structures, especially in the cities, were either destroyed or hopelessly mutilated. A special effort was also made to record the courthouse complexes in each county.

The difficulties in undertaking this survey demonstrated the vast change that swept the nation between the two World Wars. There were no professional architects available for the work, and students of the University of Virginia were recruited under a program directed by Professor Frederick D. Nichols, AIA, one of the pioneers of the original HABS. These students were paid at an hourly rate which often exceeded the compensation paid for a full day's work to qualified architects on the assignment during the depression; and travel expenses were substantial. The distances traveled to remote counties, such as Pittsylvania, and the complexities of locating the Tidewater structures which had been built along the rivers and waterways in an era of water transportation, were complicating factors.

Nevertheless more than 3,000 structures were recorded between 1957 and 1960.

The students making the inventory also attempted an evaluation of the buildings as they recorded them. Needless to say, as good Virginians they accorded the majority of them the "nationally significant" category. This, too, points out the problems of evaluation, but was remedied in this instance by a board of review of outstanding historians, architects and authorities from the National Park Service, the Trust and Virginia museums. In the final total, 76 of the more than 3,000 buildings recorded were named as nationally significant and 187 of statewide importance, the remainder in lesser classifications. Copies of the inventory were placed at the University of Virginia, the State Archives in Richmond, the Library of Congress, the National Trust, the National Park Service and the American Institute of Architects headquarters in Washington.

Where checks have been made on Virginia's inventory they have again led to the same conclusion—the losses from all causes, especially in urban areas, are mounting at an accelerating rate. From 20 to 40 per cent is an informed estimate by those who have worked in the field many years.

For the purposes of this study a checkback was made on the historic port city of Alexandria, Va., in December 1965. This was conducted by Worth Bailey, architectural historian of the HABS, and consultant to the Historic Alexandria Foundation. He was assisted by Deane Hall of the National Trust staff.

In 1941 the HABS recorded 44 buildings in the Alexandria port area. The new check showed 20 per cent of those gone, and 9 per cent in serious jeopardy. As late as 1962 a thorough census of architecturally significant buildings in the Old Towne section sponsored by Historic Alexandria Foundation evaluated 773 buildings. In the short time between the completion of the survey and the December check, 11 per cent of the buildings were destroyed or so desecrated that their significant features are no longer recognizable, and 17 per cent of the buildings are seriously threatened by Alexandria urban renewal plans and commercial development.

In the area already cleared for urban renewal no building remains standing of the group included in the most recent checkback. In the area cleared in front of City Hall for an underground parking facility and plaza stood a complex of indigenous commercial structures, locally called "Flounders" and the only iron-front building in town. In the block where Gadsby's Tavern remains the sole survivor, plans call for buildings of pseudo-Georgian design according to Mr. Bailey. Virginia as one of the states with a profound interest in its past not entirely based on pure sentiment, has become sharply aware of what the early and incomplete surveys have demonstrated. Governor Albertis Harrison in December 1965, sent out an invitation to 1000 informed leaders to attend a conference on Natural Beauty. Included in the program was an extensive discussion of man-made monuments as well.

J. Everette Fauber, Jr. AIA, who represented the Virginia Chapter of the American Institute of Architects reports their determination "to complete an exhaustive inventory of buildings within the Commonwealth that have important historic associations and architectural significance. They propose to begin their work with all the existing inventories.

"It would then be their idea to meet with representatives of the HABS, the Park Service, and the National Trust, to evaluate this material and the structures that are represented, and then to furnish the State Highway Department and other government agencies public and bodies with this inventory," Fauber continued, "along with the request that none of these buildings be destroyed or even downgraded until a *full* appraisal of their worth has been prepared and some effort at preserving them has been made."

After disheartening years of regarding the HABS and other inventories of America's architecture as a kind of death mask of an America that was, the trend over the past few years has unmistakably reversed. The urgent need for sound, impartial, professional information is being recognized, not just to maintain an orderly obituary record, but to provide a future for what survives of the past.

The active historical societies of New York State, in addition to being custodians of historical documents, genealogical data and historic house museums filled with antique objects and patriotic memorabilia are extending their work into preserving the environment those records memorialize. They have had help and advice from the state under the Division of Archives and History of the State Education Department, headed for many years by the late Dr. Albert B. Corey.

The New York Council on the Arts under the direction of Governor Nelson A. Rockefeller and a commitee of leading citizens is conducting a three-pronged attack on the problems besetting that state. Chairman Seymour H. Knox, executive director John B. Hightower of New York City and associate director William Hull of Syracuse, in an early year-book reported their reasons for placing such an emphasis on architecture in the program:

> While one may or may not choose to be part of the audience for a particular art, he cannot easily avoid his man-made surroundings in the normal pursuits of life. This environment is dominated by architecture, an unavoidable art of civilization. It seems appropriate that the Council be concerned with an art that affects and influences so many people.

And concerned it is. With a technical assistance program it is advocating Architectural Conservation, Architectural Surveys and Architectural Adaptation. Threatened buildings brought to the Council's attention by a non-profit organization are referred to an authoritative architect, or art or architectural historian, who prepares an impartial appraisal of the structure. One of the earliest and most effective uses of this phase of the program occurred in Oswego, and set a pattern for subsequent victories.

The Gerritt Smith Public Library, a crenelated, fortress-like structure built in 1866, was scheduled for demolition to provide a site for a contemporary building. The consultant's report showed evidence of the uniqueness of the structure as a prototype, not only in the state, but in the nation. Moreover its esthetic relationship to its surrounding architecture, and its role in the history of the city were significant. The report was published in its entirety, in two installments with ample illustrations in the Oswego *Palladium-Times*. The Gerritt Library remains, and an appropriate addition provides expanded facilities.

In 1965 there were 33 such appraisals rendered under the technical assistance program. One currently underway is a feasibility study by James Curtain AIA of *Hyde Hall,* the endangered mansion on Lake Otsego near Cooperstown, N.Y. located on land being developed as a recreational facility by the state.

In November 1965, a pioneer program was co-sponsored by the Council and Society for the Preservation of Landmarks in Western New York in Rochester. The meeting was combined with the annual meeting of the Society and open to the public. More than 350 attended and a panel of four outside experts and local authorities spoke of the problems currently being met in Rochester's Third Ward and in planning a future for some of its reclaimed areas.

Architecture Worth Saving in Onondaga County by Professor Harley J. McKee of the Syracuse University School of Architecture was one of the first in what promises to be a most notable series. It was hailed by Ada Louise Huxtable, architectural critic of the New York *Times,* as "the first sign of civilized maturity that can save cities like Syracuse from self-destruction." Two graduate fellows during the academic year 1963-64 had documented and compiled a list of appropriate buildings under Professor McKee's direction. From this list a panel of experts from other cities reviewed the list and recommended the 60 finally included in the study. A similar procedure was followed at Rensselaer Polytechnic Institute under the direction of Professor Bernd Foerster for the study of Rensselaer County published in 1965; and for a forthcoming one of Albany County. Professor Stephen W. Jacobs is currently directing such a study at Cornell University for Wayne County.

Studies of less extent but competent and stimulating public interest and support have been made of the stockade area of Schenectady, the cobblestone architecture of Childs and nearby areas, of Cooperstown, and downtown Buffalo.

Early in its history the Council disavowed the purely archival approach as an end in itself for such surveys, and offers a philosophy that is the essence of sound preservation policy:

It is realized that the problems of architectural conservation are not solved by establishing the historic and esthetic merit of these examples. This is a necessary first step which must be implemented in most cases by finding practical adaptive uses for these buildings.

The Philadelphia Historical Commission, created by city ordinance in 1956, and the Massachusetts Historical Commission, established by the legislature in 1963, are examples of official bodies that identify, evaluate and certify historic buildings and sites of outstanding significance to the city or state. The Cambridge Historical Commission recently issued *Report One; East Cambridge,* the first of a *Survey of Architectural History in Cambridge* which has been helpful in bringing to light a great deal of "architecture worth saving" in that area.

On Beacon Hill, the Junior League is scheduled to begin a re-survey of that historic district, which has been named a Registered National Historic Landmark. The Beacon Hill Civic Association was chiefly instrumental in securing passage of a law in the 1955 session of the Massachusetts legislature establishing architectural controls for about 22 acres of its original proprietorship.

In preparing its case, the Association authorized a building-by-building survey by students from Massachusetts Institute of Technology. It also conducted a study of the kind of laws already in effect in the first eight cities to pioneer such legislation. The results of this study, conducted by John Codman, a leading spirit in the whole effort, were published in 1956 by the American Society of Planning Officials with the title *Preservation of Historic Districts by Architectural Control.* It is still available from the National Trust which sponsored its republication.

There can be no question. As the preservationists try desperately to ascend a down escalator, which is operating at an accelerated rate, they are finding at long last state and municipal cooperation, and help from many quarters. Some of it is of the type of good intentions badly misdirected and confused; and some of the highest degree of competency.

Although not one of the initial signers of the tri-partite agreement of the Library of Congress, the National Park Service and the American Institute of Architects, the Trust has distributed upon request, hundreds of pamphlets on the value of surveys and how to conduct them. Of the more than 80 cities now affording some measure of protection for their notable architectural and historical landmarks, most of them have had direct advice and information from the Trust. So far only 14 states have not attempted surveys, but in the other 36 the surveys are unequal.

The amount of interest, financial and otherwise, shown by states and municipalities is shown on an accompanying chart prepared with the collaboration of the office of the Attorney General of Kentucky and the National Trust.

THE NATION'S CAPITAL

In our Nation's Capital, three decades after the beginning of HABS, the Fine Arts Commission and the National Capital Planning Commission decided to do something about preserving Washington's architectural heritage. They jointly appointed a Committee on Landmarks and a Landmarks Review Subcommittee, with representatives from the National Trust for Historic Preservation, the National Archives, the Library of Congress, the Smithsonian Institution, General Services Administration and D.C. Public Library. The committee found that just about half of approximately 550 buildings originally listed were gone. A few sorely neglected ones had simply decayed beyond repair. A few had had to make way for the insatiable space demands for the automobile, moving or standing. Most of them had been sacrificed to the greater convenience and profit of more modern and more spacious structures.

The Landmark Committee's preliminary list designates nearly 300 buildings, places and areas which it believes must be preserved, should be preserved if possible, or should be preserved if practicable. More than a year later there is no final list, no preservation legislation and no organization in the nation's capital, public or private, charged with the preservation of landmarks of the city. The Committee hoped that the publication of its preliminary list would in itself increase an awareness of historic treasures; the designation however, seems only to have identified them for the bulldozer.

In the spring of 1791, when the brave new capital of an empire for liberty was taking shape on the banks of the Potomac, Thomas Jefferson, the Secretary of State wrote to both President Washington and Major Pierre Charles L'Enfant of his concern for its planning. His philosophy still has a strange pertinence:

I have examined my papers and found the plans of Frankfort-on-the-Mayne, Carlsruhe, Amsterdam, Strasburg, Paris, Orleans, Bordeaux, Lyons, Montpelier, Marseilles, Turin, and Milan, which I send in a roll by the post. They are on large and accurate scales, having been procured by me while in those respective cities myself. As they are connected with the notes I made in my travels, and often necessary to explain them to myself, I will beg your care of them and to return them when no longer useful to you.

I should propose . . . that no street be narrower than one hundred feet, with footways of fifteen feet. Where a street is long and level, it might be one hundred and twenty feet wide. I should prefer squares of at least two hundred yards every way, which will be about eight acres each . . . I doubt much whether the obligation to build the houses at a given distance from the street contributes to its beauty. It produces a disgusting monotony; all persons make this complaint against Philadelphia. . . . In Paris it is forbidden to build a house beyond a given height; and it is admitted to be a good restriction. It keeps down the price of ground, keeps the houses low and convenient, and the streets light and airy. Fires are much more manageable where houses are low.

Whenever it is proposed to prepare plans for the Capitol I should prefer the adoption of some one of the models of antiquity which have had the approbation of thousands of years; and for the President's house I should prefer the celebrated fronts of modern buildings which have already received the approbation of all good judges. Such are the Galérie du Louvre, the Gardes Meubles, and two fronts of the Hôtel de Salm. While in Europe I selected about a dozen or two of the handsomest fronts of private buildings, of which I have the plates. Perhaps it might decide the taste of the new town were these to be engraved here and distributed gratis among the inhabitants of Georgetown. The expense would be trifling.

There is one other major manifestation of the growing support for scholarly and essential work in this field. The American Architectural Drawings, a catalog of original and measured drawings of historic American buildings, is a project initiated by the Philadelphia Chapter of the American Institute of Architects. Supported by a grant of $70,000 from the Samuel H. Kress Foundation, the work began in December 1964. The Preservation Committee of the chapter was under the chairmanship of John F. Harbeson FAIA. George F. Koyl FAIA is editor and Mrs. Moira B. Mathieson, assistant editor. An advisory committee of seven includes representatives of the Library of Congress, the HABS, Smithsonian Institution, Society of Architectural Historians and National Trust.

By December 1966 the initial phase of the project, supported by the present grant, will be terminated. By that time approximately 6000 noteworthy drawings will be selected, cataloged and published in a one-volume catalog by the University of Pennsylvania Press. Not only will this archive record the great sweep of American public and domestic architecture, but it will afford a documentary source for restoration of surviving examples. A continuance of the study as part of the Archive of American Architecture of the Smithsonian Institution has been proposed.

THE REGISTRY OF NATIONAL LANDMARKS

Mission 66 has not only reactivated the HABS and other major programs in preservation in the National Park Service, but it has inaugurated a descriptive and evaluative inventory of sites and buildings significant in American history and prehistory. These are proceeding on a limited budget.

For this purpose the entire field of American history has been divided into 22 major themes, each covering a particular unified topic such as Alaska Aboriginal Culture, Westward Expansion and the Extension of the National Boundaries to the Pacific, 1830-1898; Social and Humanitarian Movements; Dutch and Swedish Exploration and Settlement; Arts and Sciences; and under each a number of special sub-themes.

As each theme is studied, National Park Service historians throughout the country, under the direction of Dr. John Littleton, prepare working lists of sites and structures of potential interest; they visit the sites in question, consult with local and specialized organizations and in the end prepare a report describing the historical context, relative significance, and integrity of each. After preliminary review and submission to a National Advisory Board of experts, the Secretary of the Interior approves those classified as of exceptional value for inclusion in the Registry of National Historic Landmarks. When a site is eligible for registry, the Director of the National Park Service invites the owner to participate in the program by agreeing to preserve, to the best of his ability, the historical integrity of the site or structure, to use it for purposes consistent with its historical character, and to allow periodic visits of inspection by a representative of the National Park Service. In return for such agreement, the Secretary of the Interior and the Director of the National Park Service furnish a certificate of landmark designation, and, if desired, a bronze plaque indicating the status of the property.

To date, 673 sites have been declared eligible for the Registry, and studies are continuing. The structures or sites eligible for such evaluation are those at which events occurred that have made an outstanding contribution to, or which best represent, the broad cultural, political, economic, military, or social history of the nation; those associated importantly with the lives of outstanding historical personages, or with an important event that best represents some great idea or ideal of the American people; those that embody the distinguishing characteristics of an architectural type specimen, or represent the work of a master builder, designer, or architect; and, finally, archaeological sites of major scientific importance. An essential consideration is that each one should have integrity— "that is, there should be no doubt as to whether it is the original site or structure, and in the case of a structure, that it represents original material and workmanship." Birthplaces, graves, burials and cemeteries, as well as structures and sites primarily of significance to religious bodies, and those connected with persons of historical importance within the past fifty years, are not normally eligible for consideration.

THE LIVING IMAGE

Obviously," said Walter Muir Whitehill, in discussing the upsurge of interest in this field of surveys, "some of the certifications of local and state bodies duplicate those of the Registry of National Historic Landmarks, for what is important to the nation should hardly fail to be of significance in the community in which it stands. It never does any harm, however, to be certain that a prophet is honored in his own country. Moreover, while the National Registry cannot impose other than moral restraint upon private owners, it is sometimes possible by local action to give historic sites and buildings a degree of legal protection."

The National Trust has served for some 18 years now, as a clearinghouse of information, and as a point of appeal for those individuals and organizations who turn desperately for advice and support after the bulldozer is already at the barricade. It is beginning to find the changed climate of public opinion a powerful factor in helping the helpless. There have been more losses than victories, and more lost causes than saved. But the Trust no longer serves as just a wailing wall, and a somewhat helpless dispenser of advice to the lovelorn.

Their experience, and collaboration with colleagues in the National Park Service, the American Institute of Architects, the Federal Housing Authority and more than 650 affiliated organizations is bearing fruit. If we are to assure a future for

our past, the preservation movement must be part of broad city planning. It must not be a special interest of the local "hysterical society" to save at all costs some lesser landmark at the price of an integrated program that takes into account also, the needs of the present. As Thomas Jefferson reiterated, "the earth belongs to the living."

There are no instant answers. There is no magic formula. There are only good guidelines and a fund of information of past successes and failures. The law that will work for Charleston, S.C., may be of little help in Leadville, Colo. The principle is.

There are a few informed city planners, and we need more of them; qualified lawyers, and they are becoming increasingly interested in this field; architects who are knowledgeable. To study what they have done in their own areas is one thing; to slavishly attempt a do-it-yourself program without expert guidance is folly. The disease which afflicts the body politic of urban America cannot be cured by swallowing a universal panacea. An examination of each patient, and professional prescription is in order.

In this study many generous contributors have cooperated to place some of the remedies in our hands.

ECONOMIC EFFECT OF RESTORATION OF SINGLE FAMILY HOUSES ON CHURCH HILL RICHMOND, VIRGINIA Changes in Assessed Values 1958-1963

E. Grace Street, 2300 block, North Side, *Restored*		Assessed Value of Land and Improvements	
Location	Property	1958	1963
2300	2 apts. & exhib. rooms	$7,540	$19,100
2302	1-family house	5,020	12,500
2308	2 apts.	5,850	10,000
2310	2 apts.	5,860	16,000
2312	1-family house	5,220	12,500
2314	1-family house	5,220	11,800
2316	2 apts.	6,300	15,000
	Totals	$41,010	$96,900
E. Grace Street, 2500 block, North Side, *Unrestored (With One Exception)*			
2500	1-family house (restored)	$3,380	$7,500
2502	1-family house	3,920	4,000
2504	1-family house	3,420	4,000
2506	1-family house	5,990	6,400
2510	1-family house	4,980	5,700
2512	1-family house	4,810	5,400
2514	1-family house	5,260	5,700
2516	1-family house	6,260	6,700
2518	1-family house	6,260	6,600
	Totals	$44,280	$52,000

Percentage of rise: restored, 136 per cent; unrestored, 17 per cent, (including one restored property).
Assessment values are roughly 80 to 85 per cent of market value.

NOTE: This and the preceding chart on page 138 are reprinted by permission from *Planning for Preservation* by Robert L. Montague & Tony P. Wrenn, Chicago (American Society of Planning Officials) 1964

TRAVELERS TO OLYMPUS

Richard H. Howland

THE CAREFUL PRESERVATION OF MONUMENTS OF THE past has an ancient tradition in European countries. Pausanias, the Baedeker of the second century after Christ, is continually reporting the survival of antique buildings and their usefulness for contemporary society. His accounts also include descriptions of vanished antiquities garnered from local legends that were hoary in his own day. In describing Delphi, which was regarded by the classical Greeks as a traditional cult center of such antiquity that it was referred to as the navel of the earth, Pausanias mentions the predecessors of the great temple of Apollo. He reports that they were primitive indeed, one having been built of feathers and a successor of bronze plates. The existing temple shown to Pausanias was already 500 years old at the time of his visit, and especially notable because here might be read the sayings of the Seven Sages: "Know thyself" and "Nothing in excess."

In Olympia the traveler noted an early and effective example of historic preservation. The Temple of Hera had been built approximately 725 years previously, with archaic wooden columns surrounding the shrine itself. In the course of the preceding 700 years most of the wooden shafts had deteriorated, and were replaced from time to time by new shafts, but solidly constructed of stone.

Pausanias noted the presence of several of the original wooden columns, in the comparatively sheltered *opisthodomos*. Pausanias' successor in today's tourists' Olympia will not see any wooden shafts, of course, but he may note that the stone replacements are not all alike: Succeeding generations of preservationists executed shafts and capitals according to subtle changes of style and proportion peculiar to the various cen-

147

turies. Although all are in the Doric style, one may read the whole development of Doric proportions in the architectural fragments unearthed there 90 years ago.

Here are demonstrated the first and second great tenets of historic preservation, as enunciated in France in 1838: "It is better to preserve than repair, better to repair than restore." How sensible and sensitive were those Olympians, who maintained the continuity of a great historic shrine with repairs dating from many centuries, none of them a self-conscious reconstruction of a bygone style! Here is an early forerunner of Ruskin's and Morris' nineteenth-century Anti-Scrape philosophy. Here is an example of the continuing use of a great building with indications of all ages of its use, not artificially stopped at one particular epoch considered its finest.

The tradition continued. In Athens, at a later period, were additional instances of historic preservation, many times disclosed by today's excavators' spades rather than by ancient literary references. The famed Agora in Athens was the center of civic life for the city from the early sixth century B.C. This vast congregating place was not only an outdoor livingroom for citizens, who were like their successors today in preferring togetherness to privacy; it was also the center for political assemblies, certain religious observances, public notices and also hucksters. The tradesmen and vendors were probably for the most part ambulatory or possessed of temporary wooden stalls. In the second century B.C. commercial structures were built as permanent locations for shops and offices, and in the years soon after 47 B.C. a great new complex was erected to the east of the Agora, to house a large number of mercantile establishments and to relieve the old Agora of some of its lingering commercial associations.

The new complex, called today the Roman Agora, was very much like a modern shopping center in one of our American suburbs. Various merchants leased space in units opening from a unifying colonnade for protection from the inclement weather of the winter and the cruel sun of the summer. Various communal facilities such as restrooms and refreshment places served the customers and the shopkeepers alike. The old Agora rapidly changed from a commercial center to a cultural center. A great new concert and lecture hall was erected in the middle, paid for by Agrippa, the father of Lucius and Gaius Caesar. Here and nearby were transplanted ancient temples and other monuments, preserved by being moved bodily from suburban and other urban locations, when expanding population demands caused shopping centers or new roads or other so-called amenities to invade ancient locations.

The most conspicuous example of a huge relocated structure was the Temple of Ares. This had been constructed 400 years previously on a site at some distance from downtown, and moved to the Agora on the order of the Emperor Augustus, a

notable preservationist. The stones of the columns and walls were very carefully taken down and numbered and lettered, and skilfully re-erected between 15 and 10 B.C. just to the north of the new concert hall, which later was to become the meeting place of the Sophists and a major unit in the university complex of pre-Christian Athens. The cult of Ares flourished in its new location until the destruction of this part of Athens in the Herulian invasion of 267. The visitor today may see the remains of this temple, recently recovered in the American excavations. It is a very early precursor of the bodily transportation and re-erection of ancient monuments that are characteristic of Scandinavian preservation projects in the nineteenth and twentieth centuries, and of a number of American projects such as Strawbery Banke, in Portsmouth, N. H., at the present time.

The old Agora became more and more a relocation center for ancient monuments, as the city expanded and new housing developments and highways made it seem necessary to invade sanctuaries and established locations. The huge outdoor altar of the Temple of Ares was moved down and re-erected to the east of the temple's new site. The archaic statues of the Tyrannicides Harmodios and Aristogeiton, important civic symbols for democratic Athens, were moved to new situations near this altar and its temple. The great Altar of Zeus Agoraios, the inspirer of oratory, originally stood on a nearby hill, the Pynx, before its removal to the Agora. Other monuments now in the same area show traces of re-location.

These very active and early steps to ensure the preservation of tangible symbols of the past are natural ones, and allied with man's instinctive need to identify with his assured achievements as he embarks on an uncertain future. Dr. Samuel Johnson later expressed this in his *Journey to the Western Islands of Scotland:* "That man is little to be envied, whose patriotism would not gain force upon the plain of Marathon, or whose pity would not grow warmer among the ruins of Iona."

It is notable that Pericles purposely rescinded a hastily phrased decree, passed shortly after the Persian destruction of the Acropolis in 480 B.C., that forbade the rebuilding of the old temples in order to memorialize Persian impiety by retaining the ruins. Thirty-three years after the catastrophe Pericles repealed the decree and commenced the restoration and building program that inspired all Athenians, and created the Parthenon on top of the ruins of the old Hekatompedon. The Parthenon for the Greeks of the fifth century B.C., as for the Greeks today, was and is a magnificent symbol of national strength and pride. Its new name, derived from that of the virgin goddess Athena, recalled at the same time military strength, wisdom and the eponymons goddess of the city.

In a realistic way, in 1830, Louis Philippe capitalized on a similar identification with past glories, in naming as his new

Prime Minister the famous historian Guizot. This notable appointment served to help stabilize the new government because Guizot consciously created among Frenchmen a strong identification with the glories of French history and the achievements of their ancestors. He urged them to become chauvinistic. He capitalized on the tradition of the greatness of France. One of his new colleagues, Ludovic Vitet, developed the commission concerned with historic sites and buildings, and inaugurated the famous list of *Monuments Classées,* a model to this day.

These two illustrations, from ancient history and more recent times, may offer clues to the truth. The truth would seem to be that the preservation of significant tangible elements from the past is necessary to ensure the healthy growth of the future. Santayana has pointed out that the principal psychological difference between man and animals is memory. Those who cannot learn from the past are committed to making the same mistakes again and again. The brief inscription engraved on the Archives Building in Washington "What is Past is Prologue" carries a most important message for today's planners and tomorrow's dreamers, not a reminder for antiquarians.

There is a strong psychological need for a continuity between past and future. No healthy person wishes to dwell in a womb-like archaic habitat after birth, but the instinctive need for shelter, strength and warmth is a natural and normal desire for the human animal. Rodman Rockefeller, the head of a new international corporation intent on developing low-cost housing for the world's poor, claims that psychologists will have to help the architects in designing acceptable mass-produced shelters. He is reported to have said, in the autumn of 1965, "We could turn out houses like cars in Detroit, but people won't live in them and their governments won't let us put them up. A home is more than a roof over your head and most men dream of a solid brick house like their fathers had or like their fathers always wanted to have."

We are reminded of the universal longing of the traveler. The soldier, the human being bereft of his habitat, who feels as Ulysses did (in Elias Vassiliades' translation of George Seferis' *On a Strange Verse*):

And there comes before me,
    again and again, the ghost
    of Odysseus, eyes reddened
    by the salty waves
and his burning desire to see
    again the smoke rising
    from the fireplace of his
    house, his dog, aged
    by the long wait, standing
    by the door.
He stands like a giant, whis-
    pering through his bleached
    beard, words of our
    language as it was

spoken three thousand
years ago. . . .

Some of the genes in today's men and women go back three thousand years. All of us in the United States (with the exception of a minority) are descendants of European or African emigrants. Our heritages have been fused into a national one, with which we identify, but a pride of ethnic origin often persists and comes through to us meaningfully, and increasingly as the pressures of contemporaneity multiply. There is strength in the past and courage for the future in admitting it.

The late Roman emperor Majorian felt this identification for a remote past when he, a Christian, reacted strongly to protect the monuments of pagan Rome. Gibbon's *Decline and Fall of the Roman Empire* says this about Rome exactly 1500 years ago, in the 460's:

The fairest forms of architecture were rudely defaced for the sake of some paltry, or pretended repairs; and the degenerate Romans, who converted the spoil to their own emolument, demolished with sacrilegious hands the labors of their ancestors. The emperor Majorian, who had often sighed over the desolation of the city, applied a severe remedy to the growing evil. He reserved to the prince and senate the sole cognizance of the extreme cases which might justify the destruction of an ancient edifice; imposed a fine of fifty pounds by weight of gold on every magistrate who should presume to grant such illegal and scandalous license; and threatened to chastise the criminal obedience of their subordinate officers by a severe whipping and the amputation of both their hands. In the later instance, the legislator might seem to forget the proportion of guilt and punishment, but his zeal arose from a generous principle and Majorian was anxious to protect the monuments of those ages in which he would have desired and deserved to live.

It is regrettable that his successors allowed these efforts to lapse. A thousand years later antique Rome was again at the mercy of its predatory citizens. The rich princes and sometimes even richer prelates were pulling down ancient temples, baths and even the outer blocks of the Coliseum to provide convenient building material for their new palazzi and villas. A Latin tag: *"Quoi non barberi Barberini fecunt"* referred to the particularly rapacious Barberini family. It took the intervention of an edict of the Pope himself to put a stop to this destruction, which not only saved pagan Rome, as we know it today, but was the first piece of *preservation legislation* in modern times, the forerunner of the numerous and very helpful ordinances that in recent years have been promulgated in various European and American communities.

These concerns with the preservation of historic places in Europe, by Europeans of past generations, are paralleled by observations of a number of sensitive Americans in the eighteenth and nineteenth centuries, who were able to appreciate and value the importance of antiquity. Peter Kalm, a Swedish traveler who visited Philadelphia in 1750, noted that in the Southwark district of that city there was an old house preserved at that time as an interesting relic of pioneer days of two or three generations before. In 1818 William Strickland, a brilliant young Philadelphia architect, was employed to make measured drawings of the Benezet house, approximately a century old. As early as 1822 a trust fund was set up by Abraham Touro of Newport for the preservation of the eighteenth-century synagogue there.

Thomas Jefferson and John Adams made a notable tour of English country houses and historic sites in 1786, reported in Adams' diary and in Jefferson's letters. Their interest in the preservation of historic sites is evident in Adams' remark concerning Worcester, the site of a major defeat of Charles II in 1651, at the hands of Cromwell's forces:

> . . . Edgehill and Worcester were curious and interesting to us, as scenes where Freemen had fought for their Rights. The People in the Neighborhood, appeared so ignorant and careless at Worcester that I was provoked and asked, "And do Englishmen so soon forget the Ground where Liberty was fought for? Tell your Neighbours and your Children that this is holy Ground, much holier than that on which your Churches stand. All England should come in Pilgrimage to this Hill."

When Jefferson and Adams went to Stratford they visited the sites associated with Shakespeare with appropriate reverence, but indulged in an act of vandalism surprising to twentieth-century preservationists: ". . . three Doors from the Inn, is the House where he was born, as small and mean, as you can conceive. They shew Us an old Wooden Chair in the Chimney Corner, where He sat. We cut off a Chip according to the Custom. A Mulberry Tree that he planted has been cut down, and is carefully preserved for Sale. . . ."

The cult of relics and souvenirs was formerly a strong one, with this evidence to show that it was indulged in even by such enlightened travelers as Jefferson and Adams. It was prevalent throughout the nineteenth century and still persists, although professional preservationists and conservative tourists frown upon such practices. In the middle years of the last century the Star Spangled Banner, now the most honored possession of the Smithsonian's Museum of History and Technology, was in the possession of the family of Colonel Armistead, to whom it had been given after he retired from Baltimore's Fort McHenry. The family used to snip off pieces of this huge flag to give as souvenirs to favored friends and guests, which is the reason for its abbreviated look today, and accounts for several authentic pieces of the nation's anthem's inspiration being in private hands.

Those who have been attracted to a serious interest in antiquity through a contemplation of the isolated object are numerous, and there remains to be written a thoughtful chapter in the history of the preservation movement that assesses the interest in the relic. Pilgrim Hall in Plymouth, Mass., began in 1820 with a few objects presumably associated with the *Mayflower* passengers. It was a pioneer in its field, and much of the concern for historic preservation and the care of ancient buildings, in that part of Massachusetts, stems from early interests in these artifacts conscientiously, patriotically and enthusiastically (if uncritically) garnered by our predecessors 150 years ago. The Philadelphia Centennial Exposition in 1876 and the Chicago World's Columbian Exposition in 1897 were concerned later with an interest in our American pre-Revolutionary past, although many objects referred to as "colonial" were made years and indeed decades after 1776.

Sir John Summerson, of the Royal Commission on Historical Monuments, states a universal truth applicable to European as well as American preservationists ". . . all objects from the past are potentially meaningful. Sooner or later we shall have to face it: To modern man, *all buildings are buildings of historic interest.*"

EUROPE PROTECTS ITS MONUMENTS

Robert R. Garvey Jr.

ACH EUROPEAN COUNTRY HAS ITS OWN APPROACH to historic preservation. Each has its own legislation, its own techniques and methods.

Man has long looked upon ancient monuments as symbols of living history and has, according to literary evidence, endeavored to restore these monuments, especially since the Italian Renaissance and the rise of Humanism.

It should be kept in mind that the late eighteenth century and the nineteenth century saw the beginning and the development of modern archaeology, and the scientific study of history. Art history was also being considered in a new light. Cultural concepts were changing as quickly as science progressed. Until that time, man's acts of preservation usually did not go beyond renovation of damaged parts and replacement of various elements, sometimes in completely alien form. The thought that architectural elements had an intrinsic value was not always sufficiently considered. The main value of monuments lay in their moral, spiritual or practical significance.

Today the purpose of conservation is to preserve or to restore the monument in its original character, *its historical and artistic value being the prime concern.*

Sweden probably has the oldest legislation in the world with regard to ancient monuments. Such monuments were placed under the protection of the law in 1666. As early as 1630 King Gustavus Adolphus II had created a post as Director General of Antiquities, who was to record and collect runic inscriptions and other ancient stones and objects. Some of these inscriptions and stones are reproduced in Sweden's earliest historical documents, such as Erik Dahlberg's great pictorial work on Sweden from the end of the seventeenth century. Though the law formally protected ruins and various prehistoric antiquities, it was actually for a long time impossible to prevent their destruction. Distances in Sweden were great; and the staff was small and communications had not developed. Attempts were made, with the aid of the parish ministers, to compile lists of the ancient monuments, but these lists were very incomplete.

It was not, however, until the early nineteenth century that interest in monuments for their historical and artistic value became the rule. The movement is said to have started in the

151

papal states in 1819—the year of the pontifical edict of Cardinal Pacca which was the first example of modern legislation passed for the protection of our cultural heritage. The initiation of the new movement is also marked in that same year by the restoration of the arch of Titus formerly encased in the medieval fortifications of Rome. Most of our modern methods are based on these first two examples of legislative and technical protection.

In France, a Commission des Monuments Historiques was created in 1837. The noted author, Prosper Merimée, appointed General Inspector of Historic Monuments of France in 1841, particularly applied the two principles of legislative and technical protection and devoted himself to the conservation of ancient French monuments.

Very important was the attitude of the Greek governments after independance from Turkey had been secured. A law of 1839 declared all remnants of antiquity and the middle ages to be national property.

Today, nearly every country has a Monuments Protection Act as part of its national legislation (Great Britain and the Commonwealth, France, the Netherlands, Italy, etc.).

GREAT BRITAIN AND THE COMMONWEALTH

England and Wales began their preservation of ancient buildings or sites with the Ancient Monuments Protection Act of 1882. This listed 29 monuments—all earthworks, stone circles and the like—of which the most important was Stonehenge. They were listed in the schedule of the Act, from which the term "scheduling" ancient monuments is derived.

> In general, before a national service can impose regulations affecting private property, the property must be "scheduled." This is a legal form of notifying the owner that owing to cultural, historic or artistic values, a given site or building cannot be modified without previous authorization from the competent services.

The Commissioners of the Board of Works, as the Ministry of Public Building and Works was then called, could accept, with the monument owner's agreement, either guardianship or a transfer of ownership, when they felt the monument's preservation was of public interest by reason of its historical, traditional or artistic interest. Thereafter the monument was maintained by the Commissioners.

The Queen was also given power, by Order of the Council, to add similar monuments to the list.

The matter was carried a little further by the Ancient Monuments Protection Act of 1900. It was passed for the purpose of covering medieval buildings as well as prehistoric remains. This Act defined a monument as "any structure, erection or monument of historic or architectural interest" other than an inhabited dwelling house.

This Act led to the first acquisition of buildings other than those considered prehistoric remains: for example, Deal Castle in 1904 and Richmond Castle, Yorkshire, in 1910.

Prior to the Act, the Commissioners already had responsibility for certain buildings, but these were more in the nature of surviving parts of former royal palaces, for which the Board of Works had always been responsible. The Acts of 1882 and 1900 were limited since they applied only to those buildings or sites which the government considered important enough to accept the financial liability for their upkeep. An attempt to list ancient monuments in general was not made and published until 1921 and comprised 139 monuments in England and 70 in Wales. However, the Commissioners of Works were empowered to prepare and publish such a list of monuments (whose preservation was considered to be of national importance), with the advice of the Ancient Monuments Boards for England, Wales and Scotland, under the Act of 1913.

This Act was amended in 1931 by the substitution of the period of three months notice of intention to demolish or alter a scheduled Ancient Monument. After this, confirmation by Parliament was only required where an objection to the order was made. In the other cases, the order remained in force indefinitely. The Act of 1931 also provided that preservation orders be registered in the Local Land Charges Registry.

The Act of 1933 simplified the procedure by enabling the Minister of Works, with the advice of the Ancient Monuments Board, to issue an interim preservation notice which is valid for 21 months. At the end of that time, such notice would expire unless a preservation order was substituted for it.

As a result of the War and the aerial bombardment, public opinion began to be very concerned about the preservation of ancient monuments. A provision was therefore inserted in the Town and Country Planning Act of 1944 enabling the newly-constituted Minister of Town and Country Planning to prepare, for the guidance of the local planning authorities, lists of buildings of special architectural or historic interest. Although the Town and Country Act has twice suffered repeal since 1944, this particular section has been twice reinstated. The former Ministry of Town and Country Planning was renamed the Ministry of Housing and Local Government.

The listing of buildings of special architectural or historic interest is still proceeding and the whole of England and Wales has not yet been investigated. The term "special architecture," which applies to an overwhelming proportion of the buildings listed, has been interpreted to cover almost all surviving buildings dating from earlier than about 1700 and most significant buildings erected between that date and 1830. The interest in Victorian buildings in recent years has caused coverage of a limited number of nineteenth or early twentieth century buildings of definite quality and character.

The buildings selected are divided into two lists and three grades.

Grades I and II are both included in the Statutory List. (The difference between the two grades is the degree of architectural or historical interest.) Grade I buildings are of such interest that demolition is not allowed under any circumstances. Grade II buildings are those of such interest that they ought not be destroyed. When a building is listed in either of these grades, a notice is served to the owners and occupiers informing them that they must give the local planning authority two-months notice of any intention to demolish or to alter the building in any way that would seriously affect its character. This notice must be passed on by the Local Planning Authority to the Minister of Housing and Local Government who offers observations thereon during the two months. At the end of the two months, the owner is free to pull the building down or alter it unless a building preservation order has been issued. In the case of alterations, the two-month period enables negotiations to be made between the owner and the local authority, sometimes resulting in a mutually satisfactory method of doing the work. No compensation is payable under the order, but if the owner can prove that the order deprives him of reasonable beneficial use, he can compel the local authority to buy it from him.

Grade III, the Supplementary List, buildings are the more modest ones. They are those which would qualify for inclusion in Grade II, but have depreciated in quality. Grade III imposes no obligation on the owner or occupier. In Scotland, the whole procedure for listing a building would be similar, but separately administered.

The Ministry listing today suffers from the lack of clerical staff to convert the provisional lists into statutory and supplementary lists. However, given a substantial increase in clerical staff, the Ministry listing could be in perfect working order in a few years.

Establishing the official inventory, however, is more difficult. Special consideration is not only given to the individual quality of each building, but to its relation with other buildings. Churches are given special consideration because of record purposes, but legal provisions of the Act do not apply to them as long as they are in ecclesiastical use.

The provisions for listed buildings of the Town and Country Planning Acts are largely negative. They can prevent demolition but do not insure maintenance. The Historic Buildings and Ancient Monuments Act of 1953 was a positive step however. Always before, the authorities could prevent demolition, but could not insure maintenance. During the years following the War, it became increasingly obvious that without state aid some of the larger country houses would die from the heavy taxation and high costs of maintenance. Under the law of 1953, the Minister of Works was authorized to make grants toward the maintenance or repair of buildings of outstanding interest and their contents—with the condition that there was limited public access to the building. The Act also included monies toward the upkeep of any aminity lands. The Minister was further authorized to acquire them or to assist the local governments in doing so. Historic Buildings Councils for England, Wales and Scotland were set up to advise the Minister in making such grants. The majority of the buildings aided by grants have been inhabited dwelling houses.

These historic buildings grants amount to about $1.25 million annually. In addition, approximately $3 million is spent on the maintenance and repair of the ancient monuments under the ownership or guardianship of the Ministry.

To aid the many buildings which fail to qualify for "outstanding interest," the Local Authorities (Historic Buildings) Act of 1962 was passed. In the case of buildings not included in the Minister of Housing and Local Government's Statutory List the consent of the Minister is required.

A bill to provide for grants from both state and church funds for the maintenance and repair of redundant churches of architectural interest is being prepared now.

For a final note on the measures taken by government, the government finances Royal Commissions of Historical or Ancient Monuments in England, Wales and Scotland. They have completed, at the most, only 15 per cent of their task to record the ancient and historical monuments of the three countries from the earliest times until 1855.

Generally speaking, however, the part played by private or voluntary action through non-governmental agencies in the preservation of historic buildings has equaled, if not exceeded, the efforts of the government. Most important of these non-governmental bodies is the National Trust for Places of Historic Interest or Natural Beauty, which was founded in 1894. The Trust is now the largest landowner in the country, acquired mostly through gift or testamentary bequest. In its early days, the Trust was chiefly concerned with the protection of unspoiled stretches of coastal scenery, fenland, downs and moors. Domestic architecture, and in particular the great country homes of England, up until 1940, seemed in little danger and in no need of protection. However, since 1940, taxation radically altered their position. Owners can no longer maintain their houses. Famous buildings which survived the cannonades of Cromwell's armies, the financial panic of the South Sea Bubble and the changes of the Industrial Revolution, were seemingly rendered to the tax collector overnight.

The National Trust evolved its "Country House Scheme." This scheme enables an owner to give a house of architectural or historic interest to the Trust, together with a capital sum (or a rent-producing estate) to provide an endowment for maintenance. Because the Trust is registered as a charity, neither the property, nor the capital endowment for maintenance, are liable for death duties, and the income derived from the endowment is wholly free of tax. With this income the Trust maintains the fabric of the house, the contents of the state rooms (pictures, tapestries, etc.) and the gardens. At the same time, the Trust arranges for the donor and his heirs to continue living in the house rent-free, provided they allow public access to the gardens and state rooms on an agreed number of days every year. In this way, by a single operation, many houses and gardens are opened for the enjoyment of the public, are preserved intact as homes rather than as museums, and suffer no severance of the family connection which lends many houses much of their fascination and interest.

Another device has established close cooperation between the government and the National Trust. Estate taxes can be paid in part by the transfer of acceptable properties to the Treasury which in turn transfers such properties to the Trust.

A number of other bodies such as County Archaeological Societies also own and administer other, mostly smaller, historic buildings such as the remains of castles or abbeys.

The Society for the Protection of Ancient Buildings, which was founded by William Morris in 1877, is the oldest of the societies formed expressly for the preservation of buildings, as distinct from land. This Society has become known in recent years as the most active body, dealing with private operations, to save ancient buildings from demolition both by public propaganda and by giving advice on the manner of restoration and possible adaptation to other uses. The Georgian Group, founded in 1937, was an offshoot of the Society for the Protection of Ancient Buildings. It concerns itself with buildings dating from the Elizabethan to the early Victorian period and is a champion of these, just as the SPAB is of those of the earlier dates.

Both societies have recently been complemented by the formation of the Victorian Society which fulfills the same purpose with regard to Victorian and Edwardian buildings. It has made striking progress in reducing public prejudices in the last two years. Other societies active in the field of preservation are the Ancient Monuments Society and the Council of British Archaeology which acts as the coordinator of all local archaeological societies.

In addition, there are now more than five hundred local preservation or civic societies interested in the preservation of the character, amenities or historic buildings of areas which may vary in size, from a village to a large borough or county. The Civic Trust, founded in 1957, is the coordinator of the local preservation societies and its principle objectives include encouraging high quality in architecture, planning, etc.; preservation of buildings of artistic distinction or historic interest; and the protection of the beauties of the countryside.

FRANCE

France was the first country to show marked progress in the preservation of her monuments. Her legislation on the subject today is the most extensive. The present legislation dates back to 1913, with modifications through the years.

Buildings are designated for listing into two categories by the Minister, acting on the advice of the Commission des Monuments Historiques—*monuments classés* and *monuments inscrits. Monuments classés* are the whole or part of any building or land of public interest from the point of view of history or art. Buildings or land of lesser importance than the *monuments classés* are considered *monuments inscrits. Monuments inscrits* nevertheless have sufficient archaeological interest to render their preservation desirable. The restrictions, in either case, include not only the buildings or land designated, but also the field of visibility around them up to 500 yards.

After the owners of the buildings designated are informed of such and the designation is entered in the land charges register, the owner is entitled to a contribution from the state toward the upkeep, if his building has been designated as a *monument classé.* This matter is usually settled by a private negotiation between the owner and the Minister who provides the extent of the listing. The owner of a building can also request a listing as *classé,* after which his request is given due consideration by the Minister and his Commission. If the owner, on the other hand, objects to the classification of his building as a *monument classé,* he may appeal to the Conseil d'Etat, which decides his case. The owner can also claim compensation for inconveniences caused by this classification of his building.

In the case of *monuments classés,* no alteration, restoration or demolition may take place without the Minister's consent (very similar to Great Britain). When permission is granted, the Minister's own architects supervise the work, and in some instances, the Minister's staff actually performs the work at the state's expense.

The owner's consent to the designation of a *monument inscrit* is not required. The owner is only obligated to give the Minister four-months notice of any proposed modifications of the building. If the Minister disapproves the plan, the owner's only recourse is to get his building approved for designation to *monuments classés.* French legislation further provides that the state can contribute up to 40 per cent of the cost of upkeep of *monuments inscrits.*

The law of 1930 set up a Commission des Sites, Perspectives et Paysages in each department together with a Commission Supérieure in Paris. Their purpose is to list national monuments and sites whose preservation is of public interest from the artistic, historic, scientific, legendary or picturesque point of view. Here again, owners of the land are notified of the designation and must give four-months notice of proposed work to be done that would affect the appearance of the monument or site. The owner can appeal to the Commission Supérieure and then the Conseil d'Etat if he disagrees with the classification by the Commission des Sites. He can also claim compensation if he suffers a loss from the classification.

The foregoing legislation applies only to single buildings, and until 1962, France had no procedure for the protection of ancient towns or villages as a whole. This law, the Malraux Law, as it is often referred to, André Malraux being the minister of Cultural Affairs under De Gaulle, created a Commission Nationale des Secteurs Sauvegardés. It is hoped that in time the law of the Commission will be applied to about 1,000 historic towns and villages, but first pilot projects are being made in 14 places.

The purpose of the law is to substitute a positive approach to the problem for the State's negative actions of past years (protection through prohibitions and regulation). The law is designed to assist owners by a means of a system of loans and subsidies. The method of doing this existed in the urban renewal procedure already in use by the Ministry of Construction.

Before the passage of this 1962 law, urban renewal tended to destroy those areas in a town considered unhealthy, and build in their place modern living quarters. It has, therefore, now been decided that wherever the Ministry of Cultural Affairs considers the conservation of ancient areas in towns or villages to be necessary, the funds allocated to urban renewal for those areas shall be applied, instead to the restoration and development of the existing buildings.

Because of this, the technical services of the Ministry of Cultural Affairs work with the urban renewal services of the Ministry of Construction to determine the areas in a town which should be safeguarded. This delimitation is accomplished by taking into consideration the historic, archaeological, artistic and picturesque elements of the areas in question. They, in general, correspond with the original nuclei of the towns, from which expansion developed.

After the "protected area" in any town or village has been designated, the local authority does have the right to object. If the designation is still felt to be justified, a decree by the Conseil d'Etat will be necessary. Actually, however, the French government attaches special importance to the winning of local agreement in plans for preservation and development, since such programs would be practically inconceivable without the collaboration of the authorities immediately concerned. In fact, the arbitrary classification of an area without local agreement might quite possibly result in a stalemate.

Following the designation, the Ministries concerned have two years to prepare a plan for the area. During these two years, no new buildings may be erected nor can existing ones be eliminated or altered without the approval of the Direction de l'Architecture in the Ministry of Cultural Affairs. The proposed plan when in final form—complete with special architectural directive—will be considered for approval by the Commission Nationale des Secteurs Sauvegardés. After adoption, the plan is carried out under the supervision of the Direction de l'Architecture of the Ministry of Cultural Affairs. The procedure affecting individual monuments classés or inscrits, if they should fall within the proposed plan, will remain unaltered.

The 1962 law contains other unusual provisions, besides that regarding the financing of such restoration. The law also provides for compulsory powers of acquisition and eviction, since the owners of buildings in almost all small towns and villages of France could not afford the cost of extensive restoration. By using the urban renewal funds for replacement of substandard housing for this restoration, the state can provide up to 80 per cent of the cost of restoration. If the owners cannot or will not provide the remaining 20 per cent, they can be expropriated by agreement, or by compulsion, if necessary.

Buildings acquired in this manner form a collective enterprise undertaken on communal initiative. The owner can resume ownership upon payment of the proportion of cost due from him after the restoration is completed. If this is not agreeable, the building will be sold, again with the right of option to the previous owner. Tenants, in the same manner, can be evicted with six-months notice for the duration of the restoration, and will be found temporary accommodations elsewhere. Upon completion of the work, the tenants may return. In some instances however, they are unable to pay the increased rent due to the improvements of the building. In this case, permanent alternative accommodations will be found for them. Obviously, this is more difficult in villages than in towns, and in these cases it is a part of the enterprise of the state to aim at creating new kinds of activity which would raise the standard of living of old tenants, enabling them to pay increased rents.

THE NETHERLANDS

The first historic monuments procedures were not compiled until 1903. The present law dates from 1961. It provides that upon the advice of the State Commission for the Care of Monuments, the Minister of Education, Arts and Sciences may list sites, buildings or objects not less than 50 years old. The local authorities are the recipients of the lists and following their consideration, they may request of the Minister that certain proposed buildings be omitted from the list. The owners of the buildings make many similar objections, but these are heard by the courts rather than by the Minister himself.

In The Netherlands, too, demolition, alteration or repair of a listed building is subject to permission by the Minister of Education. If the Minister grants approval, restoration is conducted under the supervision of the State Service for the Care of Monuments by private architects obtained by the owner. According to the means of the owner and according to the importance of the building, the owner may obtain a subsidy for the maintenance of the building.

An important special provision of the relatively new law allows the Minister to list town and village views comprising groups of immovable objects, including trees, roads, streets, squares, bridges, canals, waterways and ditches which, in conjunction with one or more of the monuments belonging to the group, constitute a picture of public interest because of the beauty or character of the whole.

GERMANY

Germany began to be active in this field after the Napoleonic Wars, when Marienburg was restored and the Cathedral of Cologne completed.

While West Germany is now a federal state, there are no federal laws concerning historic monuments or their protection. However, already the constitution of the Weimar Republic contained an article (No. 150) proclaiming the protection of monuments of an artistic or historical nature by the state. This protection is now assured either through the laws of the old kingdoms, especially the Prussian law of 1919, duchies and cities of Germany or from new legislation passed by the Länder (counties or provinces) of which the present federation is composed.

For example, an Office for the Protection of Monuments (Landesamt für Denkmalpflege) was set up under the old kingdom of Bavaria in 1908, under the Ministry of Education and Culture. This Office is empowered to list those monuments of artistic or historic interest or sites of natural beauty. Demolition, alteration or sale of the site, or excavation of the site, must be approved by the Office. A similar situation exists in the Land of Nordrhein-Westfalen.

The Land of Hamburg's law of 1921 is similar, too. This Land has the Denkmalschutzamt and they with the advice of a council of twelve experts, list monuments, earthworks or movable objects of public interest for their importance to history or art history. These cannot be altered nor removed, nor can their surroundings be built on without the sanction of the Denkmalschutzamt. The Denkmalschutzamt must, though, give its decision within four months of notification. The Land can also acquire a listed monument if it is deemed necessary for its protection.

The only Land passing comprehensive legislation since the War is Schleswig-Holstein. The law of 1958 provides that the local authority, in the first instance, shall take action for the preservation of historic monuments in Schleswig-Holstein. Further, the consent of the local authorities is required for repair, alteration or destruction of a listed monument and the monument can be appropriated for its protection. However, in the case of prehistoric or early remains, their action is subject to approval of the Landesamt für Vor und Frühgeschichte. Landesamt are subject to the Kultur-Landesämter minister.

The Landesämter appoint honorary officers to advise the local authorities and the Landesämter are advised by a Denkmalsrat or council of nine members nominated by representative bodies in the state. All appeals are addressed to this latter council of nine.

In Baden-Württemberg, legislation exists to protect natural beauty, but not historic buildings or archaeological sites, except in South Baden, which had a law passed in 1947. But as the constitution of the Land provided that legislation for protecting cultural monuments could be passed, a law is now being drafted for more complete protection. Schleswig-Holstein's law is being used as the model.

Since the end of World War II, the Germans have done amazingly well, as far as the restoration of historic buildings destroyed by wartime bombing, is concerned. The rebuilding of the Goethe House in Frankfurt and of many cathedrals (Mainz) and castles (Charolottenburg) are cases in point.

AUSTRIA

Austria, another federal country, does have legislation dating back to the reign of the Emperor Francis Josephus, which was revised after World War I. A law of 1923 created a Bundesdenkmalamt to designate monuments and objects of historic, artistic or cultural significance of public interest. The unusual provision is that this automatically includes all buildings in public ownership, unless they are expressly excepted from the law. This is done at the request of the owners directed to the Minister of Education. State and Land (province) possessions are not the only possessions included in public ownership in Austria. Public ownership also includes possessions of other public corporations or institutions including religious bodies. Once again, as in most of the countries after a monument has been designated, the consent of the Bundesdenkmalamt must be obtained for its destruction or sale, especially the sale to foreigners or any alteration to it which would affect its traditional or artistic appearance. The law also provides that at the Bundesdenkmalamt's request, the local authority can forbid the erection of signs and other advertisements in the surroundings of a listed monument. There is no obligation concerning maintenance. Neither does the state contribute toward this, other than an occasional token grant for the preservation of an individual feature, such as a statue. Länder, on the other hand, however, make substantial grants for maintenance of privately-owned buildings (in this context, this may include such institutions as religious foundations which were considered to be public institutions for the purpose of the listing).

POLAND

The reconstruction of the historic quarters of Warsaw, following the liberation in January 1945, on such a vast scale was made possible by the regulations included in two laws.

The earliest Polish legislation dates from 1928 and permitted registration of whole ancient quarters or sites as historic monuments. The law was not very effective at that time, however, because the funds provided by the state were largely absorbed in the restoration of outstanding buildings in national ownership. Private ownership, which comprised the majority of the historic buildings, was left with nothing. It was not until 1937 that the Ministry of Education established a Central Inventory Bureau. By the time of the outbreak of the War, the Bureau had surveyed two provinces. This information, along with all kinds of documentary and iconographic materials, was extremely important for the reconstruction of the historic buildings and monuments. Detailed architectural measurements of most of the historic buildings were done before the War by the Conservator's Office, which also had precise photographic documentation of all historic buildings. Poland was fortunate in the fact that all these documents were taken out of Warsaw and hidden in one of the provincial towns during the War.

The second law was issued in 1945 following the destruction or damage of 710 of the 750 buildings registered as historic monuments. In fact, except in Cracow, almost all the most famous historic buildings of the country were extremely badly damaged or destroyed. While maintaining the right of private property with regard to building, this law gave the right to municipal authorities to prepare and to approve the plan of reconstruction of the town and also to take over, without any compensation, the grounds indispensable for public utility.

Also, a Directorate General of Museums and of the Protection of Monuments was set up in 1945 under the Ministry of Culture. The staff, architects and art historians, provides a regional service in every province to superintend restoration, together with Workshops for the Conservation of Historic Monuments for the actual execution of the work and a Bureau of Research to advise on methods.

The process of restoring the historic monument to the state in which it was most interesting was often applied. During the restoration of some buildings, it was discovered that sometimes it would be best to remove the later work which overlaid and obscured the original building.

In an old quarter, where narrow streets are characteristic, houses to the rear and inside the blocks are destroyed. This way, the buildings of interest are given free space which is indispensable for the health of the lodgers, just as a modern residential quarter must be well planned to insure good hygenic conditions. Many artists and scientists live in these old quarters because they prefer the atmosphere to the modern streets and squares.

The rebuilding of these groups such as market squares and even whole historic areas in Warsaw, Danzig, Wroclaw, and Posnan (from the individual building to the garden ornaments) was the concern of the Directorate.

Wooden buildings, if preservation is endangered, have provisions for subsidies to be given to the occupants, if they are inhabited, in order that they may repair the buildings. Or, another provision is the entire removal of such buildings to other sites if this presents a better chance of preservation.

Poland also provides that account must be taken of industrial and technological historical objects, such as old mills, manufacturing buildings, blacksmith shops and others, as well as objects of no special artistic value which nevertheless have a historical significance. Included in the latter are houses that have been occupied by outstanding men in the field of culture or science, by fighters for peace and progress as well as places commemorated by the struggle for independence, sites of overt and secret activity of a wider social significance and others.

As in other countries, the owner or user of the historical monument is bound to take care of its preservation. The Voivodship Conservator of Historical Monuments grants permission for any work on historical monuments and excavation sites. Likewise, no translocation of such monuments is allowed without having previously obtained his consent.

The Voivodship Conservator of Historical Monuments is entitled to command that the conservation work be carried out at the expense of the owner. In the cases when such a conservation yields no economic profit to the owner, the Minister of Culture and Art may finance the work concerned. In the case of justified anxiety that the given historical monument may be damaged or exported abroad, the latter may be subjected to temporary seizure. In specific cases, the monument may be taken over by the state, an indemnity equal to the value of the monument being granted to the owner. Archaeological excavations and findings are the property of the state. The finder of an archaeological object may be awarded a prize.

CZECHOSLOVAKIA

From the year 1918, when the independent Czechoslovak state was constituted, the provincial authorities took care of the special protection of monuments. During the years 1945-1958, the protection of monuments was reorganized with regard to the fact that the state then had the management of the essential part of the Czech cultural wealth. The present law thus dates from 1958. The Minister of Education and Culture is empowered to list property which offers evidence of the development of society, its art, technology, science or other sphere of human work and life, or any group of such things which are of similar interest collectively even if not individually.

A Central Commission for Public Monuments made up of experts acting in an honorary capacity, advises the Minister. The Commission supervises a Public Institute for the Care of Monuments and the Protection of Nature. Each Kreis or county has a similar Commission for the County established by a resolution of the County Council. Also each District Council has a similar District Commission, with a District Curator of Public Monuments who is the Chairman of the District Commission. If a Parish contains a large number of monuments, a Parish Council can appoint a similar Parish Commission.

The owner of a public monument must keep the property in repair according to the directions of the Minister and must notify the Commission of any threat or danger to it, or of any restoration work he undertakes. When monuments are in danger, the District Curator of Public Monuments is authorized to take immediate action. If an owner neglects a monument, the Minister can take the necessary steps for upkeep at the owner's expense. The Minister decides what measures are to be taken if the owner claims that he is unable to repair the building for financial reasons—this can include expropriation.

Monuments in public occupation must be used for libraries and the like after being treated with respect to their importance and consultation with the other Ministries concerned. Planning projects must take monuments into consideration and the protection of monuments takes priority over the project itself. Where a number of monuments form an important group, the Minister of Education and Culture may, after mutual agreement with other members of the Czech government and other chiefs of participating central authorities, lay down conditions controlling building in the area.

SWEDEN

The Swedish Antiquities Act states that all ancient monuments are protected wherever they are. It is forbidden to destroy them, cover them over, plant on them or do any damage to them by building or in any other way. There is an important regulation to the effect that there shall belong to an ancient monument as large a piece of ground as is necessary for the preservation of the monument with regard to its nature and importance.

The Central Office has the right to carry out all kinds of investigations and excavations. The Office can also give permission for the removal of ancient monuments if they cause the landowner or a tenant hinderance or inconvenience out of all proportion to their importance. To this permission the Office can attach conditions, including the expense of excavation.

The Act also states that a proprietor or a tenant is to make inquiries well in advance as to whether ancient monuments will be affected by the work to be undertaken.

In short one can say that the Swedish Antiquities Act is based upon the idea which prevailed throughout the eighteenth century, that the landowner has no right to use ancient monuments.

In Sweden, the preservation of monuments of historic interest relates mostly to those buildings owned by the state.

The ruins of old churches, castles and other buildings are regarded as ancient monuments and are consequently protected by the law. Buildings belonging to the state are managed by the National Board of Building and Town Planning and the oldest and most valuable of these buildings are recorded on a special list of historic buildings owned by the state. In the preservation of these buildings, the National Board of Building and Town Planning has to consult the Director General. Approximately the same rules apply to the ancient churches and their fittings.

Legal protection for old and valuable buildings in private possession is not so complete. Under the town planning and building regulations the local authorities have the duty to protect historically valuable buildings *as far as possible* and to see that they are not destroyed or damaged unless it is an imperative necessity. The restrictions in the regulations mean that they can only be applied where there is special interest in the matter and this is unfortunately not very often the case.

A new law for the protection of historic buildings was passed in 1960. Under this law a building in private possession which is particularly noteworthy can be registered by the Director General. Because of restrictive wording of the law, however, only some few buildings can be protected, and above all there is no possibility of legally protecting a street, a square or any other environment containing old buildings, of varying value individually but valuable as a whole.

A privately-owned building that preserves the individuality of the architecture of past times or the memory of a historically important event and that, considering this fact, is to be regarded as particularly remarkable, may by the Director General of the Central Office and of the Museum of National Antiquities be proclaimed a historic building. This may be done after consultation with the Board of Works, the Nordic Museum and Local Authorities. The provisions can extend to the surroundings of the buildings. The owners are notified of the listing and the listing is registered with the land charges register. Owners must obtain permission before they carry out any alteration to the buildings. If they neglect the maintenance imposed on them, the work can be done by the local authority and the cost reclaimed from the owners. But if the value of the building is reduced by the listing, the owner can claim compensation. If the owner does not wish his building listed, he can appeal to the Minister of Education.

ITALY

The number of historic buildings in Italy is so vast that it is not surprising that the Italian legislation on the subject is more concerned with buildings of such importance that they need to come directly under state ownership and control, rather than with certain limitations of private ownership, as in other countries of western Europe.

The agencies responsible in Italy for safeguarding, developing and expanding the nation's artistic, historical and cultural resources, are the operating arms of the Administration of Antiquities and Fine Arts, a bureau of the Ministry of Public Education. Other institutes which operate directly under the Bureau of Antiquities and Fine Arts are the Central Restoration Institute in Rome, the National Collection of Old Prints and Engravings in Rome, the Hard Stones Workshop in Florence, and the National Office of Photography in Rome. The Administration is the only responsible agency by law and is charged with coordinating and directing the activities of organizations with similar aims.

Buildings of historical, archaeological, ethnological or artistic interest can be listed by the Administration and their preservation thereafter becomes the responsibility of the state. The state has the right to acquire any national monument and the owner can also compel the state to do so within two months of the receipt of notification that the building has been made a national monument. Also, all subsequent transfers of national monuments from one private owner to another must be sent to the Ministry of Education.

The innumerable categories of resources classifiable as "monuments," and the matchless prestige of the evidence left on Italian soil by a civilization thousands of years old, require the government to perform tasks which will advance knowledge and critical studies, and progress in extent and depth of research and recovery activities.

Because of the delicacy of the objects of its care, this sector of the government administration is highly sensitive and affected more than any other by bureaucratic changes. The reason being that both an absolute centralization and an uncoordinated decentralization could have adverse effects on the efficiency of its action.

To insure the greatest operating consistency, the Administration of Antiquities and Fine Arts performs two separate functions. One, which concerns the teaching of arts, is now carried out by the Inspectorate for Art Education. The other, which is specifically concerned with the safeguarding of cultural assets, with the establishment and operation of museums, the holding of exhibitions, the adoption and coordination of all measures aimed directly and indirectly at promoting the knowledge and study of civilization, is a specific responsibility of the Bureau of Antiquities and Fine Arts.

It is also worth mentioning briefly that the law provides that the government, through the Bureau of Antiquities and Fine Arts, will also act for the protection of privately-owned works of art, by serving on the owner notice of the importance and interest of the work in his possession. Such notice involves a number of consequences in order to control the environment in which the work of art is located, dictating the measures required to prevent the endangering of its integrity, its appearance, prospective, lighting and decorum.

Current efforts will result in additional special legislation related to town planning problems in historical centers. Presently the town planning section of the Administration of Antiquities and Fine Arts is responsible for insuring the traditional physiognomy of the urban centers. Venice is not only protected in this manner but has in addition special legislation and it is planned that other such centers will be protected with specific laws.

Several agencies cooperate in the national effort for protection. The efforts of such groups as The Venetia Region Villas Agency or Italia Nostra Association are carried out in harmony with government agencies especially in problems having special interest in regions or urban centers.

In a world that is so rapidly changing, where countries that have recently acquired independence are developing rapidly, mention should be made of the necessity for international action in the field of preservation and restoration of monuments.

National action cannot give to our cultural heritage as a whole the care it needs to survive the coming centuries. UNESCO has, therefore, undertaken to prepare a series of international instruments, which take the form of either international conventions or recommendations and additionally operates a bureau in its control that encourages and activates programs designed to assist in the international aspects of the preservation of monuments.

Conventions are submitted to member states for ratification while recommendations are used as a basis for draft national legislation and other national programs.

Thus an international convention of the "Protection of Cultural Property in the Case of Armed Conflict" was drawn up during the course of an intergovernmental conference convened in the Hague in 1954 (fifty countries are now parties to the convention), and two recommendations have been adopted by the General Conference and circulated among the member states of UNESCO. They are "The Recommendation on International Principles Applicable to Archaeological Excavation" and the "Recommendation Concerning the Safeguarding of the Beauty and Character of Landscapes." Another recommendation entitled "The Preservation of Cultural Property Endangered by Public or Private Works" is in preparation.

In 1958, UNESCO created the International Centre for the Study of the Preservation and Restoration of Cultural Property to encourage international cooperation in activities in the conservation of the cultural patrimony of all nations—the great treasures common to humanity. Since its creation the Rome Centre has operated in close harmony with UNESCO, ICOM, and other institutes and specialized groups in Italy and elsewhere. The Centre operates a program consisting of expert consultation, publications, education and training.

The International Council on Monuments and Sites (ICOMOS) was established in 1965 by action of representatives of 26 nations at the request and suggestion of UNESCO. The purposes of ICOMOS are:

1) to promote the study and to encourage the preservation and development of monuments and sites

2) to arouse and develop the interest of the authorities and the general public of all countries with respect to their monuments, sites and cultural heritage in general

3) to constitute the international organization representing the administrative departments, institutions and persons interested in the preservation and study of monuments and sites.

Its headquarters has been established in Paris and, as yet, no programs have evolved. However, planning is under-way for programs of publications, information and collaboration at the international level.

United States participation in ICOMOS has taken the form of a National Committee composed of 12 active members representing the principal organizations concerned with the preservation of historic properties in the United States.

EUROPE: THE OLDER VISION

Each building, each artifact is a complex
of events in time and space. Our knowledge
of their spatial meaning is crude but
certain. We see things, we bump into them,
build them and destroy them casually.
But time's the dimension we've never learned
to accept or manage. It alters our world
and us: through its changes inanimate buildings
take life from human generations for whom
they testify mutely in unknown futures.
As witnesses they cannot be exchanged,
bribed or coerced. Their existence speaks
of the past, against our own presumptions
made from the present's unclear rhetoric.

A thirteenth century cistern. An old Ford.
Under the tile roofs, people live surrounded
by the past and the Fiats, Mercedes, Austins
of tourists. The inhabitants have ideas
suited to their hillsides and the demands
of life in a national monument. One must be
willing to be on show, yet rise above it.

*Making an ancient city and its pattern amenable
to the inconvenience of modern living
takes effort, and a spirited desire to keep
motor cars subordinate to people.
Why not? A few minutes drive around the clean
and open waterfront is no price for even
one old building, or the pedestrian luxuries
of wandering down old streets, gazing at cornices.*

76

Like Trajan's legions, the spiral of lost armies
winds in their triumph around the bronze
emblem of emperor and imperium, cast from cannon
and flanked by ministries; reviving for spectators
the symbols and splendors, the eagle-guarded myths.

77

78

This was Warsaw. Larger bombs, bigger guns
would have flattened it completely.
The burned-out shells, the paths through
the pathetically stacked rubble were enough.
People who love a place restore it as it was
even though the labor exceeds the effort
and the cost of a shining skyscraper.

The baroque mind conceived a blank wall
as imperfection. Vines, ribbons, cherubim
were close to its flowering vision.
The outside of the house and its furniture
were united in profusion of detail
a jungle of luxuriance, tamed and
formalized to European grace.

Nothing that's old is wholly safe
from damages by winds and rain and age:
decay comes poking in at crevices;
the roof, though seeming sound, must be relaid,
timbers replaced, and stucco patched.
Old buildings, through unceasing care
against both time and storm stay sound
to keep their graces for the future's eyes.

We want to believe in the grey stone village
and the grey stone barn on the hill above;
we want to pretend that the short green meadow
with rivery weeds, where ducks dive, playing
their tail end comedy can last a season
through sweet days of summer: trees, meadow and barn
will persist in this country the village honors.

83

*It is possible to live near the Spanish Steps and go
up and down them through each day of life: it is
possible not to notice the steps, the church or
the bright Roman sky while tourists come to see
these things: who themselves have gone unnoticing
of their native cities: Berlin, Moscow, Euclid Heights.*

*What does one do here in winter except look at the river
and the old buildings which escaped Haussman who
rebuilt the city to make revolution impossible: it is
cold on the Quai, but spring's revolution will warm
the stone which has survived war and imperious planning.*

85

*A stone tapestry woven in three dimensions: the baroque
imagination made the facade a continual changing
excitement for the beholder; each day the lights shifting,
revealing in fresh perspective each detail of form
interwoven with form, walls displaying the generosity
of merchant princes flinging to the crowd their treasures.*

Without the ubiquitous cars and television antennas
springing beyond the tiled roof, the scene
might be suspended in time, like some illustrator's
fantasy of the Netherlands for a story paced
by the lapping of water against the stone steps.

Sokolniki Park Church stands at a corner
of the park. Near it, pigeons congregate
to feed. In the hot serene Moscow summer
it shimmers as the blue serene illusion
of an iceberg floating among the trees.

*Imperium of the sea and trade routes, centered
in islands——with Venetian wealth came splendor:
the Doges' Moorish Gothic Italianate showcase,
the opulent stone confection of Saint Mark's.*

AMERICA: DISAPPEARING SIGHTS

*It is not alone what we save from the past,
but how, and with what dignity. Speaking
for our own sense of fitness: do we
value the future less than convenience?*

*Each is a temporary generation: the losses
we inflict upon ourselves for short
and seeming gain increase with time,
scaling down our dimensions. We
need old buildings in the sun to gage
our humanness against indifferent skies.*

*With tracks in the snow, history becomes
a suburb of the mind. The immediate pattern
by children crossing the lawn shows
that no one lives here: the doorsill
is clear, but the path to it isn't.
Preserved, chaste and elegant, the house
is time's dark island for the romping young.*

*In Vermont the autumns blaze suddenly
into short glory. That burning bush
of a tree by the house will soon
scrawl shadows of naked limbs
on white boards blued by the sun.*

89

John Holden Green designed the house
around which the shadows of trees
younger than itself, dapple walls
risen from decay in sun flecked grace.

Palmettoes, and the various balconies
of the ship's decks—no, the city
in riverboat elegance ready to set sail.

*Latrobe drew a small cruciform
church in a field. Beyond,
the burned White House stood
in isolated ruin.*

        *Saint John's
in the fields is now surrounded
by buildings: and a park
with Andy Jackson and other
military heroes. The shining tower,
the portico reflecting the sun,
are of a later dispensation.*

*The wealthy and important live
in these row houses and others
in Georgetown: a bohemia
too expensive for artists,
saved by its inhabitants
with single-minded vigilance.*

*In a land without titles, wealth alone
could elevate an aristocracy. Some built
well, with royal splendor, leaving
those who came after to gasp at their
golden extravagance, marvel at their taste.
These mansions are their finest monuments.*

*It is not France: the vegetation betrays
the colonial scene: the buildings remain
memorials to the American empire, sold
to escape the green devouring wilderness.*

Middletown lost the interurban railroad,
then its front yards when the highway was widened.
A few trees by the street remain. The town's lucky,
having survived the civil war and the vagaries
of progress, that impersonal disaster.

97

Behind them, the bay silvers in the sun, or
becomes wet sounds in the fog. Of the lines
lacing the city, only two are left, one
with new Swiss machinery. Although they seem
native to California, the first winding drums
were imported from Chicago, where cable cars
whipped along flat streets, speed being
relative to the nineteenth century——

Whatever else, religion built in the wilderness
austere stout buildings which outlasted their
builders and the forest. Prophecy and the wild
both tamed, they stand as a park in town.

A clock with different time on two faces
beneath the ecclesiastical spire and
four chimneys over diagonal fireplaces
mark the palace of justice, otherwise
a square block of domestic architecture
for circuit judges and the frontier court.

The bay storms, the hurricanes, wars and the
erosions of years have left the harbor
shipshape still, as any seaport town
should be, withstanding all its foes (unless
the zoning laws come tumbling down)

The double image reflects the residence—not
the house—developed by a singular hero.
He was the Enlightenment. Ingenious and
articulate, in his rural bent he was
the romantic of landscapes, the enthusiast
of views, the dreamer of the agrarian dream.

It might be P.S. Number One, somewhere back East,
or the Old High School in Illinois or Kansas.
Empty, in the desert city, it's a dead transplant,
its lifeless structure stiff in the hot soil.

History rasps around the courthouse like parched
leaves of autumn: this was early a settled land
where the first heroes of revolution found their
passions over which the years have fallen and
negligence of thought, like blown and seething snow.

Heaven, they said was at the green center
of the world's maze, where a stone award
waited the faithful. Consider the total symbols:
how they transcended this simplicity of meaning.

Stone is obdurate. Persepolis, no, nor
Rome had such fragile intricacies as
the sheet metal front with its instant
carvings and textures: a facade
in perishable luxuriance of form
aflame with the sun, splendid remnant
of an art already lost among the gilded monumen.

The great golden many tiered aviary
with promenades for people, and
mercantile levels, all guarded by
griffon gargoyles and glass
excluding weather: the nineteenth
century dream of the outside turned in.

Rising from the desert like a sudden flower
as desert blossoms after a desert rain
this church has stayed, unwithering, white
towers thrust into the infinite sky from
that barren landscape which it ruled like
something standing on the edge of the worl

107

Seen from the land, it is the seaward enigma
of voyages, the tanker from Bayway, the freighter
from Alexandria, the mysterious tramp, with
rusting sides. Seen from the sea, it signals
the beginning or the end, a bright pharos
punctuating the intervals of life.

FINDINGS
AND RECOMMENDATIONS

Part I

INTRODUCTION

IN FORMULATING ITS FINDINGS AND RECOMMENDATIONS, THE SPECIAL COMMITTEE ON HISTORIC PRESERVATION HAS attempted to develop a program to encourage federal, state and local government, and private agencies and individuals to preserve communities, areas, structures, sites and objects significant to architectural, cultural, social, economic, political and military history and which contribute to the quality and meaning of American life.

In pursuit of this objective, the Committee, which includes representatives of all levels of government and the agencies involved, has studied problems and programs related to historic preservation in the United States and in Europe. At the request of the Committee, a number of federal agencies and the National Trust for Historic Preservation have supplied studies, reports, documents and comments on numerous historic preservation activities and accomplishments. The Committee has examined contemporary European practices in historic preservation, restoration and reconstruction. It has obtained from authoritative sources in England, France, Holland, Germany, Scandinavia, Poland, Czechoslovakia, Austria and Italy legal and administrative information which could be used to evaluate European experience in relation to Amer-

ican needs and proposals for improving and developing historic preservation programs in the United States.

It is clear to the Committee that our own needs and the evidence of experience in Europe, where historic preservation is a major responsibility of government, suggest an expansion and development of our own programs, placing greater emphasis on government support of private efforts in historic preservation.

The Committee has been aided in its work by consultants and by the contributors whose work appears in the various chapters and photographic sections of *With Heritage So Rich*.

The Committee is indebted to many public officials and private citizens, in the United States and Europe, who have provided information and ideas for this study. We hope this material and our findings and recommendations will assist the growing interest in and concern with historic preservation throughout the United States.

One of the exciting conditions which has encouraged the Committee to make its recommendations is the attitude of public officials and private individuals toward historic preservation. What has been a groundswell is becoming a great wave of interest and support.

This growing interest is part of an evolutionary process which began a century or more ago with the first movements to preserve important historic sites and structures. The historical material provided this Committee, shows that this process has involved many dedicated public servants, private individuals and groups, scholars and experts.

In accordance with this increasing desire to make historic preservation a living part of our community life and development, the Committee recommends certain new programs described in this report. Along with enlargement and enhancement of existing programs, they will broaden and deepen the scope of national historic preservation activity.

FINDINGS

If it can be said that there is a new awakening of interest in the preservation of our cultural and architectural heritage, it must be added that never was the need for it greater.

Since World War II a great wave of urbanization has been sweeping across the nation. And such is the rate of growth that in the next 40 years the United States will have to build more homes, more schools, more stores, more factories, more public facilities of all kinds than in the entire previous history of the country.

Out of the turbulence of building, tearing down and rebuilding the face of America, more and more Americans have come to realize that as the future replaces the past, it destroys much of the physical evidence of the past.

The current pace of preservation effort is not enough. It is as though the preservation movement were trying to travel up a down escalator. The time has come for bold, new measures and a national plan of action to insure that we, our children, and future generations may have a genuine opportunity to appreciate and to enjoy our rich heritage.

The United States, with a short history and an emphasis on its economic growth, has left historic preservation primarily to private interests and efforts. In the older, history-conscious countries of Europe, preservation leadership has been provided primarily by government.

One of the acute shortages in the field of historic preservation is that of specially trained architects and other technicians and trained preservationists. These shortages must be remedied if the objectives outlined in this report are to be met in time and the quality of preservation activity is to be at the high level we envisage. A program of scholarships and grants-in-aid for studies is a pressing need.

Our nation began with migrations, grew with migrations, and remains a nation of people on the move. Few of us have had close ties with the land and with places and buildings. The natural result in too many cases has been a neglect of starting points and an indifference to our cultural trail of buildings and places. This is what we are trying to correct.

As is apparent from a study of various laws and programs, governmental concern for historic preservation in the United States has been limited at all levels, with some notable exceptions.

At the federal level, the laws now in effect which mention preservation directly include the Antiquities Act of 1906, written to protect historic monuments on government property; an Act establishing the National Park Service in 1916; the Historic Sites Act of 1935, which defines the national policy of preservation for public use; the Act of 1949, which established and defined the powers of the National Trust for Historic Preservation; and the Housing Acts of 1961 and 1965 which gave to the Department of Housing and Urban Development powers to use federal funds to acquire open space and to move historic structures in urban renewal areas.

The following is a summary of the various federal programs which affect historic preservation.

DEPARTMENT OF THE INTERIOR

The Department of the Interior has been responsible for a wide range of historic preservation activities for many years. It has served as custodian of prehistoric Indian villages in the Southwest, of the battlefields and fortifications of our military history, of historic buildings and places, of the evidence of our pioneers and of many other examples of the history of our social and cultural growth. The National Park Service, which is the agency within the Department responsible for this vast program, has gained worldwide renown for the excellence of its work and the service it renders to the American people and our many visitors.

The National Park Service also conducts the National Survey of Historic Sites and Buildings, which, with the help of state and local authorities, has identified thousands of historical properties throughout the United States. The Secretary of the Interior has classified 600 such properties as Registered National Historic Landmarks. Recently, the Survey has begun to identify nationally important historic districts such as Brooklyn Heights, N. Y. and Annapolis, Md. Within the past two years, 13 such areas have been classified by the Secretary of the Interior as Registered National Historic Landmarks. As the Survey continues, additional landmarks and districts are studied and recognized.

Another major program, the Historic American Buildings Survey, is of importance to the nation as a whole and to every state and community. The Survey goes beyond the study of historic sites and major historical buildings to include all examples of American architecture worthy of public concern and protection. The invaluable records of the Survey are available at the Library of Congress, and they have been indispensible aids to numbers of preservation projects. The Department of the Interior will issue a trial publication of some of the drawings and photographs for a single state (Wisconsin) in 1966: but funds are not at present available for further publication. Such publication is intended to serve the dual function of a historical presentation and a source book for architects.

Nearly half the buildings recorded in detail in the past 30 years have already been razed or destroyed by mutilation. Yet the staff of the Historic American Buildings Survey estimates that no fewer than 90,000 additional buildings should be inventoried, and that at least 18,000 of these are of such exceptional merit they should also be recorded in photographs and measured drawings. Approximately 3,000 of the 90,000 buildings are situated on federal lands and 25,000 more, located in communities throughout America, may be affected in one way or another by current federal programs and projects during the second half of the 1960's. At the current rate of progress on this Survey, it would take 75 years to accomplish its work!

The National Park Service, in cooperation with the Smithsonian Institution, coordinates the Inter-Agency Archaeological Salvage Program, involving 7 federal and many state and local agencies. This program was initiated 20 years ago to rescue irreplaceable archaeological sites destined to be permanently lost through flooding in the course of dam and reservoir construction.

The Bureau of Outdoor Recreation is authorized to provide various forms of financial assistance for historic preservation, but at present it lacks adequate funds.

Historic preservation projects of the Department of the Interior and state and local agencies have been supported by the Neighborhood Youth Corps, administered by the Department of Labor under the Economic Opportunity Act, and by funds from the Area Redevelopment Administration (now the Economic Development Administration) in the Department of Commerce.

DEPARTMENT OF HOUSING AND URBAN DEVELOPMENT

Many historic buildings and areas are in the hearts of our cities. The new Department of Housing and Urban Development administers the many activities of the former Housing and Home Finance Agency. These include, among others, federal assistance for renewal of our cities, for planning and development programs of states, counties, regions and cities, for open-space lands and for limited historic preservation assistance.

Under the Urban Renewal, Local Planning Assistance and Open-Space Land programs the Department has provided funds for planning, surveying, public facilities, open space and property acquisition for historic preservation. The Local Planning Assistance (Section 701) grants and Demonstration (Section 314) grants have been used by a number of communities in conducting surveys of historical assets and preservation potential as part of the process of preparing local comprehensive plans and community renewal programs. To date, 119 communities have utilized funds in one or more of these categories as a part of their broad preservation and renewal programs.

All of these community development programs have important roles in the preservation field and are being used to help achieve local goals for historic preservation. Under current housing and urban development legislation however, the cost of restoration and continued maintenance must be borne by a local public or private agency. No grant-in-aid or loan funds are available for the specific purpose of restoration.

Federal loan and grant-in-aid funds available for rehabilitation of historic buildings cannot be used for more than making the building habitable and marketable. Any historic design elements which do not relate to structural safety and economic usefulness are not eligible for such public funds.

Improvements needed in the Department's programs include the addition of historic sites and buildings, both within and outside the project area, to the list of acceptable local non-cash contributions to renewal costs, and an enlargement of assistance programs to include loans for acquisition and rehabilitation of historic structures and districts.

GENERAL SERVICES ADMINISTRATION

The General Services Administration is the management agency for federally-owned buildings and sites. It controls a wide variety of major buildings and areas, many of them dating from the founding of the country, including court-houses, post offices, fortifications, army camps, customs houses and every conceivable kind of structure which federal programs have required in the course of the last 175 years. The agency is responsible for safeguarding and salvaging and disposing of the huge inventory of surplus federal property, including public buildings, some of which have historic significance.

The General Services Administration and cooperating federal agencies, particularly the Department of Interior, have developed agreements for identifying the historical or other significance of sites and structures under federal management. They are also seeking means to develop workable solutions to the complex problems arising from the changing uses of such structures, and the changing patterns of government administration. The General Services Administration has assisted in the admirable efforts to preserve and restore such structures as the old State, War and Navy Building and the Pension Office Building in Washington, D. C., among others.

DEPARTMENT OF COMMERCE

The Bureau of Public Roads in the Department of Commerce, which administers the Federal Highway Program, has developed rules and guidelines for highway projects in the interests of historic preservation, archaeology and paleontology. In this connection, a circular memorandum issued May 25, 1964 by the Bureau concerning outdoor recreation and historic resources stated:

> To assure that full consideration is given to the over-all interests of the public in both the Federal-aid highway programs and programs for the protection or improvement of public recreational resources (such as but not necessarily limited to public parks, playgrounds, forests, open space, game sanctuaries, and the like) and historical resources, it will in the future be required that the plans, specifications and estimates (PS&E) for each Federal-aid highway project which affects natural or man-made resources devoted to, or included in realistic plans for, public recreational or historical preservation purposes by a public authority having the official responsibility therefor, contain a statement that the State highway department did afford to such appropriate public authority ample opportunity at the earliest practicable time to review the highway department's planning for the proposed highway location and construction. The oppor-

tunity for such a review, as a minimum, would consist of the initiation by the highway department of a direct contact between that department and the appropriate public authority preferably during the preliminary stages of plan development for the highway. In all cases these contacts shall have been made prior to the time at which the public hearing is advertised. If the officials of the appropriate public authority do not agree with the planning of the State highway department, their reason for non-concurrence shall be included with the PS&E documents, and the State highway department shall show that the suggestions of the above-referenced public officials have been examined and the plans as submitted to Public Roads provide the best possible solution in the judgment of the highway department.

INTERGOVERNMENTAL LIAISON

There have been some notable federal accomplishments in historic preservation. However, the present disposition of federal properties, the official designation of historic buildings and sites, the development of urban renewal programs, the planning of details of the federally-aided highway system and the development of national defense facilities and other federal operations, responsibilities and programs involve a series of complex activities. Each of these responsibilities and activities is the result of a separate Congressional authorization. Each is separately administered. Jurisdictional disputes in the field of historic conservation have been inevitable. Such disputes will occur again and again and provisions for their early resolution must be an important part of national programs for historic preservation.

There is no present administrative mechanism or appropriate method of liaison between federal agencies or between state and local preservation programs and the various federal agencies. The Committee on Historic Preservation recommends establishment of an Advisory Council on Historic Preservation which will adequately represent paramount interests at all levels of government and the private sector. Such a Council could reduce conflicts and improve historic preservation liaison and coordination.

Similar problems of coordination affect state and local governments. Most states and many localities can lay claim to historic preservation programs, but in too many cases, even where state and local law is sufficient and community interest is high, preservation efforts have been hobbled by the lack of appropriation of public funds for preservation—which is crucial since private property may not be acquired without fair compensation.

It is one thing to know that a threatened building is of historic or architectural importance. It is another to find the money to stave off the bulldozer and to establish and maintain an appropriate and living use for the property.

Moreover, as at the federal level, broad planning and coordination of public, state and local preservation programs are lacking.

Even in the private field, which so far has provided most of the leadership for preservation in this country, the efforts, and especially the financial outlay by private philanthropy, have been insufficient.

The focal point of private endeavor has been the National Trust for Historic Preservation, which has been engaged in a notable but limited program of education, dissemination of information, and the acquisition and maintenance of a number of historic properties. However, the largest historic property holders outside the federal government are the corporations holding and managing historic communities, such as Williamsburg, Va., Sturbridge Village, Mass., and Old Salem, N. C. The Society for the Preservation of New England Antiquities, with 57 historic structures, is probably the largest holder of scattered properties.

But sufficient funds are not available for the development and staffing of the National Trust's programs, for emergency assistance to others facing preservation crises, or for the acquisition and support by the Trust of additional properties of historic and cultural importance.

While there is a growing national interest in historic preservation, it is by no means evenly distributed. In cities we find the widest discrepancies in interest and accomplishment. In cities such as New Orleans, Boston, Charleston, S. C., San Antonio, Santa Barbara, Natchez, Winston-Salem, N. C., Bethlehem, Pa. and Providence, R. I., there has been excellent and growing support by both the business community and local government. And there are others. However, there is a longer list of cities and small towns and villages where either indifference reigns or there is outright hostility. In the latter case, preservation frequently loses the battle to stronger forces. Curiously, business leaders often ignore the economic benefits of prestige values and tourist dollars.

INTERNATIONAL COOPERATION

There is a growing interest in programs of international cooperation for historic preservation sponsored by the United Nations Educational, Scientific and Cultural Organization. These include the Rome International Centre for the Study of the Preservation and the Restoration of Cultural Property and the newly-established International Council on Monuments and Sites. The International Relations Committee of the National Trust and the Committee on Historic Preservation of the American Institute of Architects have been recommending

support of these programs for several years and also participated in the first Inter-American Historic Preservation Conference at St. Augustine, Fla., in June 1965.

It is important for Americans to share research and education programs and to participate in international meetings on historic preservation. We have much to learn and much to contribute. Support for such conferences, at home and abroad, will involve the cooperation of the Department of State which has authority to allocate funds for educational purposes.

Technical help, such as the Rome Centre can provide, is only part of the mutual education process. There must be a genuine interchange of results of research, of ideas, approaches and philosophy and it is essential that our publications, exhibitions, motion pictures and displays at international gatherings be of high quality. This suggests that consideration of international cooperation be given when the federal government appropriates funds for an expanded historic preservation program.

CONCLUSIONS TO THE FINDINGS

The pace of urbanization is accelerating and the threat to our environmental heritage is mounting; it will take more than the sounding of periodic alarms to stem the tide.

The United States is a nation and a people on the move. It is in an era of mobility and change. Every year 20 per cent of the population moves from its place of residence. The result is a feeling of rootlessness combined with a longing for those landmarks of the past which give us a sense of stability and belonging.

If the preservation movement is to be successful, it must go beyond saving bricks and mortar. It must go beyond saving occasional historic houses and opening museums. It must be more than a cult of antiquarians. It must do more than revere a few precious national shrines. It must attempt to give a sense of orientation to our society, using structures and objects of the past to establish values of time and place.

This means a reorientation of outlook and effort in several ways.

First, the preservation movement must recognize the importance of architecture, design and esthetics as well as historic and cultural values. Those who treasure a building for its pleasing appearance or local sentiment do not find it less important because it lacks "proper" historic credentials.

Second, the new preservation must look beyond the individual building and individual landmark and concern itself with the historic and architecturally valued areas and districts which contain a special meaning for the community. A historic neighborhood, a fine old street of houses, a village green, a colorful marketplace, a courthouse square, an esthetic quality of the townscape—all must fall within the concern of the preservation movement. It makes little sense to fight for the preservation of a historic house set between two service stations, and at the same time to ignore an entire area of special charm or importance in the community which is being nibbled away by incompatible uses or slow decay.

Third, if the effort to preserve historic and architecturally significant areas as well as individual buildings is to succeed,

intensive thought and study must be given to economic conditions and tax policies which will affect our efforts to preserve such areas as living parts of the community.

In sum, if we wish to have a future with greater meaning, we must concern ourselves not only with the historic highlights, but we must be concerned with the total heritage of the nation and all that is worth preserving from our past as a living part of the present.

Part II

RECOMMENDATIONS

Throughout this report the term historic preservation has been used to include the protection, rehabilitation, restoration and reconstruction of communities, areas, structures, sites and objects having historic, architectural, social or cultural significance.

To carry out the goals of historic preservation a comprehensive national plan of action is imperative. Such a plan will encourage, improve and reinforce public and private leadership.

Many individuals and private organizations have worked long and hard to preserve the physical evidences of our heritage which we are privileged to enjoy today. Public agencies have also made a substantial contribution. But to meet the current crisis and to accelerate the pace of historic preservation we need to increase the amount of government support and joint public and private efforts.

Our traditions differ from those of European countries, but we have much to learn from European experience. The weight which European governments give to historic preservation has resulted in successful programs for saving, restoring and reconstructing many different types of buildings for viable uses. There is an excellent object lesson in the European achievement in maintaining historic buildings and areas as living parts of communities and as successful economic ventures.

A national plan of action for historic preservation should include the following elements:

1) a comprehensive statement of national policy to guide the activities and programs of all federal agencies;

2) the establishment of an Advisory Council on Historic Preservation to provide leadership and guidance for the direc-

tion of inter-agency actions and to provide liaison with state and local governments, public and private groups and the general public;

3) a greatly expanded National Register program to inventory and to catalogue communities, areas, structures, sites and objects; a federal program of assistance to states and localities for companion programs; and a strong federal public information program based on the material in the Register;

4) added authority and sufficient funds for federal acquisition of threatened buildings and sites of national historic importance, and expansion of the urban renewal program to permit local non-cash contributions to include acquisition of historic buildings on the National Register, both within and outside the project area;

5) provision for federal loans and grants and other financial aid to facilities and expansion of state and local programs of historic preservation;

6) federal financial aid to and through the National Trust for Historic Preservation to assist private interest and activity in the preservation field, for educational purposes and for direct assistance to private property holders.

Detailed recommendations are as follows:

FEDERAL

1. Enact legislation to:
   a. affirm a strong national historic preservation policy, recognizing its enlarged dimensions
   b. coordinate and consolidate existing historic preservation programs

c. authorize annual appropriations for the Department of the Interior to acquire historic structures and sites of major national importance

d. consolidate the federal inventory and survey programs in a National Register and to authorize additional appropriations for the National Park Service to administer this Register

e. authorize grants to state and local governments to carry out similar inventory and survey programs in coordination with the National Park Service.

2. Enact legislation authorizing preparation, administration, publication and distribution by the National Park Service of a National Register, in accordance with carefully-prepared standards and criteria, of structures and sites, whether publicly or privately owned, of national importance because of historic, architectural, archaeological or other cultural values. Such a Register should include several categories of buildings: The first category should include our prime national monuments and Congress should pass legislation which would protect them from demolition, mutilation or alteration without approval of the advisory body which this Committee proposes. This group would include structures such as the Capitol, the White House, *Mount Vernon* and *Monticello*. Many of the buildings are at present in public hands and most of those in private ownership are in no danger. But there should be an orderly evaluation of the structures belonging in this small class which should be protected with every legal safeguard.

A second category of buildings should include structures of lesser rank which have merit and should be eligible for the broad range of assistance programs proposed in this report. Provision should be made for the government to have the right of first refusal should the owner decide to sell or demolish the structure.

A third category should include those structures of local concern whose preservation should be a matter of local decision and initiative.

3. Establish an adequately staffed Advisory Council on Historic Preservation, with membership representing the major federal departments and agencies involved in preservation matters, as well as state and local governments and public and private organizations interested in historic preservation and urban development. The functions of such a Council should include:

a. advising the President and the Congress on historic preservation as it affects the national welfare and providing inspiration and leadership for the implementation of the national policy

b. the development of policies, guidelines and studies for the review and resolution of conflicts between different federal and federally-aided programs affecting historic preservation

c. the encouragement, in cooperation with appropriate private organizations, of public interest and participation in historic preservation

d. supporting the National Register as an instrument of national historic preservation policy and insuring the coordination of the Register with activities of other agencies of government

e. making and publishing studies in such areas as adequacy of legislative and administrative statutes and regulations pertaining to preservation activities of state and local governments, and effects of tax policies at all levels of government on historic preservation, and

f. preparation of guidelines for assistance of state and local governments in drafting preservation legislation.

4. Provide by Internal Revenue Code amendment or clarify by regulation or published ruling the status of:

a. historic preservation as a public, exempt charitable activity, deductibility of gifts of historic easements or restrictive covenants to governmental units or exempt organizations engaged in preservation, and permissibility of revenue-producing adaptive or incidental uses

b. acceptance of a registered historic property for conveyance to the National Trust in lieu of an equivalent estate tax payment

c. income tax deductibility to private owners of registered historic properties for preservation and restoration expenditures within appropriate limitations

d. recognition of conveyances of registered historic properties to governmental units or exempt preservation organizations as present gifts, despite reserved life interests, provided the property is open to the public on a reasonable basis.

5. Make mandatory a preliminary review of the location and status of historic sites and buildings in relevant areas prior to the undertaking of federal or federally-aided programs or projects affecting plans for physical development. Where the review produces evidence of the existence of historic sites and buildings and that surveys made in accordance with the standards of the National Registry are lacking, make mandatory a historic survey prepared in accordance with such standards. Where necessary, provide funds for the preparation of such surveys through the Department of the Interior, Department of Housing and Urban Development, Department of Commerce, or other concerned federal agencies. Plans prepared for such development projects must take all such historic surveys into consideration, and must show evidence thereof.

6. Authorize the use of federal matching grants for acquisition by an appropriate public agency of historic structures, rehabilitation loans and grants for restoration of such structures, and recognition of public expenditures for such acquisitions as eligible non-cash contributions under urban renewal programs. Under the Urban Renewal Program, communities must match the federal grants with local contributions. In most cases, communities must put up $1 for every $2 of federal aid, although in the case of cities under 50,000 and cities in economically distressed areas, the formula is $1 for every $3 of federal assistance. However, the community has the option to make in lieu of cash, a non-cash contribution of a community benefit such as a school or sewer and water services within the project area. A little less than two-thirds of these local matching contributions are in this form. Under the 1965 Housing Act, $2.9 billion of federal grants are authorized which will be matched by between $966 million and $1.45 billion of local matching contributions. Expansion of eligible non-cash contributions to include acquisition of historic structures on the National Register both within and outside the project area would enable local communities to play a far more effective role in preservation.

7. Establish new and liberalized loan programs for private groups or individuals for acquisition and rehabilitation of historic structures and districts.

8. Enactment of a scholarship and training program for architects and technicians in the field of historic preservation, similar to the program enacted by Congress in 1964 for the field of housing and urban planning. An adequate program is of vital importance to the effective implementation of the other proposals of the Committee.

STATE AND LOCAL GOVERNMENTS (COUNTY, TOWN AND MUNICIPAL)

1. *State:* Enact legislation establishing an appropriate state agency, and enabling and encouraging local communities to establish historic preservation districts and to acquire through eminent domain (where necessary) historic structures and sites and preservation easements and restrictive covenants, and providing special property tax treatment for historic structures and preservation and restoration expenditures.

2. *State:* Establish an organizational structure capable of:
   a. providing leadership, information, standards and criteria, technical and financial assistance to local communities for preservation purposes
   b. reviewing and coordinating the programs and projects of state agencies to avoid to the maximum extent conflicts with preservation objectives

c. carrying out appropriate preservation programs, plans and studies, and
   d. establishing and maintaining an official state register coordinated with the National Register.

3. *State:* Enact legislation clarifying and encouraging the use of preservation easements and restrictive covenants for the benefit of governmental units and preservation organizations.

4. *State:* By statute or regulation, assure exemption from inheritance taxes for gifts of historic property to governmental units, the National Trust and other preservation organizations, and income tax deduction for such gifts and for preservation and restoration expenditures.

5. *State and local:* Where authorized, require by legislation and appropriate notice procedures, a waiting period before demolition or significant alteration of registered historic structures, in order to provide time for acceptable alternatives and new use solutions to be worked out.

6. *Local:* Undertake a thorough and systematic survey of historic and architecturally important buildings and areas within the community, in coordination with the National Register and the State Register.

7. *Local:* Make a comprehensive study of all available legal tools for preservation purposes, including historic district zoning and formation of architectural and historic review boards. Such studies should relate to official general plans of the locality and be incorporated in Community Renewal Programs.

8. *Local:* Provide an annual budget for expenditures to preserve and maintain those historic and architectural structures and places of importance to the community.

9. The Congress should strengthen and broaden the District of Columbia historic preservation legislation.

GENERAL

1. Historic and cultural sites, structures and objects acquired with the use of federal funds and not retained by the acquiring department or agency, or not otherwise directly disposed of, should be transferable under the surplus property disposal programs to the National Trust in fee simple. The National Trust should be empowered to lodge operational responsibility for such property with local preservation groups wherever possible.

2. In order that representatives of the Department of Housing and Urban Development, the Department of Commerce, the General Services Administration and other appropriate agencies may be allowed to sit with the Board of Trustees, the

National Trust charter should be amended to provide that the Trustees, at their discretion, be allowed to appoint additional ex-officio Trustees from among heads of federal departments and agencies.

3. Federal authorization should be provided for matching grants to the National Trust on a two-thirds federal/one-third National Trust formula for the following purposes:

  a. to provide educational and clearinghouse services and financial assistance to individuals and organizations in preservation and related fields

  b. to prepare information and educational publications, conduct meetings and conferences, finance scholarships, develop library resources, provide technical consultation and establish award programs

  c. to acquire, restore and maintain registered structures of national historic or architectural importance.

4. To assure that public funds for private historic preservation are used only for authentic needs and in accordance with established criteria, such funds should be transmitted to non-governmental organizations and private individuals only with the approval of an appropriate authority.

5. Private corporations, trade associations and labor organizations should be encouraged to identify and preserve the locations, structures and objects on which the development of their enterprise or craft has been based.

6. The great national philanthropic foundations should be urged to stimulate and assist programs for the training of architects, landscape architects, engineers, historians, designers and decorators in careers in historic preservation. In addition, they are urged to assist historic preservation research projects, publications and conference and communication media programs.

INTERNATIONAL COOPERATION

The United States should provide financial support to the UNESCO historic preservation programs including the Rome Centre, and the International Council on Monuments and Sites. In addition, federal funds should be used to support international conferences and scholarships and fellowships for international study of historic preservation.

SPECIAL COMMITTEE ON HISTORIC PRESERVATION

Albert Rains, *Chairman*
Edmund S. Muskie
William B. Widnall
Philip H. Hoff
Raymond R. Tucker
Gordon Gray
Laurance G. Henderson, *Director*

BIBLIOGRAPHY

BOOKS

ABRAMS, CHARLES. *Man's Struggle for Shelter in an Urbanizing World*. Cambridge, Mass.: Massachusetts Institute of Technology Press, 1964. 307 pp., illus., bibl.

America the Beautiful, in the words of John F. Kennedy. Elm Grove, Wisconsin: Country Beautiful Foundation, Inc., 1964. 98 pp., illus.

ANDREWS, WAYNE. *Architecture in America; A Photographic History from the Colonial Period to the Present*. New York: Athenaeum, 1960. 179 pp., illus.

BURCHARD, JOHN E. *and* ALBERT BUSH-BROWN. *The Architecture of America; A Social and Cultural History*. Boston: Little, Brown, 1961. 595 pp.

Catalog of Federal Aids to State and Local Governments. Washington, D. C.: U.S. Government Printing Office, 1954. 154 pp., illus. Prepared for the Subcommittee on Intergovernmental Relations for the Committee on Government Operations, U.S. Senate by the Legislative Reference Service of the Library of Congress.

Catalog of the Measured Drawings and Photographs of the Survey in the Library of Congress. Washington, D.C.: National Park Service, 1941. 470 pp. Catalogue supplement, 1959. 180 pp., illus., index.

CODMAN, JOHN. *Preservation of Historic Districts by Architectural Control*. Chicago: American Society of Planning Officials, 1956. 36 pp., illus. Analysis of American cities having architectural control laws. Plan for securing area controls.

COLEAN, MILES LANIER. *Renewing our Cities*. New York: The Twentieth Century Fund, 1953. 181 pp., illus.

COYLE, DAVID CUSHMAN. *Conservation; An American Story of Conflict and Accomplishment*. New Brunswick, N.J.: Rutgers University Press, 1957. 284 pp., illus.

Directory of Historical Societies and Agencies in the United States and Canada. Nashville, Tennessee: American Association for State and Local History, 1956. 140 pp., illus., index. Basic source of information about historic house museums and other preservation projects.

FINLEY, DAVID E. *History of the National Trust for Historic Preservation,* 1947-1963. Washington, D.C.: National Trust for Historic Preservation, 1965. 115 pp., illus., index.

FORTUNE MAGAZINE EDITORS. *The Exploding Metropolis*. Garden City, N.Y.: Doubleday and Co., Inc., 1958. 177 pp., illus.

FRIEDEN, BERNARD J. *The Future of Old Neighborhoods; Re-*

building for a Changing Population. Cambridge, Mass.: Massachusetts Institute of Technology, 1964. 256 pp.

GIEDION, SIGFRIED. *Space, Time and Architecture; The Growth of a New Tradition.* Cambridge, Mass.: Harvard University Press, 1954, 3rd ed. enl., 778 pp., illus., bibl.

GOTTMANN, JEAN. *Megalopolis; The Urbanized Northeastern Seaboard of the United States.* Cambridge, Mass.: Massachusetts Institute of Technology, 1964. 720 pp.

GOWANS, ALAN. *Images of American Living; Four Centuries of Architecture and Furniture as Cultural Expression.* Philadelphia: J. B. Lippincott Co., 1964. 498 pp., illus., index, bibl. Provides a comprehensive view of American architecture up to the present, with careful attention to the architecture of non-English areas.

GREBLER, LEO. *Urban Renewal in European Countries; Its Emergence and Potentials.* Philadelphia, Pa.: University of Pennsylvania Press, 1964. 132 pp., illus., index, bibl.

A Guide to the Study of the United States of America; Representative Books reflecting the Development of American Life and Thought. Washington, D.C.: U.S. Government Printing Office, 1960. 1193 pp.

HAMLIN, TALBOT FAULKNER. *Greek Revival Architecture in America;* being an account of important trends in American architecture and American life prior to the War between the States. New York: Oxford University Press, 1964. 439 pp., illus., index, bibl. The most thorough reference to American architecture before the Civil War.

HANDLIN, OSCAR and JOHN E. BURCHARD. *The Historian and the City.* Cambridge, Mass.: Massachusetts Institute of Technology, 1963.

Historic Preservation Today. Charlottesville: University Press of Virginia, 1965. 180 pp., bibl. Essays presented to the Seminar on Preservation and Restoration, Williamsburg, September 1963. Papers and comments of a group of international experts on all phases of governmental and private preservation.

HITCHCOCK, HENRY-RUSSELL. *American Architectural Books;* a list of books, portfolios, and pamphlets on Architecture and related subjects published in America before 1895. Minneapolis, Minn.: University of Minnesota Press, 1962. 130 pp., index.

HOSMER, CHARLES B. JR. *Presence of the Past—A History of the Preservation Movement in the United States before Williamsburg.* New York: G. P. Putnams, 1965. 386 pp., illus., index, bibl.

JACOBS, JANE. *The Death and Life of Great American Cities.* New York: Random House, 1961. 458 pp.

JOHNSON, THOMAS F., JAMES R. MORRIS and JOSEPH G. BUTTS. *Renewing America's Cities.* Washington, D.C.: The Institute for Social Science Research, 1962. 130 pp., illus., bibl.

LARKIN, OLIVER W. *Art and Life in America.* New York: Holt, Rinehart and Winston, 1960. 559 pp.

M'KELVEY, BLAKE. *The Urbanization of America.* New Brunswick, N.J.: Rutgers University Press, 1963. 370 pp., illus., bibl.

MORISON, SAMUEL ELLIOT and HENRY STEEL COMMAGER. *The Growth of the American Republic.* New York: Oxford University Press, 1962 (5th ed. rev. and eng.) 2 volumes in textbook edition., illus., bibl.

MORRISON, HUGH. *Early American Architecture, from the First Colonial Settlements to the National-Period.* New York: Oxford University Press, 1952. 619 pp., illus., bibl.

MORRISON, JACOB H. *Historic Preservation Law.* Washington, D.C.: National Trust for Historic Preservation, 1965(2nd edition). 198 pp., illus. Reference for individuals, organizations and public officials concerned with maintaining landmarks. Compilation of municipal and state statutes, ordinances, court decisions and enactments.

MUMFORD, LEWIS. *The City in History; Its Origins, Its Transformations, and Its Prospects.* New York: Harcourt, Brace and World, 1961. 634 pp., illus., bibl.

MUMFORD, LEWIS. *Sticks and Stones; A Study of American Architecture and Civilization.* New York: Dover Publications, 1955(2nd rev. ed.). 238 pp., illus.

Museum Directory of the United States and Canada. Washington, D.C.: American Association of Museums and the Smithsonian Institution, 1965. 1039 pp., index. Basic source of information about historic house museums and other preservation projects.

Manual of the Historic American Buildings Survey. Philadelphia: National Park Service, 1961-62. illus. Detailed guide manual for making records of historic buildings. Available on loan from HABS or some major libraries and societies.

OWEN, WILFRED. *Cities in the Motor Age.* New York: The Viking Press, 1959. 176 pp.

REPS, JOHN WILLIAM. *The Making of Urban America; A History of city planning in the United States.* Princeton, N.J.: Princeton University Press, 1965. 574 pp., illus., index, bibl.

ROOS, FRANK J. *Writings on Early American Architecture.* Columbus, Ohio: State University Press, Graduate School Studies, 1943. 271 pp., bibl. An annotated list of books and articles on architecture constructed before 1860 in the eastern half of the United States. A guide to books, pamphlets and articles on early American architecture, arranged by area, subject, and architect.

SIMONDS, JOHN ORMSBEE. *Landscape Architecture; the Shaping of Man's Natural Environment*. New York: F. W. Dodge Corp. (McGraw Hill), 1961. 244 pp., illus.

TALLMADGE, THOMAS EDDY. *The Story of American Architecture*. New York: W. W. Norton, 1927 (revised and enlarged ed. 1939). 332 pp., illus. Cited in all social histories of the U. S. and in many general histories, and included in their bibliographies.

TUNNARD, CHRISTOPHER and HENRY HOPE REED. *American Skyline; the growth and form of our cities and towns*. Boston: Houghton Mifflin, 1955. 302 pp. illus.

UDALL, STEWART L., Introduction by JOHN F. KENNEDY. *The Quiet Crisis*. New York: Holt, Rinehart and Winston, 1963. 209 pp., illus., index.

STONEY, SAMUEL GAILLARD. *This is Charleston; A Survey of the Architectural heritage of Charleston, a unique American city*. South Carolina: The Carolina Art Association, 1944 (2ed. rev. 1966), 137 pp., illus., index. Notable house-by-street index to historic buildings each with a small photograph.

WHALEN, RICHARD J. *A City Destroying Itself; an angry view of New York*. New York: Morrow, Wm. and Co., Inc., 128 pp., illus. by Feliks Topolski.

WHITE, MORTON and LUCIA. *The Intellectual Versus the City: From Thomas Jefferson to Frank Lloyd Wright*. Combridge, Mass.: Harvard University Press and M.I.T. Press, 1962. 270 pp.

WILSON, SAMUEL, JR. *A Guide to Architecture of New Orleans, 1699-1959*. New York: Reinhold Publishing Corporation, 1959. 76 pp., illus. Well-illustrated, booklet sized survey, with maps. One of a series on American cities published in connection with annual conventions of the AIA.

FOREIGN

BRICHET, ROBERT. *Le Régime des Monumenes Historiquts en France*. Paris: Libraries Techniques Librarire de la Cour de Cassation. 1952. 237 pp., illus. Rules governing and methods of management of historic monuments in France.

DINSMOOR, WILLIAM BELL. "The Temple of Ares at Athens," *Hesperia*, IX, 1940. pp. 1-52.

Housing and Urban Development in the Federal Republic of Germany. Bonn: Federal Ministry of Housing. 1961. 70 pp., illus. Commentary on problems of regulations concerning all phases of housing and urban development.

KELSALL, MOULTRIE R. and STUART HARRIS. *A Future for the Past*. Edinburgh and London: Oliver and Boyd, 1961. 151 pp., illus., index. Development of a policy of restoration,

List of Properties, 1965. London: The National Trust for Places of Historic Interest and Natural Beauty. 1965. 128 pp., illus., index. Listing of British National Trust properties, with notes on their history and architecture, as well as their availability to the public.

LORENTZ, STANISLAW. *Reconstruction of Warsaw*. Prague (unpublished paper). 7 pp. Paper concerning the problems facing restorationists concerned with the Old Town center of Warsaw, and the post World War II solutions.

Monuments Act. The Hague: Kingdom of the Netherlands. 16 pp. The Act of June 22, 1961 containing provisions in the interest of the preservation of monuments of history and art.

Pausanias, *Description of Greece*. transl. by J. G. Frazer. New York: Biblo and Tannen. 1965.

Physical Planning Act, People's Republic of Poland. Warsaw: Instytut Urbanistyki I Architektuyr. 1964. 17 pp. Regulations concerning physical planning, to include development of individual areas, establish correct spatial interrelations and for the protection of natural resources and values.

PLACHY, JUDR. FRANTISAK. *Czechoslovak Laws on the Protection of Cultural Monuments*. Prague: State Institute for the Protection of Monuments and Nature. 1965. 7 pp. Resumé of laws now in force concerning the protection of cultural monuments.

Preservation and Restoration of Monuments of Architecture in the USSR. Moscow: USSR Architecture Union. 1964. 30 pp., illus. Brief commentary on preservation and restoration in the Soviet Union and photographs of national Monuments that have been preserved.

Protection of Historical Monuments in the Polish People's Republic with Special Consideration of the Reconstruction of Towns. Warsaw: Documentation Centre for Historical Monuments. 1965. 60 pp. Collection of legislative acts regulating, or affecting the protection of historic monuments and the reconstruction of towns.

Recommendation concerning the Safeguarding of the Beauty and Character of Landscapes and Sites. Paris: UNESCO. 17 pp. Recommendations adopted by the General Conference of UNESCO at its twelfth session, Paris, 11 December 1962.

Recommendation on International Principles applicable to Archeological Excavations. Paris: UNESCO. 19 pp. Recommendations adopted by the General Conference at its ninth session, New Delhi, 5 December 1956.

Recommendations on the Means of Prohibiting and Preventing the Illicit Export, Import and Transfer of Ownership of Cultural Property. Paris: UNESCO. 1964. 13 pp. Recommendations adopted by the General Conference of UNESCO at its thirteenth session, Paris, 19 November 1964.

The System in France for the Safeguarding and Sound Utilization of Historic Urban Cites. Venice: International Congress on Historic Preservation. 10 pp. A resumé of French legislation relating to the preservation and restoration of towns, villages and ancient sections of cities.

THOMPSON, HOMER A. *The Athenian Agora.* 2nd edition. 1962.

ZACHWATOWICZ, JAN. *Protection of Historical Monuments in Poland.* Warsaw: Polonia Publishing House. 1965. 145 pp., illus. Information about the methods, achievements and the present state of the protection of architectural monuments in Poland.

ARTICLES, PAMPHLETS AND REPRINTS

APPLEYARD, DONALD, KEVIN LYNCH and JOHN R. MYER. *The View from the Road.* Cambridge, Mass. M.I.T. Press. 1964. 64 pp., illus., bibl. Published for the Joint Center for Urban Studies of the M.I.T. and Harvard University.

College Hill, A Demonstration Study of Historic Area Renewal. Providence: Providence City Planning Commission. 1959. 53 pp., illus. Conducted in cooperation with the Providence Preservation Society and the Housing and Home Finance Agency. Prepared in connection with an urban renewal project.

Criteria for Evaluating Historic Sites and Buildings. Washington D.C.: National Trust for Historic Preservation, Committee on Standards and Surveys. 1956. Discussion of historical and cultural significance of historic sites and buildings; their suitability for preservation; educational values; cost of restoration or reconstruction, maintenance and interpretation; and administration responsibility of sponsoring groups.

DALE, ANTHONY. "Listing and Preserving Historic Buildings: The European Picture," *The Architectural Review.* London, 1965. pp 97-104.

DELAFONS, JOHN. *Land-use controls in the United States.* Cambridge, Mass.: Harvard University Press. Joint Center for Urban Studies of the M.I.T. and Harvard University. 1962. 100 pp.

FEISS, CARL, FAIA., AIP. *Community Architecture: An Appeal to Action.* Washington D.C.: The American Institute of Architects, Urban Design Committee. 16 p., bibl. Comprehensive architecture of entire communities.

Final Report of the Historic Districts Study Committee. Cambridge, Mass.: Historic District Preservation Press. 92 pp., maps. Recent developments in historic preservation law and conclusions reached after review of these. A summary of Cambridge landmarks and extensive exhibits section.

GARVEY, ROBERT R., JR. "State Participation in American Landmark Preservation," *State Government,* Summer 1965. The Council of State Governments. 6 pp. The article indicates the scope of private and governmental activity in the field of landmark preservation to the present, including a listing of governmental programs through which possible preservation funds may be obtained. It urges an increase in action and emphasizes the importance of surveys, enabling legislation and financial aid as essential parts of a successful state program.

Historical New Hampshire, Vol. XVIII, No. 2. Historic American Buildings Survey, New Hampshire Catalog. Concord, N.H.: New Hampshire Historical Society. 1963. 17 pp., illus. First of revised and updated HABS lists to be published by states.

JACOBS, STEPHEN W., AIA. "A Current View of Area Preservation" Reprint from Dec. 1964 *Journal* of the American Institute of Architects. Discusses motivation for area preservation activity, federally aided local programs, social and economic issues and problems for the historian.

MASSEY, JAMES C. *Architectural Surveys.* Washington D.C.: National Trust for Historic Preservation. 12 pp. illus., bibl. Step-by-step procedure for conducting, recording and publicizing surveys. Historic American Buildings Survey and guidelines for its use.

MONTAGUE, ROBERT L., III, and TONY P. WRENN. *Planning for Preservation.* Chicago, Ill.: American Society of Planning Officials. 1964. 46 pp., illus., tables, graphs, bibl. Based on a 50-state survey conducted by the office of the Kentucky Attorney General, and the Legislative Archive of the National Trust, this work contains information on legal trends, problems and current capabilities in preservation law. Contains the first fully documented survey of the economic effects of preservation on property values, taxation and the travel industry (tourism). Appendices include sources of information and notes on the development of municipal historic district ordinances.

PETERSON, CHARLES E. "Thirty Years of HABS" Nov. 1963 *Journal* of the American Institute of Architects. 4 pp. Theory, legal basis, development of Historic American Buildings Survey.

POPPELIERS, JOHN C., editor. *Historic American Buildings Survey: Massachusetts Catalogue.* Massachusetts: Secretary of

Commonwealth Kevin H. White, Chairman Massachusetts Historical Commission. 1965. 69 pp., illus., index. Lists documentation in the Survey, 1964. Lists more than 800 structures, comprising up-dating and revision of those included in the 1941 catalogue and 1959 supplement.

Planning and Community Appearance. Report of Joint Committee of Design Control of the New York Chapter of American Institute of Architects and New York Regional Chapter of American Institute of Planners. New York: Regional Plan Association. Illus., bibl. Design philosophy, preparation of design plans and programs, existing esthetic regulations in this country and abroad, evolving legal concepts and excerpts and abstracts from existing legislation.

A Report on Principles and Guidelines for Historic Preservation in the United States. Washington, D.C.: National Trust for Historic Preservation. 1964. 24 pp., Observations on the present state of affairs, with a statement of principles and recommendations. Restoration principles, education, surveys, criteria, training, responsibility, legislation and administration.

Restoration and Preservation of Historic Buildings. Washington, D.C.: Building Reseaerch Institute. 1964. 57 pp. Papers presented at the Building Research Institute's Preservation Forum. Subjects: architecture and engineering, history research, archaeology, entomology, photogrammetry, photography, measured drawings and landscaping, pertinent data on details of restoring and preserving masonry, woodwork, paint, hardware and lighting.

ROCKEFELLER, DAVID. "The Responsibility of the Businessman in Urban Renewal." An address at a dinner meeting of the Forum on Urban Renewal, Hartford, Conn., Oct. 19, 1960.

SNOW, BARBARA, editor. "Preservation and Urban Renewal: Is Coexistence Possible?" Reprinted from, *Antiques Magazine,* Oct. 1963. 16 pp., illus. Panel of 10 experts in planning, urban renewal and preservation discuss the question.

STIPE, ROBERT E. *Civic Action and Historic Zoning*. Chapel Hill, N.C. University of North Carolina Institute of Government. 1963. Surveying and delineating historic areas in city plans. Their contribution to urban economic, social and cultural well-being.

VON ECKARDT, WOLF. *Bulldozers and Bureaucrats*. Washington, D.C.: The New Republic. 65 pp. Cities and Urban Renewal.

WHITE, HARRY E., JR. "A Discussion of Historic Districts Legislation" *Columbia Law Review*. Vol. 63, April 1963. Police Power, Eminent Domain, and Preservation and Historic Property.

Wilmington, N.C., Historic Area: A Part of the Future Land-Use Plan. Raleigh, N.C.: Dept. of Conservation and Development. 1962. Historical and architectural qualities of the city differentiated and analyzed.

WOLFE, ALBERT B. "Conservation of Historical Buildings and Areas-Legal Techniques" Chicago: American Bar Association, Proceedings. Section of Real Property, Probate and Trust Law. Aug. 1963. 11 pp. Origins of the preservation movement. Preservation legislation, determination of districts and boundaries, decisions on certificates of appropriateness, enforcement.

WRENN, TONY P. *Preservation Legislation*. Washington, D.C.: National Trust for Historic Preservation. Bibl. National Trust legislative archive; states with historic district enabling legislation and cities with historic district ordinances.

WURSTER, CATHERINE BAUER. "Framework for An Urban Society" (in *Goals for Americans*) New York: Prentice-Hall, Inc. 1960. Report of the President's Commission on National Goals, Englewood Cliffs, N.J.

INDEX

ACKNOWLEDGMENTS

The Special Committee wishes to acknowledge the invaluable assistance provided to it by the many specialists who offered their aid and to its authors who helped in providing the infinite amount of detailed work which went into the production of this book. It was especially gratifying to the Committee to receive the wholehearted and enthusiastic response from such a wide variety of sources and individuals. We would particularly like to thank the following who have given of their time and experience:

On the staff of the National Trust: Mrs. Terry B. Morton and Mrs. Linda E. Ward; and on the staff on the National Park Service: Worth Bailey, Dr. John Littleton, Dr. Murray Nelligan and Charles S. Pope, AIA. On the staff of Library of Congress: Miss Virginia Daiker Head, Reference Section, Prints and Photographs. Further acknowledgment is made to: Donald Nicoll, Administrative Assistant to Senator Muskie; Ardee Ames; Mrs. Estelle Campbell, Consultant on Photography; Robert M. Lunny, Director of the New Jersey Historical Society; and Dorn McGrath, Urban Renewal Administration, Department of Housing and Urban Development.

The Committee also wishes to acknowledge the invaluable advice and assistance received from many European sources.

It thanks those who were responsible for arranging study tours and meetings.

Among these are: AUSTRIA: Professor Dr. Walter Frodl; CZECHOSLOVAKIA: Dr. Vladimir Novotny; DENMARK: Harold Langberg; ENGLAND: Hubert Bennett FRIBA, J. F. W. Rathbone; FRANCE: Dr. Hiroshi Daifuku, Jacques DuPont; HOLLAND: Robert Hotke; ITALY: Dr. Harold J. Plenderleith, Professor Dr. Piero Gazzola; POLAND: Professor Dr. Stanislaw Lorentz; WEST GERMANY: Dr. Kurt Seeleke.

In addition, the Committee also gratefully acknowledges the assistance of the colleagues of the above listed leaders.